The Master Key

A Victorian Grimoire

SWCM - Sourceworks of Ceremonial Magic Series

Volume I – *The Practical Angel Magic* of John Dee's Enochian Tables - ISBN 978-0-954763-90-9

Volume II – *The Keys to the Gateway of Magic*: Summoning the Solomonic Archangels & Demonic Princes – ISBN 978-0-954763-91-6

Volume III – *The Goetia of Dr Rudd*: The Angels & Demons of *Liber Malorum Spirituum seu Goetia* – ISBN 978-0-954763-92-3

Volume IV – *The Veritable Key of Solomon* – ISBN 978-0-7378-1453-0 (cloth) - ISBN 978-0-954763-98-5 (limited leather)

Volume V – *The Grimoire of Saint Cyprian: Clavis Inferni* - ISBN 978-0-955738-71-5 (cloth) – ISBN 978-0-955738-74-6 (limited leather)

Volume VI – *Sepher Raziel: Liber Salomonis* – ISBN 978-0-955738-73-9 (cloth) – ISBN 978-0-955738-75-3 (limited leather)

Volume VII – *Liber Lunæ & Sepher ha-Levanah* - ISBN 978-0-955738-72-1 (cloth) - ISBN 978-0-955738-73-8 (limited leather)

Volume VIII – *The Magical Treatise of Solomon*, or *Hygromanteia* – ISBN 978-0-956828-50-7 (cloth) - ISBN 978-0-956828-51-4 (leather)

Volume IX – *A Cunning Man's Grimoire: The Secret of Secrets* – ISBN 978-0-993204-27-2 (cloth) – ISBN 978-0-993204-28-9 (leather)

Volume X – *Clavis or Key to the Mysteries of Magic* – Ebenezer Sibley – ISBN 978-1912212-08-8 (cloth) – ISBN 978-1912212-09-5 (leather)

Volume XI – *Ars Notoria* (Vol. 1) The Grimoire of Rapid Learning by Magic – ISBN 978-1912212-03-3 (cloth) – ISBN 978-1912212-04-0 (leather)

Volume XII – *Ars Notoria* (Vol. 2) The Method: Mediaeval Angel Magic – Version B - ISBN 978-1912212-28-6 (cloth)

Volume XIII – *The Steganographia Books I, II, III & IV.* Trithemius. ISBN 978-1912212-37-8 (cloth). ISBN 978-1912212-38-5 (leather)

Volume XIV – *Trithemius' Secret Library: the Antipalus Maleficiorum.* ISBN 978-1912212-46-0 (cloth). ISBN 978-1912212-47-7 (leather).

Volume XV – *Summa Sacre Magice: The Compendium of Sacred Magic.* Ganelli. Vol. 1. ISBN 978-1912212-48-4 (cloth). 978-1912212-49-1 (leather).

Volume XVI – *Summa Sacre Magice: The Compendium of Sacred Magic.* Ganelli. Vol. 2. ISBN 978-1912212-51-4 (cloth). 978-1912212-52-1 (leather).

Volume XVII – *The Master Key: A Victorian Grimoire.* W. H. Ibbett. 2nd Edition ISBN 978-1912212-55-2 (cloth). 978-1912212-54-5 (leather).

For further details of forthcoming volumes in this series edited from classic magical manuscripts see www.GoldenHoard.com

Books on Magic by Stephen Skinner

Agrippa's Fourth Book of Occult Philosophy (edited) – Askin, Ibis

Aleister Crowley's Astrology (edited) – Spearman, Ibis, Weiser

Aleister Crowley's Four Books of Magick (edited) – Watkins

Ars Notoria – the Method Vol. 2 (with Daniel Clark) – Golden Hoard, Llewellyn

Ars Notoria – Vol. 1 (with Daniel Clark) – Golden Hoard, Llewellyn

Clavis or Key to the Mysteries of Magic (with Daniel Clark) – Golden Hoard, Llewellyn

Complete Magician's Tables – Golden Hoard, Llewellyn

Cunning Man's Grimoire (with David Rankine) – Golden Hoard, Llewellyn

Dr John Dee's Spiritual Diaries: the fully revised and corrected edition of *A True & Faithful Relation of what passed...between Dr John Dee...* with full Latin translation – Golden Hoard, Llewellyn

Geomancy in Theory & Practice – Golden Hoard, Llewellyn

Goetia of Dr Rudd: Liber Malorum Spirituum (with David Rankine) – Golden Hoard, Llewellyn

Grimoire of Saint Cyprian: Clavis Inferni (with David Rankine) – Golden Hoard, Llewellyn

Keys to the Gateway of Magic (with David Rankine) – Golden Hoard, Llewellyn

Magical Diaries of Aleister Crowley (edited) – Spearman, Weiser

Michael Psellus 'On the Operation of Daimones' (edited) - Golden Hoard

Millennium Prophecies: Apocalypse 2000 – Carlton

Nostradamus (with Francis King) – Carlton

Oracle of Geomancy – Warner Destiny, Prism, Golden Hoard

Practical Angel Magic of Dr Dee (with David Rankine) – Golden Hoard, Llewellyn

Sacred Geometry – Gaia, Hamlyn, Sterling

Search for Abraxas (with Nevill Drury) – Spearman, Golden Hoard

Sepher Raziel: Liber Salomonis (with Don Karr) – Golden Hoard, Llewellyn

Splendour Solis (with Rafal Prinke, Joscelyn Godwin & Georgiana Hedesan) – Watkins

Steganographia (with Daniel Clark) – Golden Hoard, Llewellyn

Summa Sacre Magice: Compendium of Sacred Magic (Vol. 1), by Berengarius Ganelli (with Daniel Clark) Books 1 & 2 - Golden Hoard, Llewellyn

Summa Sacre Magice: Compendium of Sacred Magic (Vol. 2), by Berengarius Ganelli (with Daniel Clark) Books 3, 4 & 5 - Golden Hoard, Llewellyn

Techniques of Graeco-Egyptian Magic – Golden Hoard, Llewellyn

Techniques of High Magic (with Francis King) – C.W. Daniels, Golden Hoard

Techniques of Solomonic Magic – Golden Hoard, Llewellyn

Terrestrial Astrology: Divination by Geomancy – Routledge

The Master Key: Victorian Grimoire (with Daniel Clark) – Golden Hoard, Llewellyn

Trithemius' Secret Library: the Antipalus Maleficiorum (with Daniel Clark) – Golden Hoard, Llewellyn

Veritable Key of Solomon (with David Rankine) – Golden Hoard, Llewellyn

Bookplate in the manuscript

The Master Key

a Victorian Grimoire

being Manchester GB 133 Eng MS 44

by William Henry Ibbett

edited by Dr Stephen Skinner
and Daniel Clark

GOLDEN HOARD PRESS

2025

Published by Golden Hoard Press Pte Ltd
PO Box 1073 Robinson Road
Singapore, 902123.
www.GoldenHoard.com

© Copyright 2025 Stephen Skinner
www.SSkinner.com

2nd Edition

All rights reserved. No part of this publication may be reproduced or utilized in any form or by any means, electronic or mechanical, including photocopying, recording, or by any information storage and retrieval system, or used in another book, or by AI without specific written permission from the author. The only exception to this being fair use in a review, or the quoting of limited fully acknowledged passages.

UK ISBN: 978-1912212-55-2   *Cloth 2nd Edition*
UK ISBN: 978-1912212-54-5   *Limited Leather Edition* Copy No...........

US ISBN: 978-073878195-2   *Cloth Edition*

Table of Contents

	page
Table of Contents	7
List of Plates	8
Introduction	11
The Master Key to Ancient Mystery	19
Detailed Contents, an Index of all the Chapters	20
Book I	29
Preface	31
Origin of the word Talisman	35
Seven Tables of the Seven Planets	58
Book II	217
The Almadel	293
The Spirit Vassago	302
Bibliography	330
Index	332

List of Plates

	pages
Plate 1: Alphabets appropriated to the Signs, Planets, Numbers	37
Plate 2: Man the Microcosm or little World	45
Plate 3: Characters suited to the Latin Alphabet	55
Plate 4: Celestial Characters [suited] to the Hebrew Alphabet	55
Plate 5: Chaldean Characters suited to the Latin Alphabet	56
Plate 6: Melachim Writing of the Angels	57
Plate 7: Writing called passing the River	57
Plate 8: The Seven Tables of the Divine Names and Numbers	58
Plate 9: Table of Saturn	60
Plate 10: Table of Jupiter	61
Plate 11: Table of Mars	62
Plate 12: Table of the Sun	63
Plate 13: Table of Venus	64
Plate 14: Table of Mercury	65
Plate 15: Table of the Moon Her Compass	66
Plate 16: Seals and Characters [of the Moon]	67
Plate 17: The Characters of the Seven Angels	68
Plate 18: Characters drawn from things themselves	73
Plate 19: Joinings or Conjunctions	73
Plate 20: The Characters of the four Triplicities	73
Plate 21: Thuribalum Magica	81
Plate 22: Characters of the Behenian of fixed Stars, their Degrees	83
Plate 23: Images of the fixed Stars	84
Plate 24: Talismans which were in the Possession of Great Men	87
Plate 25: Chart of the Nine Chambers	88

Plate 26: Fig 1-6	97
Plate 27: Fig 7-11	98
Plate 28: Fig 12-17	99
Plate 29: Fig 18-20	100
Plate 30: Fig 21-23	106
Plate 31: Fig 24-27	107
Plate 32: Talismans of Aries, Taurus, Gemini, Cancer	111
Plate 33: Talismans of Leo, Virgo, Libra, Scorpio	112
Plate 34: Talismans of Sagittarius, Capricorn, Aquarius, Pisces	113
Plate 35: In the Eighth Sphere, the 28 Mansions of the Moon	120
Plate 36: Planetary table of the Cabala for extracting the English	122
Plate 37: Planetary table of the Cabala for extracting the Hebrew	123
Plate 38: A Table of the Twelve Signs	124
Plate 39: The Hebrew Notes for the same	125
Plate 40: Tables of Numeral Transpositions	126
Plate 41: Table of Even Numbers	127
Plate 42: Table of Odd Numbers	127
Plate 43: Table of Odd Numbers with a Cypher	128
Plate 44: A Right Table of Commutations - English	134
Plate 45: A Right Table of Commutations - Hebrew	135
Plate 46: The Averse table of the Commutations - English	136
Plate 47: The Averse table of the Commutations - Hebrew	137
Plate 48: Tables of Venus – Mopkel and Kompel	150
Plate 49: Tables of Venus – Cobjel and Cigmel	153
Plate 50: A Table of the Essential Dignities of the Planets	154
Plate 51: A Table of Elections of the Lunar Aspects	163
Plate 52: A Table to find the Length of the Planetary Hour	164
Plate 53: A Planetary Table shewing what hour each Planet rules	165

Plate 54: Magic Circle for the first hour of Sunday and Monday   176

Plate 55: Magic Circle for the first hour of Tuesday and Wednesday 177

Plate 56: Magic Circle for the first hour of Saturday   178

Plate 57: The figures of Divine Letters of the Seven Planets   179

Plate 58: A Four-fold Table of the names of the four Quarters   182

Plate 59: Names of the Planetary Hours, Numbers and the Angels   183

Plate 60: The Pentacle of Solomon and Peter de Abano   197

Plate 61: Sigillum Solis and Sigil of Jupiter   198

Plate 62: The true Forms & Figures of the Talismans - Dragons   269

Plate 63: The Circle of a simple construction for using the Crystal   310

Plate 64: The Lamen of Gold or Holy Table of Michael   311

Plate 65: The Almadel of Wax, Spatula, Seal & Lamen of the Spirit   311

Plate 66: The Mounted Chrystal its True size and Form   311

Introduction

The Master Key is truly an extraordinary manuscript. It was written in 1854-1860 by W. H. Ibbett. Dan Harms kindly supplied us with his biographical research, which follows:

> "William Henry Ibbett was born to Robert Greaves Ibbett and Christine (or Christina?) Jane Ibbett on July 28, 1825, and baptized on September 4 of that year. Robert is listed in the baptism record as a bookseller, but later he seems to have found a lucrative career in taking possession of goods obtained through evictions and auctioning them off. This did make him unpopular, so we sometimes see his name pop up in court proceedings and the like. This is a good thing for us, though, as it gives us details we might not find out otherwise.
>
> His son William was apprenticed to two goldsmiths, the latter of whom was Samuel Starkey, whose service he entered in 1841. We have two sets of freedom admission papers in 1846 and 1847, which likely means he could have set up shop in the profession.
>
> Instead, he seems to have gone into business with his father. Although both William and Robert occupied different addresses for their businesses over the time, the most recurring one was at 29 Jewin-Street, an address just west of St. Giles Cripplegate which is now in the Barbican Estate. William seems to have occupied 29, while Robert used 29A for his auctioneer business.[1]
>
> William was also a family man. We are missing some important dates here, but he was married around 1850 to Elizabeth Caroline Ibbett. They had two children, Ann, who was born around 1851, and William, born on September 20, 1855. Elizabeth is still with him in 1881, although the age she gives to the census taker seems to drop every time she gives it.
>
> The matter of Ibbett vs. de la Salle came before the Court of the Exchequer in 1860. Robert Ibbett had been charged by J. T. de la Salle, a landlord, with seizing the property of one Galvin to recover back rent. De la Salle had agreed to indemnify Ibbett for any risk. Robert sent his son William to recover the property, after which Galvin sued William for

---

[1] Jewin Street was destroyed by fire in 1897.

> supposedly taking additional goods illegally. De la Salle refused to pay for William's defence. I am not a legal scholar myself, but overall the judges agreed that Galvin's prosecution of William was malicious and that de la Salle should pay for costs of the lawsuit against William.
>
> Most of William's promotion in the local newspapers is not for his bookselling or auctioneering, but for selling paintings and other works of art. He also is listed as a patent agent, although he only seems to have pursued one patent in 1868 for a device "for inducing motion in mobile substances or bodies" on behalf of John Thibault Hancock of Boston.
>
> I do not have a death date for William Henry Ibbett. There is however a William Ibbett who died at the Mitchem workhouse in Croydon on December 15, 1899, but I'm not 100% sure it was him."[2]

Although Ibbett did not know Robert Cross Smith, as he would have been around six years old when Smith died (he died very young, in his thirties), I still believe Ibbett used, or viewed manuscripts that were once in the care of the Mercurii or for inspiration of his magnum opus. At the very least he would have seen works penned by Hockley. If Ibbett wasn't a member of the Mercurii, he certainly knew people who once were. As a bookseller like Denly he would have had ample access.

Although this manuscript was never published, I would guess that its contents strongly influenced the build-up of interest in the occult which helped to create the Golden Dawn roughly 30 years later in 1888. Interestingly, although it contains much of the material taught in that magical order, it also contains significant expansions on that material, along with much magical material not seen in print before.

Surprisingly it also contains information which is found in the *Summa Sacre Magice*,[3] a manuscript dating from 1346, but not to be found in other Victorian or later grimoires. In fact the present manuscript is a fairly complete magical syllabus. Its full title was:

"THE MASTER KEY.
to Ancient Mystery.
To Unlock the Secret Caverns of the Magi, and Restore to Light the whole Art of the

Occult Science
of Talismanic Sculpture.

which for Centuries have been lost, being hid under the Cloak of Mystery and

---

[2] We are thankful to Dan Harms for supplying these details of his research after our initial publication.

[3] Published in Skinner & Clark, *Summa Sacre Magice*, London & Singapore: Golden Hoard, 2024.

buried in the grave of Enigma. Elucidating the Mysterious Tables of Numbers, Angels, Spirits, Characters, Hierogliphies *(sic)* and Alphabets. Also explaining their Methods of forming by Art

Talismanic,

Images. Tablets. Amulets. Rings. Chrystals. Glasses. Lamens, &c. Enchantments, Spells, Fascinations, Bindings and preparing curious compositions as Candles & oils to produce wonderful effects

In Two Books

Compiled and Selected from the most ancient and learned Rabbies. And the most celebrated, Chaldean, Arabian, Persian, Egyptian, Assyrian, Indian, and Cretian, Phylosphers *(sic)*.
Scientifically arranged and now made practicable.

By, W.H. Ibbett."

Although the art of drawing up talismans was well known to anyone who was interested in magic, the art of 'Talismanic Sculpture' was not so common.

The presentation of this material makes page referencing more complex as it is presented in two volumes, with each volume beginning with page 1.

Volume I. Pages 1-182
Volume II. Pages 1-111

Page numbers referring to the second volume should therefore be quoted as 'II-xx' rather than just 'xx.'

Ibbett, like his peers of the late 18th century onwards, appears to have been very active in many of the social groups and occult organizations of his time, something that must have kept him rather busy with the ever-growing popularity of such ventures in Victorian England.

He was an avid collector of fine art and antiquities and would seem to have traded in both commodities, although it is unknown whether that was his main profession. Of course, Ibbett's other great passion was the occult sciences, and he would buy and sell books, manuscripts and possibly an assortment of esoteric objects. Ibbett would advertise his Occult Catalogues regularly within the occult and spiritual periodicals of that period that passed actively from hand to hand, in which one could easily find advertisements such as:

"ASTROLOGY AND OCCULT SCIENCES.

W. H. IBBETT, BOOK & PICTURE DEALER, 34, Goswell St., London, E. C., Opposite Charterhouse Wall, has on Sale a large collection of Paintings of ancient and modern art. Works on the above sciences comprising Alchemical Manuscripts, Agrippa, Barrett's *Magus*, Butler, Ball, Blagrave, Colley, Culpepper, Flud, Gadbury, Gregory, Goad, Sibley, Raphael, Wharton, Zadkiel, &c.

N. B. Extracts from White's *Ephemerises* from 1800 to the present year [1858], sent post free to all parts, on receipt of the time and date required, inclosing six postage stamps. Books on Alchemy, Magic, Astrology, and the Occult Sciences, bought or exchanged."[4]

Ibbett was not shy and he promoted the following catalogue of occult books in the same year as he was writing the present manuscript.

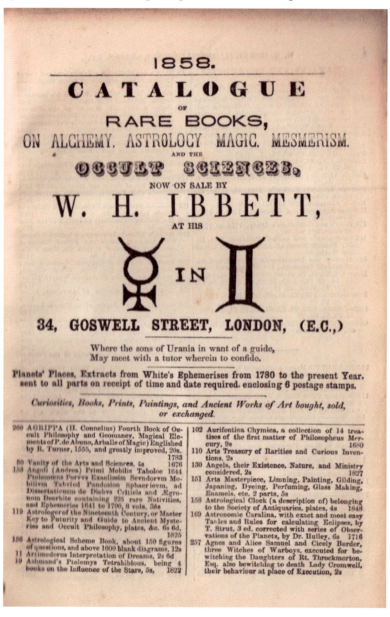

---

[4] *Astrologers' Magazine and Philosophical Miscellany* - Vol. 1, No 4. January 1858.

As shown in this advertisement the description of his home address as ☿ in ♊ portrays it as a place of clear communication and learning, as well as Mercury representing magic and the occult arts generally.[5] As indicated in the advert, Ibbett's interests also included alchemy and mesmerism.

The small verse about Urania in this advert is a certain indication that Ibbett, like Francis Barrett before him, was offering tuition or classes in astrology, and maybe magic.

Another advert: -

> *"Alchemy, Astrology, and*
>
> *Magic*
>
> ## A CATALOGUE of BOOKS
>
> *on the OCCULT SCIENCES, forwarded*
>
> *Free, on receipt of a Postage Stamp to*
>
> *W. H. IBBETT, 34. Goswell Street, London,*
>
> *E. C."*[6]

The Victorian Grimoire

The pages of this grimoire are beautifully written in English, perhaps one of the best executed Victorian manuscript I have ever seen. It certainly gives Frederick Hockley a run for his money. This grimoire contains one of the most beautifully drawn sets of the 7 Planetary Spirits, their Sigils, Angels and Intelligence seals drawn very carefully from the planetary squares which are rendered both in Hebrew and numerically. These show how the seals and characters fit exactly over the cells of the Planetary Table of Hebrew letters. This is followed by examples for specific spirits such as Barzabel. Astrological details are worked into the text, but solely for magical reasons.

Precise drawings of the structure of a thurible are sketched, followed by very sharp and clear drawings of the characters of the 15 Behenian fixed stars. The talismans related to them follow, one being for example for the Head of Algol. Various other types of talismans are drawn and explained including the Characters of the Nine Chambers and a selection of talismans owned by

---

[5] This address was just a few doors up the road from my old offices in Goswell Road which I occupied at the turn of the century, and so located in an area I knew well. S.S.
[6] *Notes and Queries*, London: OUP, Series 2, Vol. 5, Pt. 1, January-June 1858.

famous men, some familiar and others very rare. The talisman attributed to Charles 5th of Germany for example, is obviously a talisman of Mars, which the text recommends should be cut on a plate of polished wrought iron, or failing that on virgin parchment. There are talismans drafted in the name of other less well known angels such as Muriel, a protector of mariners at sea.

Although *The Master Key* sounds like a rather boastful title for a work by an almost unknown occultist, I think you will find as you read through it that there is a lot of knowledge here that needs to be preserved and used.

How active Ibbett himself was within the actual magical fraternities or spiritual groups of the time is unknown. Considering his keen interest, and the extent of his knowledge, one could speculate that he was indeed an active member. There is a strong indication that he may have been a full participating member of the *Society of the Mercurii* which was an occult fraternity that operated in London in the early 19th century. Its membership list reputedly included such names as Edward Bulwer Lytton (author of *Zanoni*), Edward Lyman Blanchard, Emma Hardinge Britten (a well-known spiritualist and occult author), her husband William Britten, George W. Graham, John Cavendish Dudley, John Palmer, John Varley, Kasper Hauser (a German foundling with a strange history), the Earl of Stanhope, Philip Henry Stanhope (an antiquarian and politician), Richard Cosway[7] (possibly a founding member), Richard Francis Burton (the explorer),[8] Richard James Morrison ("Zadkiel"), Robert Cross Smith ("Raphael"), Sir Charles Wyke, and Thomas Oxley, quite an amazing array of personalities.

A clue to his link with the *Mercurii* presents itself in several ways. It would seem that Ibbett was involved at one time with the publication of some of Robert Cross Smith's material and as a result would probably have been acquainted with him. Robert Cross Smith (1795-1832),[9] more commonly known by his pen name "Raphael" was an English astrologer, spiritualist and known to be an active member of the *Society of the Mercurii*.

---

[7] Cosway (1742 – 1821) painted a number of my ancestors, several as miniatures. S.S.
[8] Burton wrote many books, mostly as translations from Arabic and Persian, including *The Kama Sutra of Vatsyayana* (1883), *The Book of the Thousand Nights and one Night* (1885) (popularly known as *The Arabian Nights*), *The Perfumed Garden of the Shaykh Nefzawi* (1886), *The Supplemental Nights to the Thousand Nights and one Night* (seventeen volumes 1886–98) and *The Kasidah*. He reputedly knew 29 languages, and his Arabic was so good that he could travel to Mecca on Haj, disguised as a Muslim, an action and destination that was completely banned to foreigners. He was buried in Mortlake in a concrete replica tent, built just a few blocks from John Dee's old house.
[9] For more information refer to Skinner & Clark, *Clavis or Key to the Mysteries of Magic by Rabbi Solomon translated by Ebenezer Sibley*, Singapore: Golden Hoard, 2018.

The present Ibbett manuscript, a beautifully penned, meticulously laid out, and decorated work, can bear witness to the clear influence in design of this *Society*, with Ibbett using the illustration of a key on the opening title page of the manuscript,[10] a formula often used by Smith in his publications. Not only this, but within the second book of Ibbett's manuscript one can't help but notice the similarities between the decorative capitals and boarders used within it which can also be found within the *Book of Oberon*[11] a manuscript that at that time would have still been in the care of both Smith and other inner circle members of the *Mercurii*.

One small correction was made in line with Ibbett's specific instructions: the angel boxes on the Table of Mars and Table of Venus were swapped.

Ibbett started his Magnum Opus in June of 1854 and created what is essentially a complete course in magic, a master grimoire that most certainly stands head and shoulders above other grimoires of that period, and which is certainly comparable with Francis Barrett's *Magus*. The first volume of the manuscript was completed on the 8th of November 1857.[12] The second volume probably took a similar time of three years to complete. Sadly, we have no further information as to where it travelled after Ibbett's demise, but whatever its past may have been, it did eventually find its way into the collection of the *Bibliotheca Lindesiana*, the library of The Earls of Crawford and Balcarres, from Haigh Hall, Wigan, Lancashire which is confirmed by the presence of that bookplate on page **4**.

From there it was purchased by Mrs. Enriqueta Rylands in 1901 from James Ludovic Lindsay, 26th Earl of Crawford on behalf of the John Rylands Library. Today it continues to reside within the University of Manchester special collections.

---

[10] A hand coloured version of which appears on the dust jacket.
[11] Folger Shakespeare Library MS V.b.26 – Book of Magic, with instructions for Invoking Spirits, etc., 1577-1583. Published as *The Book of Oberon: A Sourcebook of Elizabethan Magic* by Harms, Clark & Peterson, Woodbury: Llewellyn, 2015.
[12] The opening page has a Victorian 'speech bubble' which proclaims "Begun June 1854." The last line of the first Book reads "Nov[embe]r 8[th] / [18]57 ☉ 9 PM." We could guess that the second Book took maybe another 3 years, giving a dating range of 1854-1860 for the whole work.

THE MASTER KEY.
to
Ancient Mystery.

To Unlock the Secret Caverns of the Magi, and Restore to Light the whole Art of the

Occult Science
of
Talismanic Sculpture.

Which for Centuries have been lost being hid under the Cloak of Mystery and buried in the grave of Enigma Elucidating the Mysterious Tables of

Numbers, Angels, Spirits, Characters, Hierogliphies and Alphabets.

Also explaining their Methods of forming by Art

——— TALISMANIC. ———

Images, Tablets, Amulets, Rings Chrystals, Glasses, Lamens, &c.

Enchantments, Spells, Facinations, Bindings and preparing curious Compositions as Candles Oils to produce Wonderfull effects

——— In Two Books ———

Compiled and Selected from the most Ancient and learned Rabbies, and the most Celebrated, Chaldean, Arabean, Persian, Egyptian, Assyrian, Indian, and Cretian, Phylosophers.

Scientifically aranged and now made practicable.

By W. H. Ibbett,

AN INDEX

of all the Chapters in this Work, and what are Contained in them

BOOK 1st

		Page
Chap 1	A Table of letters according to various Tongues shewing the true proportions Correspondencies and reduction of letters, to the Celestial Signs and Planets; and the Wonderful Power of Man	5
Chap 2	Of the Parts of Man that each Planet Governs & the diseases which each Rules	10
	Man the Micrososm or little World	11
Chap 3	Of the Diseases the Body of Man is subject to under the Twelve Signs of the Zodiac	13
	The Temporature of the Planets	13
Chap 4	Of the friendship & Enmity of the Planets	14
Chap 5	That all inferior things are subject to the Superiour	19
	Tables of Characters suited to the Latin and Hebrew Alphabets	21
	Tables of Chaldean Characters suited to the Latin	22
	Tables, Melchim Writing of Angels, also Writing Called passing the River	23
	Tables of the Divine Names & Numbers of the Seven Planets	24
	The Square Table of ♄, his Seals, Characters of his Intelligence, Spirit, & the Sigil of his day	26
	The Same of ♃	27
	The Same of ♂	28
	The Same of ☉	29
	The Same of ♀	30
	The Same of ☿	31
	The Same of ☽	32

		Page
	The Characters of the Seven Angels Ruling over the Seven Planets	34
Chap 6	The Use of the Tables of Divine Names and Numbers, and the Seven square tables of the Planets, shewing how the Magical Characters are extracted, with Examples	35
	Of Characters drawn from things themselves by certain likeness, with the Natures of the Signs, Planets & Triplicities, &c	39
Chap 7	An Ecsplainnation of the Signs Commanding, Obeying, Oposite, Fixed, Movable & Common, the four Triplisities & Seynings or Conjunctions of the Planets	40
Chap 8	Of the Trades and Proffesions & occupations of men under the Seven Planets, when well or ill situated or Fortunate & unfortunate at the Birth of the Native	41
Chap 9	Of the Seven Planets, the names of their Angels ruling their days, and their various Colours belonging to them, and an Explanation of their uses in the Talismanic Art, also the 12 Signs	43
Chap 10	Of Wonderful Phenomenous produced from certain compositions, made by Art as Lamps Candles &c	45
	The Thuribalum Magica or vessel for the burning of the Perfumes in	47
	Of the Characters of the Behenian or fixed Stars, their degrees places & natures with Talismans and Images	50
Chap 11	Talismans Medical, & Revealed, which were in the Possession of great Men in the 15th & 16th Century with full explanations	53

		Page
Chap 12	Description & Explanation of the proceeding Talismans their use & time of Making	67
	Talismans of the 12 Signs of the Zodiac	77
	Discription of the Same	80
	A Table of the 28 Mansions of the Moon their various properties &c pon the Talismanic Ant	86
	Planetry Table for extracting the names of the Angels of each Planet with the Original Hebrew Notes for Good & Evil	88
	Table of the 12 Signs with the Hebrew Notes for extracting the Good & Evil Angels	90
	Tables of Numeral Transpositions	92
Chap 13	Explanations of the Tables of Numeral Transpositions from the Unit to the Thousand & Examples	95
	Table of Right Commutations, with Hebrew Notes	100
	Table of Averse Commutations with &a	102
	Examples to the above Tables	104
Chap 14	An Explanation of the Planetry Tables of Letters, which the Ancient Cabala used for extracting the Names of Angels Good & Evil, to work any desired effect from the Seven Planets and twelve Signs	105
Chap 15	An Explanation of the Tables of the Seven Planets their squares, Compass & Numbers, with their Divine Names Intelligcies & spirits and their Characters set over them, with the names of their Angels of their days, their Sigels Planets & Signs governing them	110
	The different Characters of Good & Evil Angels, drawn out of the table of the Square of ♀ with the different Characters of the Transpositions both from the Numeral & Commutation Tables as examples to Fig. 1. 2. 3 &c from the Word Love.	119

22

		Page
Chap 16	A Table of Essential Dignities &c of the Planets with explanation	120
Chap 17	Demonstrating the use Nature & Reason of The Faces of the Planets	123
Chap 18	The Impediments of the Moon, to be observed in the Talismanic Art	127
	Explanation of the Table of Elections of the Moon, with table of aspects to the Planets	129
Chap 19	Table to find the Length of the Planetry hour for every 10 days in each Month through the Year	130
	A Planetary Table shewing what hour each Planet rules every day & night in the Year	131
	The Seven Planets. Called the 7 governors of the World & their Names in this Art by the Magi	135
Chap 20	Of Imprecations & Joinings many words together as Sentences & Verses, and of the Virtues and the Astrictions of Charms	139
	Five Magic Circles as drawn by Art	142
	The figures of the Divine Letters of the Seven Planets, which are used by the Ancients in framing all kinds of Talismans Seals &c	145
Chap 21	Of the Sacred Characters of the Seven Planets and their use in the Talismanic Art	146
Chap 22	A four fold table of the names of the four Quarters, their heads, their Angels, and of the Sun & Moon for this Art	148
	Table of Names of the Planetry hours, numbers, & the Angels ruling both day & night	149
Chap 23	The Angels ruling the day, the Air & Heavens their ministers, & to what quarter of the World they belong. The Perfumes their offices, and Conjurations	153

		Page
Chap 24	Four Examples for framing four Circles for the four Quarters of the Year, Spring Summer Autumn & Winter, with their uses	161
	The full Explanation of the Wonderful Pentacle of Soloman, with three other Originals	163
	Various inscriptions to be engraved in the outside Circles of Talismans,	171
Chap 25.	How to Make the Renowned Electrum for all Magical & Talismanic purposes. as Lumans, Bells, Speculams, Images, Rings Seals Tablets &c	173
Chap 26	Of Holy Pentacles, Sigils &c their nature, how made & Compounded, Also the use made of them in this Art	174
	Verses from various parts of the Psalms appropriate to the Talismanic Art	181

BOOK. II.

Chap 1	Of the Four Elements	1
Chap 2	A three fold Consideration of the Elements	2
Chap 3	The Wonderfull natures of Fire & Earth	4
Chap 4	The Wonderfull natures of Water Air and Winds	6 / 6
Chap 5	The Various kinds of Compounds what relation they stand to the Elements, and what relation there is betwixt the Elements themselves & the Souls, senses and Dispositions of Man	9
Chap 6	Of the Virtues of things Natural, depending immediately upon the Elements	11
Chap 7	Of the Occult Virtues of things, how Occult Virtues are infused into the several kinds	

			Page
	of things by the Idea's throught the help of the Soul of the World, And the rays of the Stars, and what things abounds most with this Virtue	12
Chap	8	How it is that particular Virtues are infused into particular Individuals even of the same Species. and Shewing from whence Occult Virtues of things proceeds	14
Chap	9	Of the spirit of the World, what it is and how by way of Medium it unites Occult Virtues to their Subjects	18
Chap	10	Of the Composition and Harmony of the Human Soul, and of the necessary Observations, for all Magical & Talismanical experiments	21
Chap	11	The Divine Gifts recived by Man from above through the several Orders of the Intelligences of the Heavens above by the power of Mans Soul, in the mind reason & Imaginations	26
Chap	12	Of the Sun and Moon, and the Considerations of their most potent & wonderfull Power in all Magical purposes	30
Chap	13.	Of the Twenty Eight Mansions of the Moon. & their Virtues, the true motion of the heavenly Bodies to be observed in the eight Sphere, Planetary hours &c	33
Chap	14	The Composition of Fumes appropriated to Each Planet, to be used as occasion may Require, as Recommended by the Ancient, for perfecting the work	37
		Prayers &c to be used on begining or making any Talisman	39
Chap	15	Of the Images in the Zodiac, What virtues they receive from the Stars, obeying the will of the Operator	41
Chap	16	Of the Images of the Faces of the Signs & of Images without the Zodiac, Called fixed Stars	43

Chap 17	Of the Images or Talismans made under the Head & Tail of the Dragon, called the Moons Nodes	50
Chap 18	Of the Images or Talismans made under the 28th Mansions of the Moon, & their wonderfull Properties & Effects.	51
Chap 19	Of the virtues of places, and what Places are most suitable & appropriated to every Star or Constellation	58
Chap 20	Celestial observations particularly to be observed in the Manufacturing of some Images, Rings, Talismans, Tablets, & with Examples	59
Chap 21	Of Talismanic Rings, their Metals, Compositions and Manner of making them according to the ancient custom of the Magi, with Examples	65
Chap 22	Of certain Images, whos likeness resemble no kind of Celestial figure but only the likeness of that which the Imaginative fancy of the Worker desires	66
Chap 23	An Account of some Wonderfull Talismans which has been found in the Eastern countries & their natures and power accounted for by some of the most Learned Philosophers	71
Chap 24	Divination Per Crystallum, containing the Divination by the Crystal or Berill Glass, from an Ancient M.S. in the Library of Queen Charlotte of Buckingham Palace, called the Book of Solomon the Almadel	75
	The Conjuration	80
	The Divine Call	82
	The Spirit Bassago how to call & obtain him in a Glass or Chrystal Sphere	84
	The Bond or Obligation of the Spirit Bassago	87
	Prayers &c to be used for the same purpose	89

		Page
Chap 25.	Of The Power and Virtue of Resemblance and Imagination through the Arts & Sciences	94
Chap 26.	Three Doubts of the Existance Efficacy, & Virtues of Talismans, obtained and retained by the Influences of the Stars. Answered	100
Chap 27.	A few Useful remarks to all Curious readers Shewing them how to find out by Similitude the Virtues of things so that a General and proper Judgement may be Assertained through the whole System of Nature	108

The MASTER KEY to Ancient Mystery.

BOOK. I

The things that hath been, it is that which shall be, and that which is done is that which shall be done, and there is nothing new under the Sun;   Solomon. Eccles – 1.9.

PREFACE

To enable the curious researcher satisfactorily to investigate and reap much profit from this Celestial and sublime Science I have Selected from the Works & Traditions of the Ancients. The wonderfull effects produced by Talismanic Sculpture, which has been hid for Centuries under the Cloak of Mystery and buried in the Grave of Enigma – And have removed that cloud and opened that Grave, for those whose delight it is to contemplate and Study the surprising works of Nature and who are desirous of becomming Adepts in the Occult Science, But the Sceptic will be dis-appointed & left destitute in the shade of their own Ignorance, You therefore Sons of Wisdom search diligently in this Book, which is a Cabinet of choice Secrets, for to You only do I offer them. For it cannot be expected that every Man is endued with the same degree of Knowledge or follow the same pensuits, can we supose that Sir Robert Peel, who is a Great Statesman is equally as great in Chemistry, as such it is most illiberal for any Man to condemn anothers Works because he is Ignorant of them. Shall the whole Art of Physic be condemned, because an eminent Physician commits an Error or Arithmatic be cast aside because an intricate question cannot be resolved, It is a hard matter to show a reason why the Glo-worm Shines by night; why the Needle points to the North or why the little Remora, stops a Ship upon full Sail, by hanging upon the Keel, yet the first two is obvious to –

the Eyes of all men, and the last experienced by many Nav-
-igators. I believe few will deny, that the Heavens as Med-
-iums, produce upon and in the Earth the growth of Veg-
-etables and Minerals. Now if Some veneriferous Veg-
-etables or Mineral, being taken into the Body of Man
hath power to destroy life, or Some other, endued with a
Cordial property hath power to restore decayed Nature;
Much more then may the Influence of the Stars, which gave
Such Vegetables or Minerals their Nature & Being, effect the
Death or preserve the life of Mankind

("January 21st 1693. The moon having been eclipsed that
night, the greatest part of the sick died, about the very
hour of the eclipse, and Some were even struck with
Sudden death" – Dr. Mead on Planetary Influence,)
which the Scripture doth evidently manifest, "That the Stars in
their Courses fought against Sisera" (Judges. 5. 20.) which also
Testify the Truth of Magic; for Moses being skilled in Magic
Commanded Aaron to cast down his rod and it became a Ser-
-pent, and Pharoah called the wise men and the Sorcerers
and they cast down every man his rod and they became Serp-
-ents. The Waters Changed into blood. The bringing forth of
Frogs &c. was also done in the presence of Pharoah by the
Enchantments of the Magicians of Egypt (Exodus. 7 & 8) which
is proof that the Egyptian Priests, Miracles to have been as
Real as those of Moses. Balaam was a Magician and used
Enchantments (Numbers 23 & 24) and Elisha commanded Gehazi
to take his staff, and go his way, and if thou meet any man salute
him not, & if any man salute thee, answer him not again, and
lay my staff upon the face of the Child (2d Kings. 4. 29.) by the same
power did Elisha Cause the head of the Iron axe, which was lost
to rise to the top of the Water (2 Kings 6: 5 & 6) but some will have it

that Talismans being made of Metal &c are Material and dead
and as such can possess no power, I answer, of what power or virtue
did the Prophets bones possess (which was dead & Material) which as the dead
man, touched he revived and stood up on his feet (2ᵈ Kings 13, 21) –
Sensitive as I am of the deep rooted prejudice which exists
against works of this kind, and in an age when every-
-thing is dispised which does not in the least Contribute
to the gain of Gold, while the people are led by a
Spurgeonite Clergy on the one hand, who are forever Ranting
in opposition to each other, Preaching up Passive obedience, while
themselves live in Luxury, and on the other, by the Medical
faculty, whos opinions is like the wind ever changing; That
gave so much Satisfaction, at the late trial at the Old Baily
where The Public was astonished to hear one doctor swear
his belief that death was caused by 'epileptic convulsions
with tetanic complications'; another that it was the natural
result of 'angina pectoris' a third and fourth, that they
did not know the cause of Death, It is not surprising
when such men out of mer Curiosity examine such works
which are scarce, their attention is arrested at the Sight of
a Number of Tables Characters Hieroglifics &c and being
desirous of Som information, Studies Closly, but finding
unnoticed or wrapt up in Mystry that part he is desir-
-ous of obtaining, Feels disapointed, Throws aside the
art with disgust and ever after considers it as meer
fables and all that have to do with it as Cheats and impostures

  The mind of Man is so deprav'd that what,
   It cannot comprehend 'twill seek to blot,
Wether what I have here don will advance this
Science of Talismanic Sculpture, must be left
to the Readers Judgment, but I flatter myself

he will find Rules Explanations of the Tables with Examples, that cannot be met with elsewhere, and have this advantage, that he may Consult them with the greatest Rediness, for which I have examined the works of both Ancient & Modern Authors, and have brought the whole within a narrow Compass, However I shall think my time (which has been the leasure hours of Night-) well employed, if it Conduce to advance this Sience and tends to place the Practice on a more Certain Foundation.

The Origen of the Word
Talisman

There is nothing in the world at large or in the whole Buisnefs of Philosophy that hath more perplexed our New Philosophers than this subject concerning Images Figures &c as Talismans made under certain Constellations the Manufactoring of which is called Talismanic Sculpture. by the Ancients this science was Divinely Contemplated, but now in disrepute through the Ignorance of the times, Therefore now let us consider the Origin of the word Talisman as is handed down to us by the ancient, They are in Hebrew מגן Maghen i.e a Scutcheon or Shield in Chaldea Egyptian, and Persian צלמניא, Tsilmenaia – which signify a figure or Image. In Arabick הטלמם. Talisman or טלסם Tsalisman, and in Greek ςοιχεία the Hebrew word Maghen though it signifies a Scutcheon or any other thing, noted with Hebrew Characters, the Virtue of which is like that of a Scutcheon. and though these Characters according to the opinion of those that are most versed in these Theological Mysteries ans some kind of Imperfect Image that is Graven Carved or Painted, Maghen therefor properly signifies any piece of paper parchment or any other Matter marked or noted with Certain Characters – drawn from the great name of God Tetragrammaton or. the Great Name of God, of four Letters or from any other as will be shown in the Body of this work This word also Signifies though Improperly by these very figures and Images which we speak of, because that these as well as the Characters of the Tetragrammation serve as they say instead of a Buckler and Shield of defence against Enemies

Diseases, hurts &c. The Chaldea word Tsilmenaija or Talismoüth comes from the Hebrew צלם Tselem which signifies an Image, and the Arabic word Talismam may likewise have derived from the same root Talismam being corrupted from צלמם Tsalimam by the Transposition of one letter only. But the truth of this Conjecture is yet uncertain as it is not yet known from whence it first sprung. For the word Maghen signifies nothing but a Scutcheon which is very commonly known to all. Therefore is it very indifferent to me from whence the name first sprung I shall call them Talismans, and endevour to prove by an Argument at the end of the work Theire existance and power from the Celestial Influence in three different ways i.e first from the Influence of the Stars, by the power of Resemblance and by numerous experiments on Animals Vegatables Minerals &c

Alphabets appropriated to the Signs, Planets Numbers &c
Plate. 1.

1	2	3	4	5	6	7	8	9
5	♈				B	B		
7	♉				Γ	C		
8	♊				Δ	D		
9	♋				Z	F		
30	♌				K	G		
40	♍				Λ	L		
50	♎				M	M		
60	♏				N	N		
70	♐				Π	P		
90					P	R		
100	♒				G	S		
300	♓				T	T		
2	♄				Α	A		
3	♃				Σ	E		
4	♐				H	I		
20					I	O		
80					O	V		
200					Y	Icon		
400	☽				Ω	Vcon		
1	Terra				☉	K		
6	Aqua				Ξ	Q		
	Aer				Φ	X		
10	Ig ms				X	Z		
	Spus				Ψ	H		

Chapter 1

A table of Letters according to various tongues showing the true proportions, correspondencys, and reductions of letters to the Celestial signs and planets and the wonderful Power of Man.

The Omnipotant God, after he made the Heavens the Earth, and all things therein; he made Man after his own Image; and to compleat his work, he gave to Man Mind and speech, he also gave him dominion and power over the Earth, the Beast of the Earth, the Birds of the Air, and the Fish in the Sea; And Man first escercised that speech, by giving proper names to all, God also by his divine providence, divided the speech of Man into a diversity of languages, which languages, according to their diversity have received various and proper Characters in writing, consisting in their certian order number, and figure, which were not so disposed by mere chance, or by the week judgement of Man, but from the divine <u>intelligences</u> whereby they should agree with the Celestials, their bodies and virtues. But of all the writings that of the Hebrews is the most sacred in all the figures and characters, The points of Vowels and tops of accents is more consisting in matter, form, and spirit, In the seat of God which is the Heaven, where the position of the Stars where first made (and the most learned Rabbies testify) after them in figure are formed the letters of the Celestial Mysteries, as by their figure, form, and signification, such is the numbers signified by them, as also the various harmonies of their conjunctions, they have undertaken by the signature of their letters, the forms of their characters and their signature, simpleness, composition, seperation, crookedness, directness, defect,—

6

abounding greatness smallness crowning opening shutting order, transmutation joyning together to gether and revolution of letters and of their points and tops and by the supputation of numbers by the letters of things signified to explain all things how they proceed from the first cause and how they are to be again reduced down to the same the Rabbies also divide their Hebrew alphabet viz into what they term twelve simple seven double and three mothers which signifies the characters of the twelve Signs of the Zodiac the seven planets and three elements Fire Water and Earth for Air is accounted by them no element but as a glue or cement and a spirit of the elements to these they appoint tops and points which by those the aspects of the planets and signs together with the elements the working spirit i e the mind and the speech of Man and the Air the truth of all things have been and are brought forth so by these characters of letters and points signify the things brought forth the names of all things are appointed the regular names of all things explained and carry with them every whare their essence and virtues which changed by us at our pleasure loose all power and activity as our language bears no kind of affinity in either number weight or measure without which nothing can be produced Therefor the ancient Magi com̃mandeth that they are kept without corruption in their own characters however barbarous or ancient they may appear to us for in them are concealed the mysteries and conveyances of the omnipotency and revealed to man from above for out of them breath forth the harmony of the Godhead and being consecrated

by divine assistance all creatures above fear them
those below tremble at them the Angels Reverence them
all evil spirits are afraid of them every creature doth
honour and every Religion adore them therefore they
with fervency enable man by their power which in
them are the foundation of the World and of all
creatures that is therein which are named by it and
by their revolutions every creature and thing in exis-
-tence receive its name also every saying being and
virtue which he receives from above to work wonder-
-ful things above nature the appearances of which
must strike the ignorant with astonishment and judge
it to be supernatural agency. I shall now explain the
several meanings which the Ancient Magi made the
comparison of these letters to the planets Signs &c First
the Aloph א Vau ו and Yod י they being the three
letters of original pronunciation, without which no
language can be formed; but from which all language
springs; they therefore placed the א for the Earth, being
the Mother of all the Creation out of which all things first
sprang; the ו to the Water which assists all Vegetation,
and nurishes the same and the י to the Fire, because it is
in every thing and invigorates all, without which, for
want of vital heat, every thing would perish; as such
י ו א represents the three Elements, Earth, Water and fire;
the Air being accounted no Element, but termed by the
Philosophers a Medium or Glue receiving every thing into
itself, joyning things together, and is the resounding Spirit
of the Worlds instrument; receiving into itself the influencies
of all the Celestial bodies, and communicates them to the
other Elements, The seven double ת ר פ כ ד ג ב which are

(without what the Hebrews calls dagash) are very soft in their pronunciation, which softness is the production of harmony They therefore attributed them to the seven planets, they containing in themselves in their numbers motions and periods perfect harmony which is termed Celestial harmony. The other twelve ש ק צ ע ס נ מ ל י ט ח ז ה; are called simple letters, and those they have placed to the Signs of the Zodiac they, being recipient or receivers of the Planets called their Houses in which they perform and distribute their various powers, either good or Evil; as Ourselves in our own houses, perform what we think requisite, either for the Good of ourselves, or for the good, or evil of others; by giving power to our coleagues as our instruments, to exe--cute our desires, in such manner do the Planets act by our wills Preceeding I have given the Alphabets, first the number answering to each Planet, Sign &c the second line are the twelve Signs, seven Planets &c The third is the Afsyriac Characters answering the Signs Planets &c The fourth line is the old Hebrew Characters, answering the same, The fifth line is the Modern Hebrew answering in the same manner The Sixth is the Greek Characters placed in the true order The Seventh is the Latin Char--acters or letters all which are placed exactly corresp--onding the Signs Planets, numbers &c and in the same correct manner can any other Alphabet be placed for this Science but the English, that being deficient in character, which must render it imperfect. therefor nothing can be produced therefrom to answer any effect. As such I would advise my curious artist, to work by the Alphabets all--ready noticed in the preceeding Page, which will be quite sufficient for any Practioner to perfect himself

in this sublime Science. The eight is an alphabet of Charac-
-ters or scales which by its use as the others in which
the Magi rendered their works Mysterious; also the
ninth which are the Characters of the Stars that they
called Celestial out of which alphabets the Characters
of the Behenian; or first Stars for this science are
compounded Therefor from these letters numbers were
first founded and from numbers harmony was produced and all harmony consists of sounds or voices or
from voices as singing which is produced by the breath
for sound is a breath and the voice is animated —
breath speech is a breath pronounced with sound from
the voice signifying something the Spirit of which pro-
-ceedeth from out of the mouth with both sound and
voice voice is sent forth from the inward cavity of the
breast and heart by the assistance of the Spirit by
which together with the tongue forming and striking
the narrow passages of the mouth and by the assistance
of the other vocal organs articulate sounds were pro-
-duced and from those articulations the elements of spee-
-ch first originated by which interpretations the
secret motions of the mind are laid open. The
formation or nature of the human voice is very obscure and
cannot be comperehended in what manner it is made or what
it realy is I never knew either an ancient or modern
Philosopher who could ever account for it. A modern
Philosopher, from him I never can exect it for he is too
much busied to obey that great command of Man
know thy self All music consisteth in voices, in sounds
and hearing sound without air cannot be audible though
it is necessary for hearing yet as air it is not nor can

it be perceived by any sense for sight seeth it not being of no color nor the ears unless from voice nor the small unless oderiferous &c nor the taste unless it be Sapid, nor the touch unless it be cold hot or solid &c. Man is composed of the Elements, is evident his name first given him by God is an indelible proof of truth, which cannot be doubted, For God Said let us make Man after our own Image, and God made man from the Earth and Breathed into him the Breath of Life, and Called his name Adam Now it may be asked, why called Adam more than any other name, that can have no Analogy? To this I answer the name given to every thing on the Earth has an affinity and that the very name Adam given to man proves of what he really is and of what he is compounded i.e This Hebrew name אדם Adam. The first letter signifies אפר Epher i.e Dust the second letter דם. Dam i.e Blood and the third מרה Marah i.e Bitterness: which Intimates that Man is nothing but Bitterness and Sorrow Corrupt Blood and Sin & lastly but Dust and Ashes

Chap 2

Of the Parts of Man, that each Planet rules; and the Diseases of Man, that each Planet governes.

The twelve parts of man Governed by the Signs, are ♈ the Head ♉ the Neck ♊ the arms ♋ the Breast ♌ the Heart ♍ the Belly ♎ the Navel ♏ the Secrets ♐ the Thighs ♑ the Knees ♒ the Legs ♓ the Feet, When Planets are in these Signs Fortunate, diseases are Prevented and Cured by this Art as hereafter follows And if they are unfortunately Plased, Diseases not only follows. but are encreased to a Degree

Man
The Microcosm or little World.

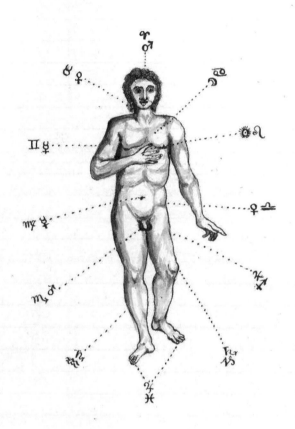

The twelve Parts of Man which are governed by the twelve Signs of the Zodiac

♄ Rules the Spleen, Right Ear, Bladder, Bones and Teeth
Diseases, of the Stone, Deafness, Dropsey, Scurvy, Canker Consumption, Black Jaundice, Quartan Ague, Leprosy Cholic and Rheumatism

♃ Rules the Lungs, Ribs, Arteries, Liver, Pulse, Gristles and expulsive faculty.

12

Diseases Pleurasy, Cramps, Appoplesy, Inflamation of the Liver, Shortness of Breath and Convulsions

♂ Rules the Veins, Left Ear, Head, Miseriacks, Secrets and Attractive Faculty,

Diseases, Pestilence, Imposthumes, Putrid fevers, Yellow Jaundice, Erysipelas, Blotches, Bloody flux, Tartarian Agues, Fistulas, Wounds (but chiefly in the Head and Face) and the Small Pox

☉ Rules the Right eye, Heart, Vital Spirits and Sinews

Diseases, Swoonings, Palpitations, Heart Burning, Bad or Sore Eyes, and all disease the Eyes are Subject to

♀ Rules the Womb, Reins, Privites, Neck Breasts and all answering to Generation,

Diseases, all Diseases in the Womb, Fits of the Mother, Gonorhea, Priapism, Stranguary, flus of the Stomach Quinzey, Lues benerea,

☿ Rules the Imagination, and the whole Intellectual Faculty, or Part, Memory Tongue, Hands and Fingers

Diseases, Phrensy, Meagrims, Deprivation of Sense Lethargy, Duting, Hoarseness, Phthisick Impediment of the speech, Tongue and Rheum,

☽ Rules the Brain, Left Eye of Man and the Right Eye of Woman, the Bladder Intestines and Stomach

Diseases, Eppilefsy or Falling Sickness, Cholic, Menstrous, and Oppilations

Note By the ☽ being Combust with the ☉ all and every specie of Insanity is caused

Chap 3
Of the Diseases the Body of Man is subject to under the Twelve Signs of the Zodeac

♈ All diseases of the Head, as Vertigo Lethargy Epilepsy Apoplesey, Head Ach Tooth Ach Pimples in the face &c

♉ Rheums and Defluxions, and all Diseases in the Throat, Quincey, Kings Evil &c

♊ All Putrefaction of the Blood Corruption, Aches, Dislocations, wind in the veins and all Distempers belonging to the Arms

♋ Indigestions, sharp Defluxions on the Lungs Coughs and all Defects in the Breasts Ribs and the Plurisy,

♌ All Choleric Diseases, Burning fevers Yellow Jaundice Tremblings Qualms &c

♍ All defects of the Gastric Vessels Obstruction of the Spleen and Hypochondriac, Melancholy

♎ All Imposthumes, or Ulcers in the Kidneys or Reins. Retention of Urine Gravel, Stone Heat in the Kidneys, and all Diseases Common to those parts

♏ Stone in the Bladder, Running of the Reins, venereal Disease Fistulas, and all other diseases the Secrets are subject to

♐ Fistulas Sciatica, Falls from Horses and all hurts by them and from all other Beasts Similar

♑ Leprosy, Itch and Scabs, Corruptions &c and all Diseases the Knees, are liable to, Sprains Fractures &c

♒ Gouts, Cramps and all Infirmities of the Legs

♓ Aches Lameness Gout in the feet Corns, and all Diseases of the Feet

The Temperature of the Planets

♄ . Is Cold and Dry, Melancholy and evil
♃ . Is Hot and Moist, Temperate and Good
♂ . Is Hot and Dry, Choleric and evil
☉ . Is Hot and Dry, and Choleric
♀ . Is Cold and Moist, Phlegmatic and Fortunate
☿ . Is Convertible, in Nature and Mutable
☽ . Is Cold and Moist, and Phlegmatic

Chap 4

Of the friendships. and Enmity of the Planets

It is now requisite to know, that all things have friendships, and enmities from the largest to the smallest, hath something that it fears and dreads as an enemy, and that is destructive to it, and on the contrary something that cause it to rejoice in, and is delighted by its presence, and by which, it receives strength, So as in the elements, 🜂 is an enemy to 🜄 and the 🜁 to the 🜃 but yet they agree amongst themselves, Such is the Nature of the Celestials ☿ ♃ ☉ and the ☽ are friends to ♄, but ♂ and ♀ are his enemies. ♃ is in friendships with every Planet, but ♂ who is his his inveterate enemy, and ♂ is in enmity with all, but ♀ she is his only friend ♃ and ♀ love the ☉ but ♂ ☿ & the ☽ are his enemies ♀ is in friendships with all but ♄ whom she hates ♃ ♀ and ♄ are friends to ☿, The ☉ ☽ & ♂ are his enemies, ♃ ♀ & ♄ are friends to to the ☽, But ♂ and ☿ are her enemies, There is another kind of enmity which is much the strongest i.e. when they are in ☍ Houses as ♄ to the ☉ and the ☽ – ♃ to ☿ – ♂ to ♀, and their enmity is the strongest whose excaltations are ☍ as ♄ and the ☉ of ♃ and ♂ of ♀ and ☿ But their friendship when agreeing in nature substance and power. To them the strongest as ♂ with the ☉ – ♀ with the ☽, as ♃ with ♀ – Their friendship also whose excaltation is in the house of another as ♄ with ♀ – ♃ with the ☽ – ♂ with ♄ and the ☉ with ♂ – ♀ with ♃ and the ☽ with ♀. These dispositions therefor of friendships and enmity are nothing else but certain inclinations of things, the one to the other, desiring such and such things if it be absent, and a desire of moving towards it, unless it is hindred by another power, and to acquiese and delight in it when obtained, Shunning the Contrary, and dreading the approach of it, and not resting in, nor being content with it,

15

Therefor in rendering service to Man and curing diseases incident to his Body, which are soly caused by the Situations positions and transitions of the Planets, and their Aspects, in the twelve signs of Zodiac — As the Physician prescribes a Mixture of various things to cure the disease, So must the Practitioner of this Science, first Study well the Natures and effects of the Planets and Signs; after which make various Compounds of the same, in Talismans to work various Cures &c

For Example to performe Cures by the Talismanic art, we will say the Dropsy, this disease is well known to be a Watery Complaint Search for the means that may be proper to answer the desired effect, Therefore this disease consisting in Moisture, Take a matter to engrave upon opposite, i.e hot and Dry which must be a Metal under ☉ or ♂ which is Gold and Steel, as such, the substance is something Hot and Dry, Then choose for the Ascendant to work under, a sign hot and Dry likewise which if the ☉ is chosen, Gold must be the Matter and the Sign must be ♌, if ♂ is chose, Steel must be the Matter and ♈ the Sign to work under, and as it is necessary to choose some Star to which the Malady belongs, look in the tables of diseases under the Planets, and under ♄ is found the dropsy — but as it is necessary to have for Sympathy some very moist Star, Take the ☽ in her vain For as in curing the Bite of a viper by mixing some of its fat with the Antidote, In the same manner do they persue in curing and expelling all Watery humours, by making use of that Star which hath the greatest Affinity with the Watery humors, Also observing the Sign which relates to that part of the Body affected. This is the Counsel of a most Learned Physician

Oportet Medecum, Obsque defectu Scire, ubi axis Polaris ubi sit linea Meridiontis ubi oriens uby occedens &c

16

Now, that the Signs have more agreement with and have stronger influence upon one Part of the Body than another we are certainly taught by daily experience, for it is by Planets transitions in the Signs that the Sudden Changes of the Weather takes place, and the verious parts of the Body of Man is afflicted, and according to his Nature and temparature such are his afflictions If he is by Nature Cold and dry, his disease will tend to that nature. If he is Cold and Moist his disease will will be of that nature If he is Hot and Moist his afflictions will be of that Nature, and if he is Hot and dry such will be the nature of his disease, For these are the four temperatures of mans Body, and of these do the four Cholars consist, which are in the Composition of Man which Cholers are Governed by the four Triplities who are the Governors of the Seasons of the year Spring, Summer, Autumn, and Winter, Therefore according to the nature Man and of what Choler his Body abounds with most, that Choler is too great redundancy afflicts the Body, The Yellow Choler for instanstance if generated in the Body too much effects the whole system visibly (this commonly called the Bile) and if not kept under the secretian becomes deranged by their equilibrium being disturbed the Stomach being charged with such sharp humours becomes vitiated and rejects its nourishment, the Blood than in the grand resovoid of Nature, becomes tainted and in that state it is carried through the Anteries from thence conveyed into the vessels &c. and the Blood being thus tainted the whole Body becomes Diseased, and turns as Yellow as Saffron, which is called the Yellow Jaundice, Now by the tables of Diseases. you'l see ♂ is the Author of this disease and ♋ that of Indigestion, there ♂ passited in ♋ which Sign Governes the Breast &c. and ♂ you'l see by the Table has his fall there, therefor the Sign is injured by his presence and he is injured by being so posited he then in his regular course must pass through ♌ which governes the Heart, he there still remains injured and being in ♌ which Sign his Hot dry and Choleric, and ♂ hot Dry and Choleric the Body is overpowered by fever, tremblings quantoms and the Yellow Cholar. becomes more prevelant. if not got under the most extreems dangers follows as Hypochodriac &c. Now ♌ being a hot dry and Choleric Sign, the ☉ who is the planet belonging to it, he ruling the Heart vital Spirits Nerves &c The ☽ Ruling the Brain. she being Cold and Moist & Phlegmatic and she being posited within 8 degreet 30' before and after the ☉ let me ask what disease a man would be subject to under such Positions. If a Man is deranged in his Intellects you Call him a Lunatic again If a man hath the Sephyle you call it venerial the former derives its term Luna the ☽, and the later from ♀ See the Plate, P.11. ♏, ♂, which ♂ &c. the sign ♏, rules the parts of generation, and ♀ rules with her Sign the Navel &c ♀ being the friend of ♂ one Masculine the other feminine by the uniting of Sexes, and the act of Copulation the above mentioned disease is obtained, and that only when ♂ is in a peculiar position in the heavens with ♀. You see by the Plate, P.11. ♈ ♂ governeth the head, the ☽ and ♋ governs the Breast &c the ☉ & ♌ the heart &c, under the unfortunate position of these Planets, and the ☽ being in Combustion of the ☉, which is within 8° 30' before and after him. a man under such positions are always Lunatics, and every time the ☽ is thus situated he is then most violent

Thus Curiously contemplate the properties and principles of all things, and weigh correctly in the Scales of Nature the two chief points. Sympathy and antipathy. Attraction and

18

Repulsion, the two Waters, Divine and Human, The two Testaments, the two commands of Love, the two first dignities, the two Intellectual Creatures, an Angel and the Soul, the two great Lights of Heaven, the two Solstitis, the two equinoctials, the two Tropics, the two Elements which produce a living Soul i,e Earth and Water and lastly Number Weight and Measure by which every thing exist and Subsist, and by which are the Roots and foundations of all the Arts and Sciences possess yourself with the true knowledge of these Taking for your   Guides
The Three Theological Virtues, Faith, Hope, and Charity, and all is at your Command, Therefor Ask and you shall have, seek and you shall find
<u>Knock and it shall be opened</u>
The Triplicities of these signs, answer one to the other and agree with the Celestials, so do they agree in the members of the Body of Man, which is sufficiently manifest by experience, because if the feet are wet and cold, it immediately strikes into the belly, and breasts from which cause they are always affected and diseased. As the Signs governing both are of a Cold Nature which are ♍ and ♎ for which reason is why (in Medicinal application) when applied to one generally helps the other and by warming the feet, when a pain of the Belly is violent helpeth the pant and the pain very soon ceases Remember therefor this order and consider that all things, which are under any one of the Planets have a certain particular Aspect or inclination to those members attributed to that Planet, and especially to the signs which are called the houses, and exaltations These are the only situations requsite to work under in this

Science which is to tend to the general good of Mankind and is termed Sympathy

Chap 5

That all inferior things are subject to the Superior Heaven is a superior and greatest, and therin is contained Things Terrestial, but as in their cause only, and in a Celestial manner, The Earth is an inferior, and also Cont--aines things Celestial, But in a Celestial manner as to effect only, and from the strong impression the power of the ☉, makes on perticular things we call them Solary, also from the strong impression the power of the ☽ makes on perticular things we call Lunary so it stands good on the Animal, vegatable and mineral Kingdom, on which The ☉ ☽ and other Planets, makes strong impressions of their virtues, From whense it is that all kinds of things receive more operations, and properties as to their Natures, of the Planet they are under or governed by So it is with mans Body, it being divided into twelve parts and each part placed under the dominion or governed by one of the Twelve Signs of the Zodiac consequently all things which are under its influence. Sympathetically acts (wether animal vegatable or Mineral) and is good for that part of the Body, the Sign governs, As for Example ♌ governes the Heart of Man, which is the Sign belonging to the ☉, as such all Solary things are good for the Head & Heart by reason that ♌ being the House of ☉ and ♂ his Exaltation – (See the table Page 120) So things under ♂ are good for the Head and part of generation, by reason of ♈ and ♏. ♈ governing the Head and being the House of ♂ and ♏ also being his House, But to know how mans Body, is distributed to the Planets and Signs (See Page 11 Plate) the figure of a Man with the twelve Signs and Planets, that govern and rules each part

20

According to the Arabian system or doctrins the
☉ rules and have dominion over the Brain heart the thighs
marrow, right eye and the Spirits, also the tongue mouth
and the rest of organs of the senses & powers of imagination
☿, the splene, stomach, bladder womb right ear and the
faculty of Common Sense
♄ the liver and fleshy part of the Stomach
♃ the abdomen, and navel, (Hammons attributed to him) the
ribs, breast, bowels, blood, Arms, the right hand, the left ear
and all the natural powers
♂ the veins kidnies gall Bladder buttocks Back and motion
of the Sperm, and all the irascible powers. (some say the blood
♀ the kidnies, testicles, secrets, womb the seed and cupiscible, powers, as also the fat, flesh, belly breast navel
and all parts which serves to venereal acts, also the
Os sacrum, the back bone and loins, also the Head
mouth, from which is given & received the token &c of Love
☽, she challenges the whole body & every member thereof
according to the verity of the signs, But yet they ascribe
her to the Brain the seat of the intellectual faculty the
lungs, spine stomach Menstrues and all other excrements
and the left eye and also the power of increasing.

The Square, Oppositions &c

In this Seisence have quite a contrary effect, as it is by □ &c
that cause the disease in the Body, the ☽ □ by ♂ in ♋ his house disease
the Breast ♋ being a watery sign and ♂ a hot Planet cause hot and moist
the ☉ in ♌ □ by ♂, ♌ governing the heart and ♌ a fiery sign and ♂ hot
cause a hot and dry disease. As you see by the table of Diseases (Page
10 to 19) these diseases are produced by the before mentioned Causes, which
are evil, and the same is cured by the Good aspects, These
effects produced is from what is termed Antipathy

Characters suited to the Latin Alphabet

A+1	B+2	C+3	D+4	E+5	F+6	G+7	H+8	I×9
♏	♐	♏	♍	♌	♓	♈	♈	♉

K+10	L+20	M+30	N+40	O+50	P+60	Q+70	R+80	S+90
♋	♎	♍	♍	♎	♐	♀	♏	♉

T+1'	V+2'	X+3'	Y+4'	Z+5'	ω+6'	T+ 1' for 100	V+ 2' for 200	X&c 3' for 300
♏	♉	♍	♍	♍	♍			

Celestial Characters to the Hebrew D°.

9- ט	8- ח	7- ז	6- ו	5- ה	4- ד	3- ג	2- ב	1- א
∪	⊓	ᛏ	φ	⊓	⊣	⊣	З	⋈

90- צ	80- פ	70- ע	60- ס	50- נ	40- מ	30- ל	20- כ	10- י
⋎	⊙	⋎	⋃	⋋	⋊	⋈	⌒	△

		ת	ש		4'- ת	3'- ש	2'- ר	1'- ק
4' for 400	3' for 300	2' for 200	1' for 100		⋎	⋃	⋎	⋎

To find what Character belongs to a Sign, Planet &c you must enter the Table N° 1 (all Characters suited to the Hebrew) in the Line N° 5 which is the Hebrew Alphabet, corresponding to the Numbers, Signs, Planets, &c

22
Chaldean Characters suited to the Latin

A··1	B··2	C··3	D··4	E··5	F·6	G··7	H··8	I··9
Γ	Γ	V	V	Γ	Γ	Γ	Ρ	Ρ
J·Cons·10	K··20	L··30	M··40	N··50	O··60	P··70	Q··80	R·90
ㄱ	ㅓ	ㄱ	ㄱ	ㄱ	ㄱ	ㄱ	ㄱ	ㄱ
S··1'	T··2'	V··3'	V·Cons·4'	X··5'	Y··6'	Z··7	8'	9'
L	ㅏ	ㅏ	ㅏ	ㅏ	ㄴ	ㄴ	ㄴ	ㄴ
1000	2000	3000	4000	5000	6000	7000	8000	9000
J	ㅏ	ㅅ	ㅅ	ㅁ	ㄷ	ㅁ	ㅁ	ㅁ
1510	1511	1471	1486	2421	1801	1803	1807	1811
ㅍ	ㅍ	ㅍ	ㅍ	ㅍ	ㅍ	ㅍ	ㅍ	ㅍ

To find in what manner these Alphabets agree in Characters &c with the Signs Planets &c you must observe those which are suited to the Latin alphabets, that you enter the table of numbers Signs Planets and Alphabets and under N° 7 which is the Latin Alphabet, you must enter the letter, and look to the left, in a line to the numbers, and there you will find the number Sign and Planet, that corresponds with the letter you want See Plate of Page 3

Melachim Writing - of Angels

9. ט	8. ח	7. ז	6. ו	5. ה	4. ד	3. ג	2. ב	1. א
⋈	▢	V	N	Π	Y	U	♄	
90. ץ	80. פ	70. ע	60. ס	50. נ	40. מ	30. ל	20. כ	10. י
⚚	✳	⋈	⋕	H	J	⌒	⌒	
9ꞌ. ץ	8ꞌ. ח	7ꞌ. ז	6ꞌ. ס	5ꞌ. ן	4ꞌ. ח	3ꞌ. ש	2ꞌ. ᶜ	1ꞌ. ק
4ˢ for 400	3ˢ for 300	2ˢ for 200	1ˢ for 100	V	⌣	✠	⋈	▢

Writing called passing the River

9- ט	8- ח	7- ז	6- ו	5- ה	4- ד	3- ג	2- ב	7- א
ᴼ⊦	⌐	⌒	E	⅂	J	⊓	⋈	
90- ץ	80- פ	70- ע	60- ס	50- ן	40- ם	30- ל	20- ך	10- ו
Π	Υ	⸮	⌒	□	3	7	⊓⊓	
9ꞌ- ץ	8ꞌ- ח	7ꞌ- ז	6ꞌ- ס	5ꞌ ן	4ꞌ- ח	3ꞌ- ש	2ꞌ- ᶜ	1ꞌ- ק
5 to 9 are finals	4ˢ for 400	3ˢ for 300	2ˢ for 200	1ˢ for 100	E	V	Ɔ	△

The above two Alphabets or Characters are Suited to the Hebrew alphabet and to find in what manner they answer to the Signs Planets &c, you must refer to the table of Signs Numbers & Planets at Page 3 Plate

The Seven Tables of the Divine Names and Numbers of the Seven Planets

of ♄

3	Ab.		אב
9	Hod.		הד
15	Iah.		יה
15	Hod.		הוד
45	Jod ha vov ho. (Jehovah extended)		יוד הא ואו הא
45	Agiel.	Intelligence	איאל
45	Zazel.	Spirit	זאזל

of ♃

4	Aba.		אבא
16	hoh.		הזה
16	Ahi.		אחי
34	Elab.		אלאב
136	Jhphiel.	Intelligence	יהפיאל
136	Hismael.	Spirit	הסמאל

of ♂

5	He the letter of the holy name		ה
25	jhi		יהי
65	Adonai		אדני
325	Graphiel.	Intelligence	גראפיאל
325	Barzabel.	Spirit	ברצבאל

of ☉

6	Vau, the letter of the Holy name		ו
6	He (extended) the letter of the Holy name		הא
36	Eloh.		אלה
111	Nachiel.	Intelligence	נכיאל
666	Sorath	Spirit	סורת

Of ♀

7	Aha	אהא
49	Hagiel. Intelligence	הגיאל
175	Kedemel. Spirit	קדמאל
1225	Bni. Seraphim Intelligencies	בגישרפים

Of ☿

8	Asboga, eight extended	אזבוגה
64	Din.	דין
64	Doni.	דני
260	Tiriel. Intelligence	טיריאל
2080	Taphthartharath. Spirit	תפתרתרת

of ☽

9	Hod	הד
81	Elim	אלים
369	Hasmodas Spirit	השמודאי
3321	Shedbarschemoth, Schartathan the Spirit of Spirits	שדברשהמעתשרתתן
3321	Malcha, betharsisim hed baruah Schehalim the Intelligency of the Intelligence	מלכא.בתרשישים.עד.ברוח.שהקים.

Table of Saturn

 ♄ His Compass

Seals and Characters

of ♄   Intelligence   Spirit

The Angel of the day his Sigil. Planet, the Sign governing the Planet

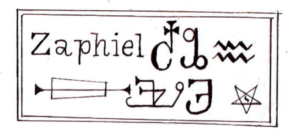

The Angels of Saturday
Zaphiel. — Machatam. —   Uriel,
צפיאל ✶   אוריאל
כסאל or Cassiel

Table of Jupiter

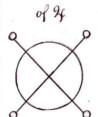

♃

His Compass

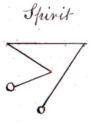

Seals and Characters

of ♃   Intelligence   Spirit

The Angel of the day, his Sigil, Planet, the Sign, governing the Planet, and Name of the Sixth Heaven

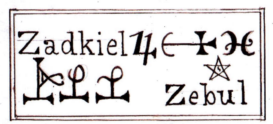

The Angels of Thursday
Zadkiel — Casliel — Asasiel

28

Table of Mars ♂

11	24	7	20	3
4	12	25	8	16
17	5	13	21	9
10	18	1	14	22
23	6	19	2	15

His Compass

Seals and Characters

of ♂   Intelligence   Spirit

The Angel of the day his Sigel, Planet, and Sign governing the Planet and the Name of the fifth Heaven

The Angel of Tues-day

Camael —— Satael —— Amabiel

במאל ×
ממאל or Samael

Table of the Sun

6	32	3	34	35	1
7	11	27	28	8	30
19	14	16	15	23	24
18	20	22	21	17	13
25	29	10	9	26	12
36	5	33	4	2	31

His Compass

א	לח	גד	ל	גב	א
ל	ח	כח	כז	יא	ד
כד	גג	ית	יו	ר	יט
יב	יז	כא	כג	כ	ית
יב	כו	ש	י	כט	נה
גא	ב	ל	ד	הג	לי

Seals and Characters

of ☉ — Intelligence — Spirit

The Angel of the day, his Sigil the Planet. Sign governing the Planet, and the Name of the fourth Heaven

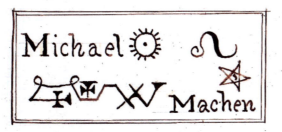

The Angel of Sunday

Michael —— Dardiel —— Huratapal

מיכאל ×

Table of Venus

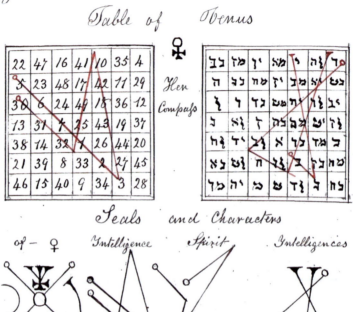

Her Compass

Seals and Characters

of — ♀   Intelligence   Spirit   Intelligences

The Angel of the day, his Sigil, Planet, the Sign governing the Planet, and the Name of the Third Heaven

The Angels of Friday

Anael _ _ _   Rachael _ _ _ _ _   Zadkiel

הנביא ✝

31

Table of Mercury

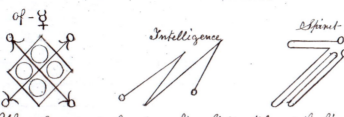

Seals and Characters

The Angel of the day, his Sigil, Planet, the Sign, governing the Planet, and Name of Second Heaven

Raphael ☿ ♊ ♍
Raquie

The Angels of Wednesday
Raphael ____ Miel ____ Seraphiel

א רפאל

32

Table of the ☽ Her Compass

37	78	29	70	21	62	13	54	5
6	38	79	30	71	22	63	14	46
47	7	39	80	31	72	23	55	15
16	48	8	40	81	32	64	24	56
57	17	49	9	41	73	33	65	25
26	58	18	50	1	42	74	34	66
67	27	59	10	51	2	43	75	35
36	68	19	60	11	52	3	44	76
77	28	69	20	61	12	53	4	45

Hebrew Numbers

לז	עח	נט	ע	כא	סב	יג	גד	ה
ו	לח	עט	ל	עא	כב	סג	יד	מו
מז	ז	לט	פ	לא	עב	כג	נה	יה
יו	מח	ח	מ	פא	לב	סד	כד	נו
נז	יז	מט	ט	מא	עג	לג	סה	כה
כו	נח	יח	נ	א	מב	עד	לד	סו
סז	כז	נט	י	נא	ב	מג	עה	לה
לו	סח	יט	ס	יא	נב	ג	מד	עו
עז	כח	סט	כ	סא	יב	נג	ד	מה

Seals and Characters of the ☽ Spirit

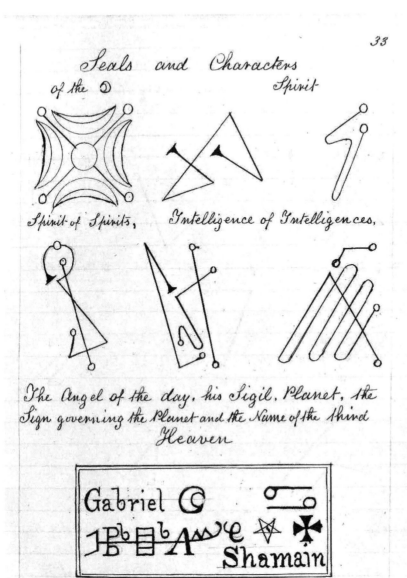

Spirit of Spirits,   Intelligence of Intelligences,

The Angel of the day, his Sigil, Planet, the Sign governing the Planet and the Name of the third Heaven

Gabriel ☾   Shamain

The Angels of Monday
Gabriel ——— Michael ——— Camael
גבריאל ——— מיכאל ——— כמאל

The Characters

of the Seven Angels ruling over the Seven Planets, Drawn according to Art from the Seven Square Tables

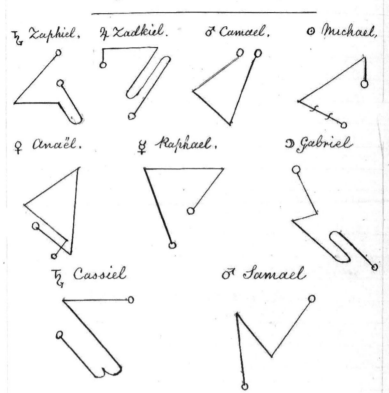

As there is a difference in opinion among the Rabbies, which are the angels of the days of Saturday of ♄ and Tuesday ♂, I have drawn the Characters of both, that the artist may use which he most prefers, —

The use of the Tables of Divine Names and Numbers, and the seven Square Tables of the Planets, shewing how the Magical Characters are extracted — —

Chap 6

1st Example of ה‎ג

I shall now begin with the Square Table of ה‎ג, In this Table of Divine Names and Numbers I see his mean Number is 3. i.e. Three squares in a line and three lines in the square each way, the Divine Name answerable to that is Ab, which opposite are the Hebrew Notes ב א, Aleph and Beth, the first and second letters in the alphabet as such their Numbers is when added together 3. The next Number, I find is 9 - v.e. that three times, three is nine, which is the number of squares contained in the Square or table the Divine Name answering to that is Hod, opposite to which the Hebrew notes are ד ה. He and Daleth He the fifth and daleth the fourth, letter, when added together makes that number 9, The next number is 15 -i-e the numbers added together in each line in the Table and also, designaly make fifteen, The Divine name to that number is Jah, the Hebrew notes are ה‎י Yad and He. which Yod being the tenth letter and He, the fifth added makes the number 15, The next of that is Hod extended, the Hebrew notes to which are ד‎ו‎ה, He, Van, daleth, He the fifth letter Van the Sixth and daleth the fourth which added as before makes the number 15, The next is 45 and the Divine name is Jehovah which is יהוה but extended to יוד הא ואו הא which is Yod 10. Van 6. daleth 4. He 5, Aleph 1. Van 6. Aleph 1. Van 6.

36

He 5, and Aleph 1, which numbers added as before makes the numbers 45. The product of the whole numbers of the table of Saturn. The next is Agiel, his Intelligence which answers to the same number, the Hebrew notes of which are אגיאל. Aleph 1. Gimel 3. Yod 10 Aleph 1. and Lamel 30, and when added make the number 45. now to obtain his true Character according to Numbers and Art, I examine wether any of the Hebrew letters in point of their numbers are beyond the Compass of his Table, to which I find, by setting them down thus ל 30. א 1. י 10. ג 3. א 1, I now enter the Table according to succession of the numbers begining with the figure 1 and (0) signifying the begining of the Character. I then trace a line to the square where the figure 3 is continueing it back to the figure 1 because 10 is beyond the compass therefore I leave out the Cypher and enter the 1 only, and as the same figure follows I return it back breaking the curve signifying that the square is entered by two figures of one number and in continuation of the same line I trace to the Square where the figure 3 is because 30 is above the Compass of the table. therefore I leave out as before the Cypher which being the last letter I terminate it with an 0 as the begining and my Character is now completed as you'l see in red lines in the Square table of ♄, the Character of which is in full placed underneath and is called the Character of the Intelligence of ♄ precisely in the same manner is the Character of his spirit obtained. Note, always observe to touch with the lines the left hand points of the tops of the squares within the square of the number required. unless the same square is entered more than once, then they must be curvated and formed according to the Artist, only particularly take care that all lines belonging to one square do not enter into that of another, as that will alter the numbers of the Characters, likewise take care that all letters bearing the numbers beyond the Compass of any of the tables, the Cyphers must be omitted and entered as before by the figure only

2nd Example of ♂

The Character of his Spirit whos name **Barzabel** I draw down the Hebrew note thus ⟨ 30. 2. ℵ 1. ⅄ 90. ⅃ 200. 2, Now seeing that there are to be entered two figures of one number, I enter them, as see table of figures, continuing the line from 2 to 9 then trace back to 1 and from 1. touch the square of 2 and from thence to the top of the Square of 3 and then it terminates with 0 and the figure or Character of his Spirit is Completed

3rd Example of ☿

This is a compound Character of Characters or a Conjunction of two therefor the first part or Letter must be entered in the with an 0 and the line Continued to the extremity with a break see the figure in the table of ☿. The next word must be begun with a break also as two end to join and the line must be continued through all the squares till it is termanated which must be finished with an 0 as the former, it is then Compeated

4th Example of the ☉

This Character is that of Michael the Angel of his day, the Hebrew notes are ⟨ 30. ℵ 1. ⅃ 20. ` 10. ⅁ 40, which are Mem, Yod, Caph, Aleph and Lamed, now 40 being

38

above the compass of the table I omit the Cypher and enter the 4 making an O, for the begining and as the 4.10.20 are in a line I draw my pencil through making points at the squares (see the Character of Michael) then continue the line from 20 to 1 and from 1 to 30 and finish it with an O as before then the Character of Michael is completed. In the same manner are all the other Characters drawn forth, and in the same manner and by the same rules may every other Character be drawn from any Language or office thing or matter, to work any effect either Good or evil to answer any design at the will of the operator in this Art.

Note, where your Characters begin as that of the spirit of the ☉. or terminates with two figures of the same numbers in one square they must always be broken as see figure of the ☉. Also where many lines return backward and forward many times into any two opposite squares they must be carefully kept within the compass of the Square so entered. see the character of the Spirit of ☿. when any acute Angles are formed from the entering of any figure the left hand Corner on the top of the Square. shou'd be touched if possible if not as near as possible. but under the above observ-
-ations the fancy of the Artist may be displayed

Characters drawn from things themselves by a certain likeness with the natures of the Signs Planets &c

Commanding ♈ * ♉ * ♊ * ♎ * ♌ * ♍   Opposite
Obeying   ♎ * ♏ * ♐ * ♑ * ♒ * ♓

F + M + C   Four Triplicities
♉ * ♈ * ♊   F + ♈ * ♌ * ♐   hot and dry
♌ * ♎ * ♍   A + ♊ * ♎ * ♒   hot and moist
♏ * ♎ * ♐   W + ♎ * ♏ * ♓   cold and moist
♒ * ♑ * ♓   E + ♉ * ♍ * ♑   cold and dry

+ Fixed, Moveable, Common, Fiery, Airy, Watery, Earthy.

Joinings or Conjunctions

☌ of ♃ ♄
☌ of ♄ ♂
☌ of ♃ ♂
☌ of ♃ ♄ ♂
☌ of ♀ ♂ ♃
☌ of ♃ ☿

The Characters of the four Triplicities

Fire | Air
Earth | Water

Chap 7

Explaination of the Signs Commanding, Obeying, Oposite, Fixed, Movable and Common, the four Triplisities and Joynings or Conjunction of the Planets

---

<u>Signs Commanding</u>, mean that whatever work is begun under their Afscention when free from any bad Aspects and belonging to the Signs Obeying must if well managed according to the rule laid down, yield to the operators will

<u>Signs Opposite</u>, mean that whatever work is began under the ☍ of either the Signs or Planets, if for good will fail but if for evil will succeed as the mind of the operator desires and all Planets suffer detriment in Signs opposite to their own

<u>Fixed Signs</u>, mean that when the ☉ enters therein the weather is than more permanent, i.e. In this Art whatever work is began under any of the fixed Signs will be lasting and not easy to be removed These Signs all work of long duration must began under

<u>Movable Signs</u>, means that when the ☉ enters therein the Season of the Year and weather is moved or changed, So in any work performed under these Signs capable of Changing (the Person thing &c) the nature of the same, Work done under these signs are of Short duration

<u>Common Signs</u> are between movable and fixed as such in this Art very little regard is paid to them (only occasionally These Signs are neither very short nor very long,

The <u>Characters</u> of the <u>Triplicities</u> are used at the will of the operator when framing a Talisman under that Triplisity applicable to the work he has in hand, therefore with other Characters &c they are formed; the same by the conjunctions of the Planets

Chap 8

Of Trade and professions under the Seven Planets when Well or Ill situated, v.c. fortunate & unfortunate at Birth

1st of ♄.

<u>Fortunate</u>, a Person skilled in occult antiquities, things and callings. by Water and any thing relating to the same Sailors, Plumbers, Ship Carpenters &c and all things belonging to the Earth as carriers, Broom men, Brick makers Brick layers Undertakers and bearers of Corpis Horstlers Plough Men Scovengers Colliers Ditchers Carters, Chandlers, Gardners Herdsmen, Dyers of Black Cloth &c Shepards Coachmen and Cow-herds

<u>Unfortunate</u>. Lowly Labourers, emtyers of privies Sewer Men &c Diggers of Coalpits, and all base sorded occupations

2nd of ♃.

<u>Fortunate</u> Signifies. Judges, Counsellors,, all Ecelesiastical men as Priests. Levites. Chancellors, Lawyers, and all who follow the Law from the highest, Schollars and Students in general. Clothiers Woolen Drapers,

<u>Unfortunate</u> Mountebanks Quack-salvers, Empyries, Cheats and all men who will take Bribes to do dishonourable Actions

3rd of ♂.

<u>Fortunate</u>. Conquerors Userpers, Tyrants Generals of Armies and Soldiers, Physicians, Apothecaries Churgians, Marshalls, Butchers, Gunners, Watchmakers, Barbers &c all trades where sharp iron tools are used, Curriers Tanners Gamesters Dyers of Colours, Bakers Carpenders Cooks, Cutlers Taylors, Smiths, Alchymists, Chymists &c

<u>Unfortunate</u> Hangmen thieves & Pickpockets, Serjents Cutters by the Highway Jailors, Murderers and all evil cutthroats

42

4th of the ☉

<u>Fortunate</u> Emperors, Kings Monarchs, Princes and all High People, Gentlemen, who hold high offices under the Crown Coiners, Goldsmiths and all trades tending to the nature

<u>Unfortunate</u> Tyrants Userpers Constables, Head Borough's and all such as have any petty or Userped Authority

5th of ♀

<u>Fortunate</u>, Musicians in general, Gamesters, Embroiders Jewellers Linnen drapers, Perfumers, Painters of Pictures, Engravers Silk mercers and such occupations as serve for the Adorning of Women, &c. Women, Wives, Mothers, Virgins &c

<u>Unfortunate</u>. Common Fidlers, Pipers Ordinary Painters Women Taylors Glovers Upholsterers &c

6th of ☿

<u>Fortunate</u> Astronomers, Astrologers, Philosophers, Mathematicians, Secretaries, Diviners, Merchants, Sculptors, Modellers, Poets Orators, Embassadors, Commissioners, Schoolmasters, Advocates, Attornies all Ingenious Artificers, and Learned Men in general,

<u>Unfortunate</u> Scriveners, Accomptants, Sollicitors, Clerks, Carriers, Messengers, Footmen, Thieves, Money lenders, Userers, and all Petty Fogging Persons whatever

7th of the ☽

<u>Signifies</u> all Common People, and having no specifiac Professions belonging to her only what belongs to the water She being as it were the looking glass of Nature, receiving all lights &c from the other Planets and conveying the same down to this Terrestial Globe, therefor in this Science she is used as an Aider or Asister in all works communicating not only her own power in all her changes but also the powers and properties of the other Planets by way of

Conception bringing them forth to the inferior World, as being next to itself, for all the Stars have influence on it being the last receiver which afterwards, communicateth the influence of all the superiors to these inferiors, and pours them forth on the Earth, Therefor her motion is to be observed before the others, she being as the Parent of all Conceptions which it diversely issues forth in these Inferiors according to the different complexions, motions situations and different aspects, to the planets and all other Stars, and though it receiveth powers from all the Stars, yet especially from the ☉, as often as it in the ☌ with the ☉ it is replenished with vivifying virtues, and according to the aspect it Borroweth its complexions, The first Quarter being Hot and Moist the Second Hot and Dry, the third Cold and Dry, and the Fourth Cold and Moist, and from it in the heavenly Bodies beginneth the series of all things, which <u>Plato</u> calleth the <u>Golden Chain</u> by which every thing in Nature is linked together.

Chap 9

Of the Seven Planets the Names of their Angels ruling their Days and the Colours belonging to them, and their use in this Art, Also the twelve Signs.

♄ ..	Cassiel	Pale Leaden or Lead Colour.
♃ ..	Zadkiel	Ash. greens. purple and Blue.
♂ ..	Samael	Red, Yellow or Saffron.
☉ ..	Michael	Yellow or Gold.
♀ ..	Anael	Light Blue or White.
☿ ..	Raphael	various Purples.
☽ ..	Gabriel	Silver, White, pale green and Yellow

Of the Twelve Signs

♈	Machidael	White and Red or mixed
♉	Asmodel	White and Citron or Mixed
♊	Ambriel	White and Russet or Mixed
♋	Muriel	Green and Russet or Mixed
♌	Verchiel	Red or Green
♍	Hamaliel	Black speckled with Blue
♎	Zuriel	Black dark Crimson or tawney
♏	Barahiel	Brown
♐	Advachiel	Yellow or green tending to Red
♑	Hanael	Black dark Brown or Russet
♒	Cambiel	Azure or Sky Blue
♓	Barchiel	A Glittering White

The Characters of the Angels of the Planets I have given in page 84 also the true method of extracting them, which in the same manner must be extracted the Characters of the Angels of the 12 Signs, from their Hebrew Notes

Of <u>Colours</u> In Page 59. it is explained according to Art But further it was highly recommended to those Persons whos Signs or Planets that they were under, to wear such Colours, as Belongs to the same holding of it by way of Sympathy. As such to the different Planets &c they give (according to their natures) their Colours, To ♄ Leaden Black Lucid Earthy, Brown, he being an ill disposed Malencholy Planet, To ♃ Saphire and airy colours and those which are green clear purple, darkish golden and mixed with Silver which are all pleasing to the eye, He being the author of Sobriety and temperance, To ♂. Red and Burning fiery flaming, Violet purple, Bloody and Iron Colours He being the author of Mischief, Anger haste, Choler extra-vagance and heat, To ♀ ☿ and the ☽ all white fair curious, greens, muddy betwixt Saffron and purple, & being the author of Voluptuousness and Pleasure, & being the author of wit Fancy Ingenuity and Invention and the ☽ Being the mother of all Conception Therefore whatever Planet she apply to in this Art she strenghthens the same, and under such upplication be it what it may, such power will be concenterated in the work in hand, according to the oper- -ators will

Chap 10
Of Wonderful Phenomenons produced from Certain Compositions as Lamps Candles &c

The following are the compositions and methods the ancients used. called Celestial Effects

Take the skin of a Serpent when fresh killed and twist it up like Catgut then take the blood and fat thereof and mix with some hard Tallow to make it a substance and make a Candle using the skin for the wick, The whole of this must be done under the Ascension of ♏, and when this candle is lighted the whole room if small will appear full of serpents. The same may be prepared as a Lamp both lighted in the hour of ♄

Another method, kill a snake, take the Skin as before, and Beat the flesh and blood with just sufficient of Wax to fix it, then as before make a Candle in the hour of ♃ under the ascendent of ♏, and lighted in the hour of ♂

In the hour of ♄, ♒ ascending, Take a Quantity of flies and boil them with a sufficient quantity of Wax and as before a Candle, and when lighted will be seen thousands of Flies.

Take a bottle full of Oil. and when the Grape is in flower in the Hour of the ☉ put into the bottle, the

46

Flowers, and suspend the bottle to the Branch of the Vine with yellow silk, covering it from the wet and let it remain till the grapes are ripe, then take down the bottle, and the Oil whenever lighted there will appear to the sight quantities of Grapes as if growing.

<u>Take</u> of paison which comes from a Mare after Copulation and Boil the same with Oil, and Burn it in a Lamp lighted in the hour of the ☉ in a dark room, and a most wonderful appearence will take place. The same effect may be produced from the fluid of a she Ass after Copulation, preparing as before, and lighted in the hour of ♄

Take the Blood of a Lapwing and mix with it the herb Centory, with a portion of Honey and prepare it in the hour of ♄ and light it either as a Candle or Lamp and very strange appearence will follow

Put the Olive Oil into a Lamp, mixed with Glass in very fine powder and light it in the hour of ♄

Take Olive Oil as before but put around the wick powdered Sulpher, and strange appearences will follow

Take the Head of a black Cat and bruise it to a pulp and boil the same with olive Oil, then strain of the whole fat or Oil, prepare & light this in the hour of ♄

Thuribalum Magica

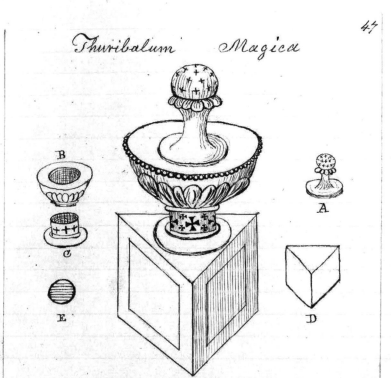

This Thuribalum and Tripod should be of the following proportions and forme. The vase consisting of three Parts. as A The Cover which has a tube up it and a hollow ball on the top, perforated with 9 Crosses to let the Perfume escape, The body B has a small grate as E on which the fuel rest on when put into the Body B, The Bottom C is a vacume for the admission of the air to keep the fire burning, therefore from the passage or currancy of air from C to A answers as a pair of Bellows, The Tripod or Stand D the top and Bottom must be an exact triangle, and the sides must be a perfect square equal to the triangle each way and may be made either Solid or hollow of some hard wood as Pane tree. Ash or any other; When this Apparatus is completed

48

Consecrated and Exorcised It must be covered over with a new fine White Linen Cloth, and kept from the prying Eyes of the Curious unless you choose to show it to a friend of your own Nature one after your own heart following the same persuits thursting after Occult Knowledge

The Fire which must be burned in this Thuribulum must be Charcoal produced from the Tree or wood which bel--ongs to the Planet, (or which is under it) also the Perfume as the greater the Sympathy the greater and most power--full is the effect produced, The Planetry hour also must be observed, and that the first hour or Sunrise for the beginning of any Experiment, and if the experiment is likely to occupy more time, leave of exact at the end of that Planetary hour and begin the moment the next comes in and so proceed till you have finished the work you had began, devoting your whole thoughts or even your whole Soul in the accomplishment of your object, and suffer no interruption whatever – nor let no living Soul see or know what you are about, but be as silent and secret as the grave, if not your labour will prove fruitless and youl meet with nothing but disappointment, For St Paul saith, trust not thy friend which lyeth in thy bosom". Therefore in all things sacred, Secrecy is the Soul of Nature;

Characters of the Behenian of fixed Stars Their Degrees, Places and Natures

Characters	And Natures	Places	Natures
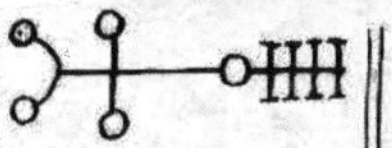	The Head of Algol	18°„ ♉	♄ ♃
	The Pleiades	22°„ ♉	♂ ☽
	Aldaboram	3°„ ♊	♀ ♂
	The Goat Star	13°„ ♊	♃ ♄
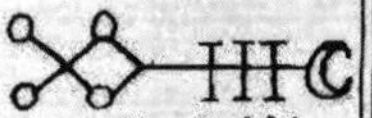	The Great Dog	7°„ ♋	♀
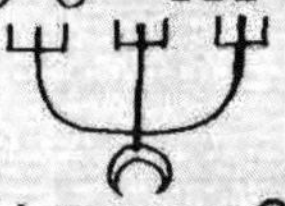	The Lesser Dog	17°„ ♋	♂ ☿
	The Heart of the Lion	21°„ ♌	♃ ♂
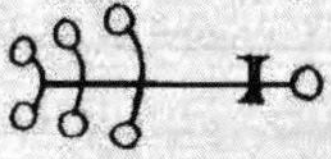	The tail of the Bear	19°„ ♍	♀ ☽
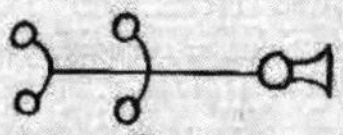	The Wing of the Crow	7°„ ♎	♄ ♂
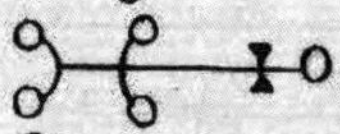	Spica	16°„ ♎	♀ ☿
	Alcameth	17°„ ♎	♂ ♃
	Elpheia	4°„ ♏	♀ ♂
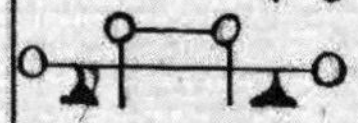	Heart of the Scorpion	3°„ ♐	♂ ♃
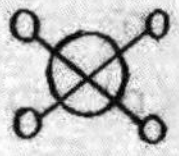	Vulture falling	7°„ ♑	☿ ♀
	Tail of Capricorn	16°„ ♒	♄ ☿

Images of the fixed Stars

The Ancient Magi also made Talismans &c of the fixed Stars, for the Head of Algol, In the Centure they formed the Head of a man with a Bloody neck, They asfer whoever it is made for and bear it will allways be success-full in presenting petitions, It preserveth every member of the Body from injury, a Defence against witchcraft and neflecteth all evil Maclinations upon our enemies, Under the Constellation of the Plaïdes they made (in the same way) a lamp in figure and they that it encrease the light of the eyes as to enable the bearer to afsemble and see Spirits and to reveal secret things, Under Aldaboram they made an Image of a Flying Man for Riches and Honours Under the Goat they made an Image of a Man playing on a musical instrument. this they say makes a Man highly hon- -our'd and exalted by people of high rank. and in Medical application cures the tooth ack, Under the greater dog star they made the Image of a Hound with a young Virgin this they say bestowes. honor good-will and the favour of Man and Aerial Spirits, and gives power to pacify and reconcile Men, Under the lefser Dog Star they made the Image of a Cock it confereth of both Spirits and Man it gives power against witchcraft and preserveth Health Under the heart of Leo they made an Image of a Lion or Cat it appeaseth wrath and gives favours Under the tail of Ursa Major they made an Image of a Bull or a Calf this they say is good against incantations, and secures the bearer in his travels against harm, Under the Wing of the Crow they made the Image of a Raven or Snake, this gives the Bearer the power of driving away evil Spirits or gether them together it defend the Malice of Men, Under the Spike they made an Image of a Bird or a Man loaded this confereth Riches, and cause the Bearer to overcome his enemies. Under Alchameth they made the Image of a Horse or a Wolf, this is good against all feavens, Under Elpheia they made an Image of a Hen, or Man crowned this bestows on the Bearer the Good will and love of all Men, Under the heart of Scorpio. they made an Image of a Man in Armour, or the figure of a Scorpion, this gives understanding and memory, and aids the power against evil Spirits, by driving them away and it also binds them at the bearers will. Under the Vulture — they made the Image of a Vulture or a Hen this gives great power of every Beast of the Earth. Under the Tail of Capricorn they made the Image of a Hart or Goat this gives to the Bearer prosperity

These are some of the fixed Stars which they command to be engraven on their Stones or Compound Metals, They observe that if. very correctly framed and finished by, ant, they may be formed by a pen on Parchment, the pens made from such Bird as belongs to the Star, if for Beasts or the Stars formed from the Beast the Ink must be the Blood of that animal, and the burnt ashes of the Hairs — mixed — the Parchment must be pure called Virgin made from the Skin of young Kid or from the skin of young Cats, before their eves are opened which is the third day, this parchment must be well cleansed in ether and dried only in the ☽ beams when she is at the full and kept in the dark for use, and the Talisman must go through all operations as is hereafter mentioned, then kept secret, wrapped in a piece of fine new linen, and at any time when an effect is desired the Bearer must fix his whole soul on the object of his wishes, what he most earnestly desires and by a secret occult power, he will be struck with astonishment

Note. That in making the Compositions for Talismans for the fixed Stars, you must observe their natures which is according to the degrees in the Signs Example The Head of Argol is 18° of ♉ and is the nature of ♀ and ♃ because in the Table of essential Dignities Page 120 you'll see in the line of ♉, ♀ is in her own terms, for the first 8°, but from 8° to 15°, are the terms of ☿, and from 15° to 22 are the terms of ♃ consequently the begining on 18°- the Ascension of the Head of Argol, ♃ having his terms from 15° to 22° by begining your Work on the Eighteenth degree Ascending which will be four degrees belonging to ♃ to make up the twenty two and from 22° to 26° being the terms of ♄ they have each four degrees as such they are of an equal power – therefore the Compound to be wrought upon must be equal in Mixture, I see ♂ has his terms also in ♉ from 26° to 30°- and I will ask the reason (as he has 4° in the same sign – Whe he is not taken) I answer, because ♂ being in enmity with ♄ and ♃, and his nature being totally opposite, evil cannot be mixed with good or day with Night. but if ♂ had been a Planet in friendship with the other two his nature and aid might have been taken Therefore by the same rule you may discover whether one Planet hath more power in a Constellation than another — for if one Planet bears two or more degrees than another according to what it is — he must have his greatest share in the Compound to be wrought upon and also of Characters &c. The same by all the other Stars and Planets Signs &c

<u>Note</u> According to the Natures of the fixed Stars, which the table of Essential dignities fully explain, of such proportions, must be the Material, proper chosen, with the time place, Work &c and the framing of their Characters which are done by the Tables of the Squares of the Seven Planets

Chap 11

Talismans which were in the Possession of Great Men

a	b	r	a	c	a	d	a	b	r	a
a	b	r	a	c	a	d	a	b	r	
a	b	r	a	c	a	d	a	b		
a	b	r	a	c	a	d	a			
a	b	r	a	c	a	d				
a	b	r	a	c	a					
a	b	r	a	c						
a	b	r	a							
a	b	r								
a	b									
a										

A — IN HOC VINCE ☧

B — (pentagram)

C — (seal with Hebrew)

D — צמנה

D — בוזז

54

This was very much esteemed amongst the Ancient Cab-
-ilists, as containing the twenty seven letters of the Hebrew
alphabet, which they have formed in Similitude of the
same, and used them as Characters in this Art they
have divided it into three Classes, i.e. A.B.C. — they then
have divided into what they call nine Chambers when
they term the nine orbs of Heaven, which characters
they also term the nine orders of Angels, The first
Chamber contains Unites as you'l see by the Hebrew Alphabet
i.e. the first א which is one, the tenth which is י and ק which
stands for 100, which they term unites as they the begining
of numbers by the addition of Cyphens, Therefore they stand
as three ones — which added together makes the number 3
The second Chamber begins with ב which is the second

letter in the alphabet, the second letter is ב which is the number 20, the third is ר which is the number 200 as such they
take away the cyphers, and reckon the two's by adding them
as, two four Six, or by multiplying them by 3 as 3 times 2 is 6,
the number three being what is termed the Holy number
which is the number of the trinity, The third Chamber begins with ג which is the 3rd letter, the second is ל which stands
for 30 the third is ש which stands for 300, they then take
away the Cyphers by which means the three's are left — they
multiplyed by three as before produce the number 9 which
is attributed to the ☽. and the same rules must be observed
by the other six Chambers, and by multiplying by 3 the
numbers of the nine chambers you'll find them as follows
3, 1 are 3, 3. 2 are 6, 3.3 are 9, 3.4 are 12, 3,5 are 15. 3,6 are 18,
3,7 are 21. 3,8 are 24. and 3,9 are 27 which is the complete number of the Hebrew Alphabet. The first 3
chambers are the seals or marks of Simple numbers
The second 3 are (being tens) the seals or marks of
Celestial things, and the third which are hundreds —
signify all inferiour things The first are intellectual
the second Celestian and the third elemental These
Chambers are framed by the intersection of four Par-
-allel lines intersecting themselves into right Angles,
which forms the direct figure of the Cross that our
Saviour was Crucified on. which figure was so reverenced
by the Ancient Philosophers that they have formed very
curiously an Alphabet from the figure and made use
of it in Secret and Sacred things, as simple and compound
Characters, and from framed the Names of and Char-
-acters of the different Angels. The Alphabet of the
Cross and the formation of names compounded
I shall endeavour to explain which is as follows

Cross   The Cross Desected and Numbers from the parts

One • over either of these figures signifies unites, two : signifies tens, three ∴ signifies hundreds which for any particular name compounded short that signifies and beans any extent in numbers these points are called Notariacon and their use is as follows. To frame the Characters of the Angel Michael which in Hebrew is thus מיכאל, but in the Characters of the Cross is thus ⌐∙ ⌐∙∙ ⌐∙∙ ⌐∙∙∙ ⌐ this Character is framed of five figures with the use of the Notariacon explained. It is thus contracted from the same figure into three figures ⌐ ⌐∙∙ ⌐∙∙ after which it is contracted into three letters leaving out the Notaracon and is thus formed into a Talisman, and the Characters thus placed, drawing on the top of the Character his Sign ♌, the ☉ his Planet, Yayn the name of hour ruling, in the Circle on the top Varcan which is his King, and Tus Andas and Cynabal, are his three Ministers, which youl see by the Tables of the Names and Angels of the Planetary hours and Days, Thus did they frame from the different Alphabets these Characters

      Hebrew   Greek   Latin

The Arabians made use of these Characters very much and were very partial to them, as their representations are not like any other Characters or human signs, but we not knowing their quality which was never yet signified or mentioned in any writing — must work from their names and as our fancies devote consecrate to them figures & marks by which we cannot compel them to us but by which, by art we must rise up to them, viewing them with adoration then with a firm belief un doubted hope and quickening love we must call upon them in Spirit and in truth by their true names and Characters, and then we may obtain from them the virtue and power we most earnestly desire,

The Characters preceeding this Chapter are not to be received only by revellation which can be found out no other way, as the ancients assert that there are from some secret work, breathing out a harmony of some Divinity or that they are procured by some certain agreement or compact in language betwixt Spirits & Angels. That mark A was a mark or sign shewed to Constantine which is called a Cross the Characters compounded from some alphabet (which I conceive must be from the Greek according the Characters) the same as the word Michael and the motto In hoc vince. i.e. in this overcome — Now in decyphering this Character according to art I find it compounded as follow X signifies the Element called fire — which is either burning, hot bright shining heavenly. P signifies the sign ♑, belonging to ♄. his nature is to kill and slay all and to lame every member The I signifies the ☉, and nature of the Spirits of the ☉ is to raise men to the highest pinnacle of honour, and this Character ⌣ which can mean no other but ♌.

58

— signifies the ☽ and the nature of her Spirits are to obtain Honor and Riches. Therefore it appear to me that this Talisman was compounded by An† and made under the above mentioned Constellations & Planets to produce the effect. That marked B is one that revealed to Antiochus by Sirname Soter is, the figure is a Pentangle which signifies health, In the faith and virtue of which tradition tells us that both kings obtained great victories. That mark'd C was received from an Angel by Judas surnamed Machabeus, in faith of which he fought and overcome Antiochus Eupator, which Characters signifies the name of Iehovah of seventy two letters of equal name and number and means thus. who is there amongst the strong as Iehovah. The Talisman marked D They say if properly made will protect the Bearer from Mischief of evil Spirits and men, and all dangers from Journies, waters enemies and arms the Characters are composed from the first five verses in Genises and means the representation of the Creation of the world

The Talisman marked E, they also say that if properly framed is a most sacred one and efficacious against all diseases of Man and must be made of pure Gold, The fore part is the four Squared names of God from the highest to the lowest from which those holy Names or Seals arise the intention of which is inscribed in the Circumference. on the Backpart, inscribed the seven lettered name Araritha which is extracted from this verse

אראיתא ✡ אתהרודה" יהוה המוהוולהראל ✝

and round the Circle is written the interpretation. They recommend that if you write the Characters on Virgin Parchment (which in a great number of experi-ments will have a wonderfull effect) you must write with Ink made from the smoke of a Consecrated wax taper and holy water i.e. also consecrated. These they recommend to be worn as Ligatures suspended by such things as belongs to the different Planets observing their Colours, if for ☉ it must be suspended by a Yellow Silk or Gold Thread in the Hour of the ☉ - name the intent of the thing and what it is for - if for any disease They recommend to name three seperate times the names of the disease, repeating some part out of the Scriptures which containes every thing applicable to all your wishes

Note. (Paracelsus) Says., The Imperial Talisman of Constantine A. Must be of pure Iron on the day of ♂ which is Tuesday and in his hour, which is the 1st and 8th of that day the ☽ in ✶ or △ to ♂ and must be engraven at the same time, and in the increase of the ☽. Which give victory over Enemies, the person for whom it is made must Retire to some secret Place and fumigating it with the Magical suffumigation of the Spirit of ♂. which consist of Red Sanders, frankincense and Pepper, and suspend it from some part of the body where it will be kept Clean and Secret or it may be worn on the finger as a Ring, the Characters being engraven inside, He also places the character of ♂ where the Red dot is in the Circumference.

The Talisman. Marked F of Charles the V.th Emperor of Germany. The Characters are strongly cut upon a Plate of Polished wrought Iron and are chiefly the symbols of ♂ in his dignity in good aspect with ☽ and benefic Planets. The wearer sustained by the Martial Star was presumed to be invincible in battle and protected from offensive weapons The Imperial chieftains relied upon its virtues with success. The Talisman marked G. The Good Angel Muriel presiding when this impress is cut upon a plate

60

of pure Silver, the mariner who bears it about him shall be protected from all perils of the Sea, and return safe in health from his voyage.

That marked H Is a martial Talisman is ensures success in military expeditions protects the body and renders ineffective the assaults of an enemy and is wrought under ♂

That marked I is a Talisman prepared under mixed Stellar influences of a commanding but benevolent kind and is as a safeguard against the effects of lightning and stormes preserving the wearer from sudden accidents and death resulting from stormes

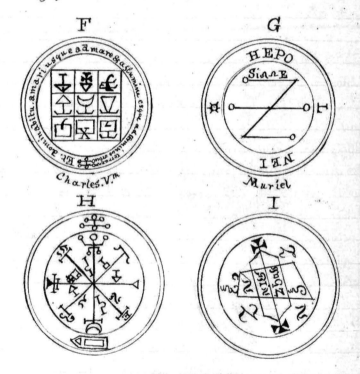

Note, the Inscription of F. Et dominabitu a mari usque ad mare & a flumine usque ad terminos orbis terrarum

The Number three is an incompounded number a holy number and a number for as we read in Medea

She speak three words, which caus'd sweet sleep at Will
The troubled Sea, and raging Waves stands still

and in Pliny it was the custom in every Medicine to spit with three deprecations and hence it was cured, for this number conduceth to the Ceremonies of God and Religin that by the solemnity of which prayers and Sacrifices were allways thrice repeated. This number was highly esteemed by the Ancient Magi. Wherefore Aristotle in the begining of all his speeches concerning the Heavens, calls it a Law to which all things are disposed. Tresmegistus saith that by this number the world was perfected: Hemarmene, necissity, and order (i.e) a concurrence of Causes which is commonly called Fate, and the execution of them to the fruits or increase, and a due distribution of the increase. The whole measure of time is included in this Number (i.e) the Present the Past and to come. Also all magnitude is included in it. A Line, Superfice and Body. Every Body consists of three intervals, Length Bredth, and Thickness. All Harmony containes three consents of time Deapason, Hemiolion, and Diatessaron, There are three kinds of Souls. Vegatative Sensitive and intellectual, And as the Prophet saith God orders the World by number Weight and measure. Ther are three powers of intellectual Creatures Memory, Mind and Will. There are three quaternions of Celestial Signs. Fixed, moveable and Common. There are three faces, and heads to every Sign of the Zodiac, There are three Persons in the Supersubstantial Divinity. There are three times of Nature, Law and Grace. There are three Theological Virtues. Faith, Hope and Charity. Scripture tells us that

Jonas was three days in the wales Belly and that our Saviour was as many days in the Bowels of the Earth, and it is further said that Christ to cure the Blind spit three times in the Palm of his hand and anointed the Eyes of the Blind and they were instantly restored to sight and Virgil saith

   I walk a round
* First with these threads, in number which three are
 'Bout th' Alter thrice I shall thy Image Bear
 After which
† Knots Amaryllis tye! of Colours three
 (Then say) these bonds I knit for Venus be,
 In the same place
‡ As with one fire this Clay doth harder prove
 The wax more soft; so Daphnis with our love

Note. The meaning of the Ancients by this Number is that whatever you undertake, that the Ceremony must be performed three seperate times, before it can be Perfected, and that by the Number Three many wonderful things can be produced proviso that the Cogitations of the Operators mind is strong and firmly fixed, with a most ardent desire to posess or accomplish the work his mind has resolved upon, and all things will yield to his power

* which means a Charm in Love by suspending the Image of the fair one of his heart.

† which he means the operation of the Charm to bring into action the desired effect. in the hour of ♀ a time suitable to the purpose, using such colours appropriated to the Planets required to the aid of the operator.

‡ Means after he has moulded the image of the Person as near as posible, he holds it over a fire of such meterial as belong to ♀ as Myrtle &c repeating the verse & naming her name, effects to which desired by him &c

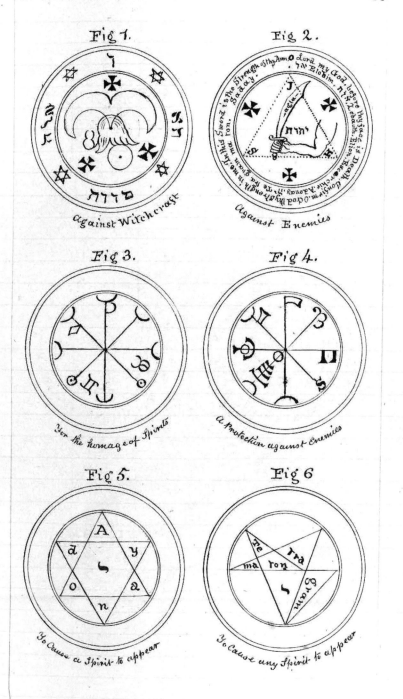

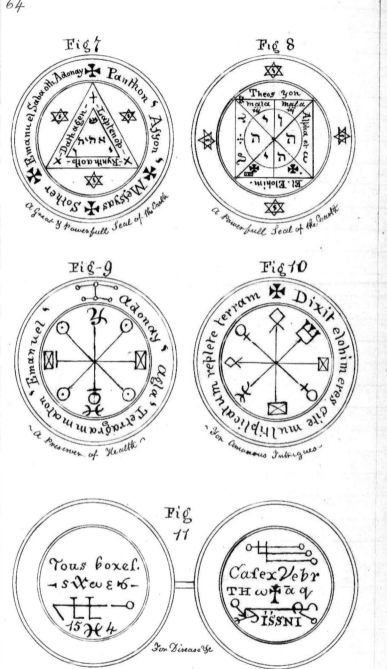

66

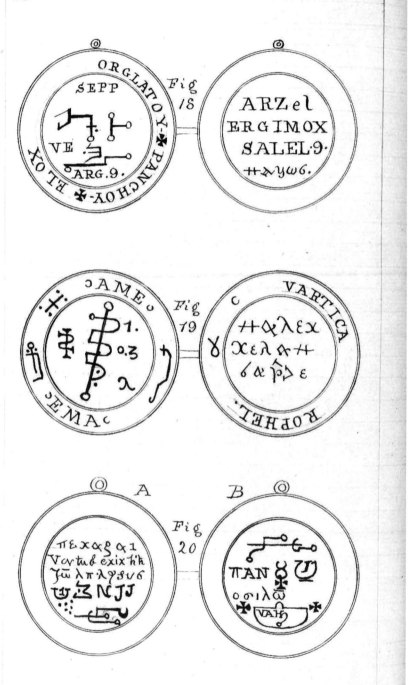

A Discription and Explanation of the Proceeding Talismans, the Power of which have been Proved
Chap 12

Fig 1. This is a Talisman, made against the Possesion of an Evil Spirit, or what some say an Evil Tongue, which is commonly called Witchcraft. It is made under the ☉ when free from bad aspects, and in his hour, when the ☽ incresing. It may be either engraved on a Plate of Gold, or formed on a piece of Virgin Parchment, with Ink made from the Ashes or Blood of a Solar Bird, and a pen made from the Quill of the same; when done it must be wrapped up in a Piece of new linnen, and suspended by a strip of Kids Skin and in the hour and Day of the ☉, hung on the Neck of the Person by a young Virgin

Fig 2 Is a Talisman of defience; and whoever bear it, it will defend him from all harm from his enemies, and defeat their Machination. It must be made in the hour and Day of ♃, when he is free from all impediments, and when the ☽ is increasing, it can also be form'd under any fixt Star, Mansion of the ☽ - which is appropriate for it with all observations necessary in this Art. The Aid of the ☉ will not be amiss

Fig 3. This Talisman is made under the ☽ when in her greatest Strength, in Exhaltation &c. or under one of her Mansions, appropriate, and She increasing in ♉; and whoever bears this, all Spirits will do homage to him when requested. Some part when the ☉ is happily situated in ♊ and ♉

Fig 4. This is a Talisman of Defience, and Whoever bears it need fear no foe as no harm can come to his Person as by its power the Evil disigns of his Enemies will be frus--trated, the time and manner of making is as before men-

mentioned on this occasion

Fig 5. This is a Great Character which should always be worn. it is called the great Seal of God and is very potent and is used on all good occasions and to make all things prosper invoke by this Seal.

Fig 6. This is the greatest and most powerfull of all Characters, being the Seal of the great Jehovah and is made as above

Fig 7. This is a most potent Talisman of Spirits without which none will appear and is called a Seal of the Earth the making and proper time will be seen in the Body of the work

Fig 8. This is a Talisman as before a Seal of the Earth

Fig 9. This Talisman is a Preserver of Health and must be made under ♃ in his hour and day at sun rise, he being free from all impediments and in a favourable aspect with the ☽ increasing, and worn suspended by the neck

Fig 10. This is a Talisman favouring amourous intrigue and must be made under ♀ in her day and hour and when in a Favourable aspect to ♂ if possible

Fig 11. This Talisman is one of Pices and is made in the month of Febuary when the ☉ enters first therein. The Composition for this Talisman must be One Dram of Gold two Drams of Silver, Four drams of tin, one dram of Soft Iron, One dram of Copper, these must be put together and Cast, if ♃ well situated and free from impediments in the 8th House, and if possible finish the Work under ♃, and it must be put on in the Day and hour of ♃. This Talisman is most efficacious to overcome and restrain anger, a cure for the Apoplexy Cholice, and other disorders Similar in Women as in Men, It also will aswage the Gout, Spasms, and diseases in the feet, and for that, should be worn under the Navel

Fig 12. Is a Talisman of very Valuable and must be made of fine Lead in the Hour of ♀ when the ☽ enters the Sign ♈ in the form described and the figure must be engraved in the hour of ♄. Then upon a piece of Copper the same Size as the other. When the ☽ touch's the Sign ♑ in the hour of ♄ engrave thereon the Characters as in Fig 13 when finished leave them till ♀ comes to a Conjunction with ♄. then at that instant unite the two engraved faces together, fixing then at their edges by a little Soft solder and cover them with Virgins Wax, and sow them up in a piece of Silk with some herb under ♀. in the day and hour of ♀ hang them round the neck, and whosever wears this it greatly assists in recovering the lost Sight, taken away Pains of the eyes and Causes the Sight of both young and old to be clear

Fig 14. This is a Talisman of Victory, and must be made under the Eight Mansion of the ☽ and must be engraved on a piece of Pure Tin and whoever Bears it will not only be victorious in all war like Pursuits but defeat all his enemies, when Warlike instruments are so decided. It must be performed with Saturnine things

Fig 15 This Talisman is to be made under the Eighteenth Mansion of the ☽ and must be engraved on a plate of Copper. and whoever Bears it it will cure bad fevers, Pains in the Belly. It must be perfumed with Hartshorn They also do assert that wherever it is buried no Snakes Serpents or any venamous thing will live while the Image is there

Fig 16 This is a Talisman made when the

70

☉ and ☽ enters the Sign ♏, they Say that whoever Beans this, it will cure the Cramp, and diseases belonging to ♄. They also say that where this is buried no Snake Serpent or venomous thing will live; and it-it-is made when the ☽ enters ♎ it is certain cure for Saturnine disease, especially if ♄ is there as he has is Detriment.

Fig 17. Is the reverse of it when made in the former Manner. but if made in the latter way the reverse must be appropriate to it.

Fig 18 Is a Talisman against Driness in the Brain and other diseases in the Head, Take of ☉ ʒp of ☽ ʒii of ☿ ʒi of ♃ ʒiii well refined, Let them be all melted together in the point of the new ☽. then pour them out and make a plate, which must not be put into the fire any more. When ♃ is in ♓ his own House. let these Characters be eng-raven of the one Side of the Lamen, and on the reverse let these words be written as in the figure. and in the superior part of the Circumference, then let there be made a Ring of Pure ☉ and affixed thereunto when the ☽ is declin-ing for it to be hanged by: it matters not in what day the Ring is made so that it be done in the hour of ☉ Let it be hung about the Neck, in the point of the new ☽.

Fig 19 Is a Talisman against the Palsey (a great secret of Paracelsus) Take of pure ☉ ʒii of pure ♄ ii. and first when the ☉ sets going under the Earth in the same hour, Melt the ☉ in a new meltingpot. and immediately after the Sun is set Cast the ♄ in and forthwith pour them out. keep this mass. afterwards when the ☽ is in 12 degrees of ♌ melt again. and it will appear like bell metal, to which add 3 drams of ☿, but let it be long in melting. then when the ☽ comes into the 12 degree of ♏. melt this matter again. and Cast it into it one dram of ♃ and presently Cast it into a mold because it admits not of any impression of the humour then keep it till ☉ enters ♈ which is on the 10 of March Then engrave the characters on both sides as in the figure, You must begin and finish them in the hour of ☉. It needs not what day only let the ☉ be in ♈ as is above said, The Lamen is to be Kept, and when the Palsey taketh any one let the time, day and hour be diligently enquired of the beginning of the Disease: and the same hour of the day let the Talisman be hanged about his Neck

Note Paracelsus also states that the Aurum Potable be administred to the Patient, which will be found in this work.

Fig 20 Is A Talisman against the Stone and Sand in the Reins ℞ of ☉ ℨiii of ☽ ℨiii of ♃ ℨi of ♄ ℨifs Let all these be melted in a clean Meltingpot on Sunday at 10 of the Clock before noon ☽ increasing, which being melted. Cast in Saltpeter & Tarter, afterwards let them be Cast into the form of A Lamen, and let it be Cut and polished in the hour of ♂ and day of ♀, but as yet let nothing be engraven thereon, and in the point of the new ☽ begin the Sculpture, and make haste that the side marked A may be finished in that hour, Then let this be safely kept untill some day of ♃ when the ☽ is in good aspect with good Planets as ♃ ♀ or ☿, then let the words and Characters be engraved on the other Side B. in the hour of ☿ Then let the Lamen be hanged about the Neck of the Patient, when the ☽ is decreased on the day and hour of the ☽. the Ring ought to be made of ♂ to which the Lamen is hanged. let the Patient drink wine every morning wherein the said Seal hath been steeped all night, and afterwards hang it about his Neck again This doth wonderfully expel the Stone, for which thing also Spirit of Roman Vitrol is good in Water.

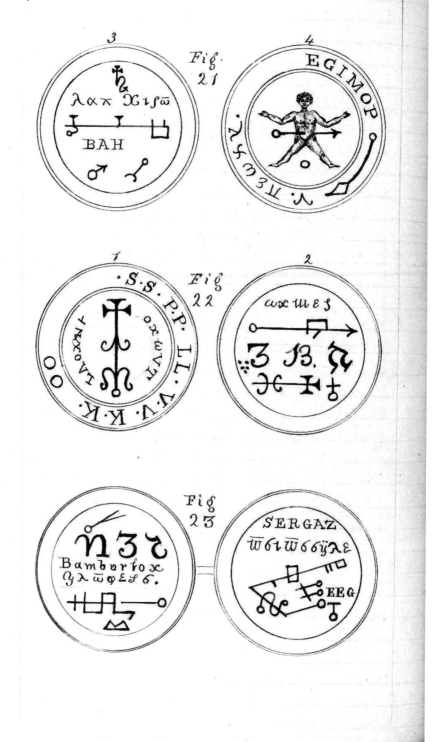

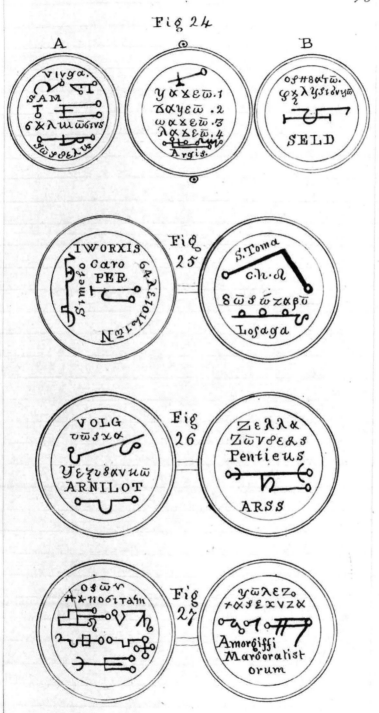

74

Fig 21 Is a Lamen against the Gout. Take of pure ☉ & ☽ and filings of ♂ each ʒi of ♄ ʒii. Let them be all melted together add some Borax, then pour the matter out on a smooth stone, that it may make a thin Lamen, for it cannot be worked with the Hammer. When ♄ is in ☌ with ♂ in the same hour let the Characters be engraven on two seperate pieces in the same hour on one side only, and let them be so kept that they touch not one another. Then make a Sigil of pure ☉ very thin when ♀ is in ☌ with ♄ or ♂ and engrave the Signs as in figure 22. But note that the Seals are to be conjoyned together when there is a ☌ of ♀ & ♄. the second face of the ☉ Seal marked 2 is to be turned against the engraved face of the superior Seal which hath the Planet ♂ and is Marked 3. but if ♀ be in ☌ with ♂ then the second face of the Seal of ☉ is to be turned upon the face of the Superior Seal N°4 which hath the image of a Man. and when the ☽ comes to the 6 degree of ♋ in the same order as is before shown let the Sigils be both joyned together the Seal of ☉ being placed in the middle and fastened together with a ♂ wire and let the patient hang them about his neck (Paracelsus also anoints the Members of the Patient with this Oil)

℞ of Mummy, Mastic, Red Myrrh, Olibanum, Ammoniacum, Opoapnex, Bdelium, each ʒii Vitriol ℔ii Honey ℔ii Xanter ʒi ʂ Aquavitæ gal iii Let them all be Distilled together into an Oil. Then take little Flies such as are bred in the dead Carcases of Horses. and make an Oil of them being well bruised. with this Oil of Flies mix ʒii with ʒiv of the other Oil. will mix and Distill again. let this oil be preserved

Fig 23. A Seal against Contractures. Take ☉ thrice refined by Antimony the weight of a Ducat. and melt it when the ☽ is in the 19 or 20 degrees of ♑ and cast into it as soon as Molten 30 grs of ♀ in filings under the same hour. which being done let it remain untill the ☽ is in the same degree of ♍. Then Melt it again and cast in 30ᵈʳᵐ of ♂ filings. pour it out and keep it till ☽ is in ♌ and then fashion it for the Sculpture which must be done in the hour of ♃ Let this Seal be engraven on both sides which must be sewed up in a fine Cloth and is to be hanged about the Neck by the Cloth only. and not by its own body in the day and hour of ♃ in the increase of the ☽

Fig 24 Is a Seal to provoke the Mensture and is made of pure ♀ in her hour and is to be bound with a String upon the back of the Woman at the beginning of the back bone upon the Testes, laying the engraved side to the flesh in the hour of the ☽, But if Nature suffer through too much Fluxes make one of Pure ☽ in the hour of the ☉ on both Sides to be Engraved as A & B Let it be sewed up in Silk and bound upon the Navel. turning the side B next her body, and afterwards when the Flux begins to stay let her wear it 30 days. and then take it off for if she wear it any longer their is danger lest they be quite driven away and so cause a greater hurt

Fig 25 Is a Sigil for the Leprosie and is made of pure ☉ in the hour of ♄, but engrave the Characters in the hour of the ☉ when the ☽ is in ♌ and ☉ in the same Sign which usualy happens in July, Let it be hanged about the Leper in the hour of ♀ the ☽ increasing, let him also drink wine wherein the same Sigil hath some time steeped, it must be renewed every year in July as this Sigil looseth its force in a Year. The Leprosie working so strong in the body of Man

Fig 26 Is a Sigil for the Vertigo. In the hour of ♂ and day of ♃. the ☽ in ♈ which is the last aspect of ♂. but see that she hath no evil aspect from any other Planet

76

Take of ☉ ʒ ſs of ♂ ʒ ii of fine ☽ ℈ v all properly refined and melted together and wrought into a very thin Lamen and Engrave as in the figure when the ☽ is in 12 degrees of ♉ and apply it to the Patient in the hour of the New ☽, on the very point that it first begin with

Fig 27 Is a Sigil For the trembling of the Heart, first in the day and hour of the ☽ take of ☽ ʒ ſs which put and keep in a melting pot untill the hour of ☉ which is the 4th hour following in the order of unequal hours, then melt it and Cast in two ounces of ☉. let them Cool in the melting pot, till the hour of ♀ melt them again and Cast in two drams of ♀ and pour it out and work it with a hammer into a Lamen and prepare it for engraving. Then when the ☽ and ♀ beholds one another with a good aspect Engrave these two Signs ⟨sigils⟩ ♑. afterwards in the point of the new ☽ engrave these three characters under the other two ⟨sigils⟩. then let it rest from that new ☽ untill the next full ☽, and in the point of the full ☽ on the same side over all the Signs let the words be engraved as in the figure. This being done mark when the ☉ enters ♌ and in the same hour of his ingress inscribe the characters as in the next next figure on the other side, which must be gun and finished in the same hour, This Sigil is to be hanged about the Patients Neck in the hour and point of the full ☽ next his flesh upon his Heart

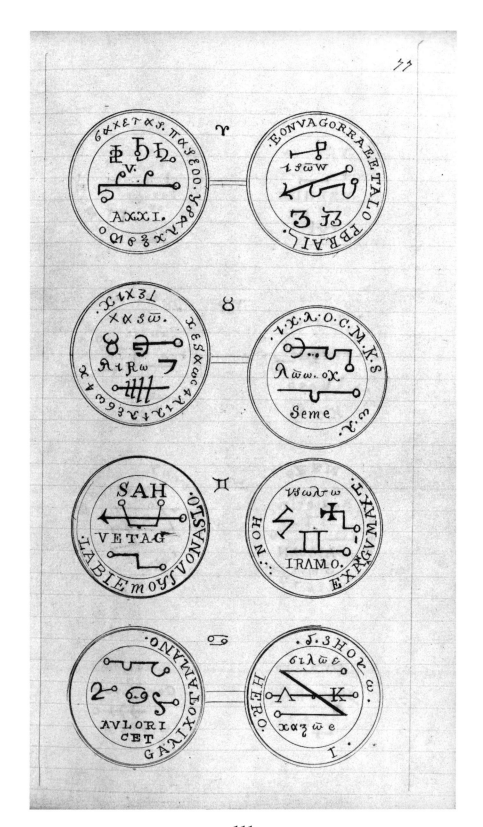

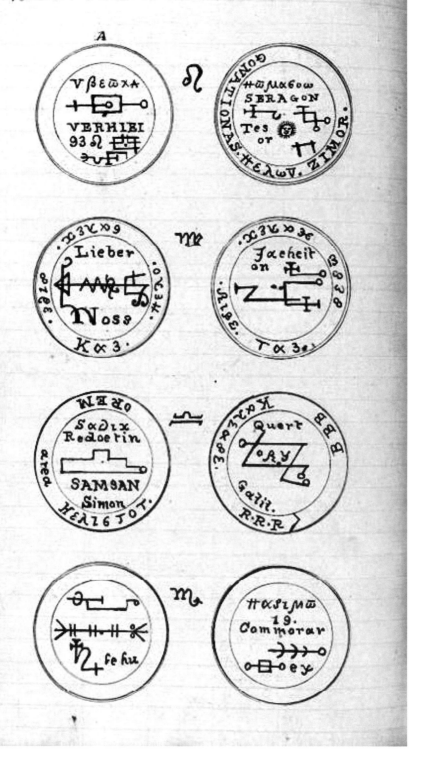

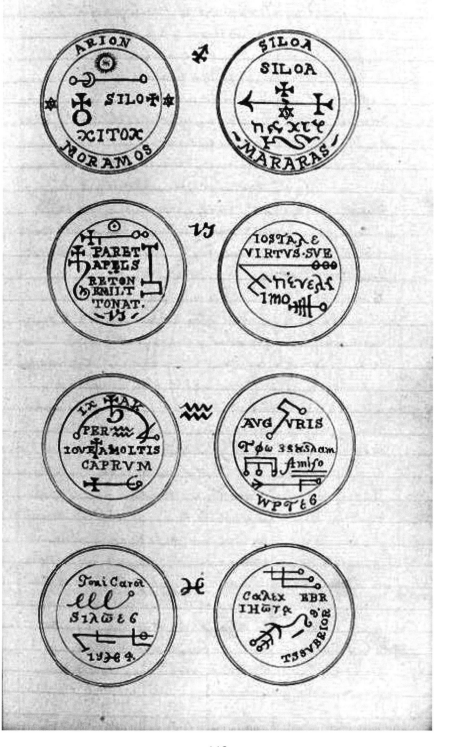

The Talismans of the Signs of the Zodiac

♈ Take of ♂ ʒ p. ☉ ʒ ii. ☾ ʒ i. and ♀ ʒ p. in the day hour and very point wherein ☉ enters the first degree of ♈ (which happens about the 10ᵗʰ of March) and all to be melted with a violent fire, but first the ♂ must be reduced into filings. They being all melted and prepared, on the day of ♂ and the ☾ being in the 9 or 10 degree of ♈ in the same hour it must be finished, but it must be applied when ♂ is in the 8 or 9 house of Heaven. This Seal is said to cure all Fluxes and Catherres descending from the Head upon the Brain, and drieth up all Flegm of the Head and all Diseases which appertain to the Head, it amendeth all Maladies thereof, being worn, night and day, the Sign of ♈ being turned next the Brain.

♉ Take of ♀ ʒ i. ♃ ʒ i. ♂ ʒ p. and of ☉ ʒ ii. Melt and mix all together the ☉ being in ♉ which happens about the 8ᵗʰ day of April, and in the very point of ☉ ingress into ♉ this Seal must be begun and finished, or else the whole will be frustrated, and when the ☾ is in 10 degrees of ♉ it is to be applied. The Nature and Property of this Sigil giveth a most excellent Remedy to them who have lost their Generative Virtue, if it be so hanged that it may touch the Navel. The Sign ♉ being turned next the flesh, it gives the best help to Man or Woman.

♊ Take of ☉ and ☾ each ʒ i. Let them be both melted the ☉ entering ♊ which is about the 10 or 11 day of May. There are two Lamens to be made out of the mixture whereupon the Signs &c are to be engraven on one Side, and both are to be connected together with a band of the same matter about half an inch asunder, that they may not touch one another with the plane faces, that a pipe of the same metal may be interposed that may hold a goose quill full of ☿ when the work is complete let ☿ be poured in the Quill and stoped with mastick the day and hour of ☿ the ☾ decreasing. The Signs are to be engraven when the ☾ is in the Sign ♌ or ♓, but must be applied when ☿ is in the first house or heaven, the air mild. The face of the Seal that hath the Sign ♊ is to be worn upon the naked Skin.

To know the power of this, Seek the Virtues of ♊ in producing Diseases, and Judge according.

♋ Is of pure ☾ in the hour when the ☉ enters ♋ which is about the 10 or 11 day of June. but the ☾ must not be afflicted by any evil aspect or Planet. engrave the Signs ♋ in the hour of the ☾ increasing. in the same hour they must be begun and finished. This Seal must be applied in the day and hour of the ☾ decreasing. and must be kept very clean. The Virtue thereof causeth happy Journeys. it is good against the Dropsie and all diseases proceeding from moisture or superfluous Flegm.

♌ Is of pure ☉ melted and wrought when the ☉ enters the first degree of ♌ which is about the 13 or 14 day of July and perfected before the end of the hour. afterwords when ♃ is in ♓ the Signs ♌ are to be engraven on one side as in the first figure marked A and the other side is to be engraven when the ☾ is in the House of ♃ that is in ♓. Note after the melting of ☉ it must not be put again in the fire. Let it be applied in the day and hour of the ☉ It hath a most excellent virtue, it causeth great Favour to men and women that wear it. it is good against Quartain Feavers, The Liquor is also good to be drunk wherein it hath been infused all night. It is especially approved against Pestilence. and all inward inflamations, and against all Diseases of the Eyes. Coming from heat, and all evil which are called flying Humons. it is also good against Burning the Seal being applied upon the place, draweth out the fire.

82

♍ Is made of ♀ 5i. ☉ 3ʃ. ☽ 5ii and ♃ 3ʃs and melted on the day of the ☉ in August when the ☉ enters into ♍ and reduced into a thin Lamen in the hour of ☿ well aspected let the Characters &c be engraven and finished in the same hour. Let it be applied when ☿ is in the first house of heaven, the Air clear and serene in the hour of ☿.

♎ Is made of pure ♀ when the ☉ enters ♎ which sometimes happens on ☉ day in September, according to the progress of the Year, and this is to be noted, That when ♀ is the ruling Planet or Reservator of the Year, the Sigil will be of much more virtue, especially, if those wear it, who were born under the same Planet. and if it be made and prepared for them, when ♀ is in ♎. The Signs &c are to be engraven, afterwards in the day and hour of ♀. and applied in the first or eight hour which ♀ governs. It is an admirable Remedy against all bewitchings of women, which hinder the act of generation especially in those whom they hate. and is most profitable against all griefs of the Secret members.

♏ Is made of pure ♂ in the day and hour of ♂ when the ☉ enters ♏ which is in October. and in the same hour let one side of of this Lamen marked A be engraved with his Character, afterwards when the ☉ is entered into ♈ let the other side be engraven It may be applied at any time It is a most Remedy against all poyson and Diseases thereby inflicted. it is excellent for Souldiers, Captains and such as are in daily Controversies

♐ Is made of pure ♃ in the hour of the ☉ ingress into ♐ in November, on the first degree of the ingression, let it be signed in the hour of ♃. and applied in the same hour the ☽ increasing. There must be a Ring of ☽ to hang it to and must be kept very clean. But it must be left off in the time of Copulation. or else it looseth its virtue. For its strength and Power is as before done concerning the Sign ♊.

♑ Is made of ☉. for ♄ hath no operation with other Metals. There must be made a Ring of ♀. and together with the Seal, are to be made in the hour when the ☉ enters ♑ and is furthest distant from us. Let the Seal be engraven on the day and hour of ♄ in good aspect with some other Planet. It must be applied when the ☽ is decreasing or diminished in light, but the hour of the aspect, wether it be of the ☽ or any other Planet, matters not. This Sigil is called Seal of Favour. and throughly heals the Itch or Scurff in the Thighs (Paracelsus cured these Diseases by this, without any other means)

♒ Is made of ☉ ℥ ſs. ♄ ʒ ii. and ♂ ʒ i when the ☉ enters ♒ in the month of January. in the same hour, and when ♄ is in the Ninth house let the Signs be quickly engraven. you must not apply it till the ☉ is under the Earth, and in the Hour of ♄; and then it is good, being hanged about the Neck, against Contractures. Cold Diseases, and Sinews Shrunk. it will preserve the Memory and Good to get Favours amongst Men. is good against Poyson. no venemous spider will remain upon it

♓ Is made of ☉. ♂. ♀. ☽. of each ʒ ii and of ♃ ℥ ſs. all melted together when the ☉ enters ♓ in February. and the Seal formed and Engraved in the same hour of the ☉ ingress. Let it be applied when ♃ is well placed in the eight house of heaven and in the day and hour of ♃. This good to Loose and expel Cholera. of which do grow many Diseases, as, Contractures, the Palsie. Shrinking of the Joints. Burnings &c it mitigateth the pain of the gout. taketh away the Cramp, and all griefs proceeding from Flures. This Seal ought to be hanged down low upon the Navel.

Note, some of the Learned, state. Whatever the effects are to be must be wrote around in Latin. And a Verse out of the Scripture must be taken appropriate

They may also be reduced to a Seal or Ring, where there

84

is no reverse, by taking the inscription from out the outside Rim and placing it at the back. the Ring should be hollow and some herb or plant belonging to the Planet. must be concealed. Some of the Learned put on the reverse of their Talismans. the Tables of Squares with Characters and Letters. which often they placed Single Letters. i.e. the first letter of each word, which the whole sentence contain's. which is the reason that is so difficult for one Artist to find out the meaning of anothers work

The proceeding Talismans. Are Originals and very Ancient. and having given the Metals they are to be made of and the exact Method. To render my information complete to the reader I shall now Explain in what manner the Talismans framed from, and with the Square tables on them also See Page 26. for their discription and effects. The Talisman of ♃ composed of his Square table see Page 27 It must be made of Pure Tin. The form as before shown but in the middle Circle must be Placed the full Table of Squares and Numbers on the reverse which you'l see by the Table page 24 which contains all the divine Names belonging to him with their Numbers. In the vacant part of the circle put therein his Characters — and names of angels belonging to him out of his Table Page 151 in form as you'l see Page 164. On the reverse side the Image of the Planet must be Engraved. i.e. A man clothed in a Saccerdotal habit holding a book in his hands in the act of reading. On his head a Star with five Points in the center the Character ♃. and put thereon such Characters suitable to him and the intent made for. the Office it is to performe in Latin or Hebrew. and if for a good purpose It must be made in the Day and Hour of Jupiter when

85

fortunately aspected and free from any impediment. The Moon entering into the first degree of Libra

This Talisman whoever it is made for it conciliate Love and favours, drives away Cares, and cause prosperity in all undertakings in Business and every thing belonging to ♃ If it is made under an unfortunate ♃, every thing will prove Contrary, then the Character of the Spirit must be put in the Square

In the Eight sphere e̊/y 28 Mansions of

m	s	d	ʹ	ʺ		
1	♈	1	-	-	begins	It causeth discords and Journies
2	♈	12	51	26	‹‹‹‹‹‹	For finding treasures & retaining Captives
3	♈	25	42	52	‹‹‹‹‹‹	Profitable to Sailors Huntsmen and Alchymists.
4	♉	8	34	18	‹‹‹‹‹‹	It causeth the destruction & hindrances of Buildings, fountains wells. Creeping things and discords.
5	♉	21	25	44	‹‹‹‹‹‹	It confirmeth Buildings, gives health and Good will
6	♊	4	17	10	‹‹‹‹‹‹	It is for hunting beseiging towns. revenge of Princes. destroys harvests & fruits. hinders operations of Physicians.
7	♊	17	8	36	♃ 7¼ st	It conpeneth gain & friendships. good for Lovers. scareth flies and destroyeth Majesteries.
8	♊	30	0	2	‹‹‹‹‹‹	It causeth love. friendships. it driveth away and afflict captives. confirming their imprisonment
9	♋	12	51	28	‹‹‹‹‹‹	It hindereth harvest and travellers. Sows discords between men.
10	♋	25	42	54	‹‹‹‹‹‹	It strengthens buildings. yields Love - benevolence and help against Enemies
11	♌	8	34	20	‹‹‹‹‹‹	It is good for voyages, and gain by Murchendize and for the Redemption of Captives
12	♌	21	25	46	‹‹‹‹‹‹	It giveth prosperity to harvest & Plantations but hinders Seamen. is good for servants. Captives and companions.
13	♍	4	17	12	‹‹‹‹‹‹	It is good for Benevolence. gains voyages Harvests and freeing of Captives.
14	♍	17	8	38	♃ 2¼ nd	It causeth love of the Married. cureth the Sick. good for Sailors but hinders Journies by land.

the ☽. For Magical purposes,

15	♎	0	0	4 ⋘	It is good for getting treasures it helpeth forward divorce, discords and destruction of houses, enemies and hindereth travellers
16	♎	12	51	30 ⋘	It hinders journies, wedlock, harvest, merchandize but prevaileth on the redemption of Captives.
17	♎	25	42	56 ⋘	It bettereth a bad fortune, make love durable strengthens buildings & help Seamen.
18	♏	8	34	22 ⋘	It causeth discord, sedition, conspiracy against Princes & Great men, revenge on enemies, freeth Captives and preserve Edifices
19	♏	21	25	48 ⋘	It assist in besieging & taking Cities Towns and driving men from their places
20	♐	4	17	14 ⋘	It tameth wild Beasts, destroys the wealth of Societies, & Compelleth a Man to come to a certain place
21	♐	17	8	40 ⋗ 3¼ ʳᵈ	It is Good for harvest, gain buildings, and travellers, and causeth divorce,
22	♑	0	0	6 ⋘	It promoteth the escape of Captives and cures diseases
23	♑	12	51	32 ⋘	It causeth divorce, liberty of Captives and healeth the Sick
24	♑	25	42	58 ⋘	It is Benevolent to the Married Causeth Victory to Soldiers, and hurteth the execution of government that it may not be exercised.
25	♒	8	34	24 ⋘	It helps revenge, destroys enemies maketh divorce, for spells against copulation, and bindeth every member of Man from performing its duty
26	♒	21	25	50 ⋘	It causeth a union & friendship of Men, and destroys prisons and Buildings
27	♓	4	17	16 ⋘	It is good for harvest, Revenues, Gain, heals the infirm, hinders buildings, causes danger to seamen & cause mischiefs on whom you please
28	♓	17	8	42 ⋗ 4¼ ᵗʰ	It is good for harvest & Merchandize, secures travellers through dangerous places, and cause loss of treasures.

Planetary table of the Cabala for extracting the names of the Angels good or Evil
English

	of good	♄	♃	♂	☉	♀	☿	☽	1799	
1	A	A 1	B 2	C 3	D 4	E 5	F 6	G 7	U	400
2	B	H 8	Ie 9	I 10	K 20	L 30	M 40	N 50	V	300
3	C	O 60	P 70	Q 80	R 90	S 100	T 200	V 300	T	200
4	D	U 400	A 1	B 2	C 3	D 4	E 5	F 6	S	100
5	E	G 7	H 8	Ie 9	I 10	K 20	L 30	M 40	R	90
6	F	N 50	O 60	P 70	Q 80	R 90	S 100	T 200	Q	80
7	G	V 300	U 400	A 1	B 2	C 3	D 4	E 5	P	70
8	H	F 6	G 7	H 8	I 9	J 10	K 20	L 30	O	60
9	I cof	M 40	N 50	O 60	P 70	Q 80	R 90	S 100	N	50
10	I	T 200	V 300	U 400	A 1	B 2	C 3	D 4	M	40
20	K	E 5	F 6	G 7	H 8	Ie 9	J 10	K 20	L	30
30	L	L 30	M 40	N 50	O 60	P 70	Q 80	R 90	K	20
40	M	S 100	T 200	V 300	U 400	A 1	B 2	C 3	I	10
50	N	D 4	E 5	F 6	G 7	H 8	I 9	J 10	I cof	9
60	O	K 20	L 30	M 40	N 50	O 60	P 70	Q 80	H	8
70	P	R 90	S 100	T 200	V 300	U 400	A 1	B 2	G	7
80	Q	C 3	D 4	E 5	F 6	G 7	H 8	I 9	F	6
90	R	J 10	K 20	L 30	M 40	N 50	O 60	P 70	E	5
100	S	Q 80	R 90	S 100	T 200	V 300	U 400	A 1	D	4
200	T	B 2	C 3	D 4	E 5	F 6	G 7	H 8	C	3
300	V	I 9	J 10	K 20	L 30	M 40	N 50	O 60	B	2
400	U	P 70	Q 80	R 90	S 100	T 200	V 300	U 400	A	1
	1799	☽	☿	♀	☉	♂	♃	♄	of evil	

Planetary table of the Cabalar for extracting the names of the Angels good or Evil
Hebrew

	1799	☽	☿	♀	☉	♂	♃	♄	of good
400	ת	ז	ו	ה	ד	ג	ב	א	1
300	ש	ג	ט	ל	כ	י	ט	ב	2
200	ר	ש	ר	ק	צ	פ	י	ג	3
100	ק	ו	ה	ד	ג	ב	א	ד	4
90	צ	מ	ל	כ	י	ט	ז	ה	5
80	פ	ל	ק	צ	פ	ע	ס	ו	6
70	ע	ה	ד	ב	א	ת	ש	ז	7
60	ס	ל	כ	י	ט	ח	ו	ח	8
50	נ	ק	צ	פ	ע	ס	נ	ט	9
40	מ	ד	ב	ב	ח	ש	ר	י	10
30	ל	ג	י	ט	ח	ז	ו	כ	20
20	כ	צ	פ	ע	ס	נ	מ	ל	30
10	י	ג	ב	א	ת	ש	ר	מ	40
9	ט	ט	ח	ז	ו	ה	ד	נ	50
8	ח	פ	ע	ס	נ	מ	ל	ס	60
7	ז	ב	א	ת	ש	ר	ק	ע	70
6	ו	ט	ח	ז	ו	ה	ד	פ	80
5	ה	א	ס	נ	מ	ל	י	צ	90
4	ד	א	ה	ש	ר	ק	צ	ק	100
3	ג	ה	ז	ו	ה	ד	ב	ר	200
2	ב	ס	מ	ל	כ	י	ט	ש	300
1	א	ח	ז	ר	כ	פ	ע	ת	400
	of evil	♄	♃	♂	☉	♀	☿	☽	1799

A Table of the Twelve Signs.
From which the Names of the Good and Evil Angels are Extracted.

good g-	♈	♉	♊	♋	♌	♍	♎	♏	♐	♑	♒	♓	⊗
1	A 1	B 2	C 3	D 4	E 5	F 6	G 7	H 8	I 9	J 10	K 20	L 30	U 400	400
2	B 2	L 30	K 20	J 10	I 9	H 8	G 7	F 6	E 5	D 4	C 3	B 2	A 1	V 300	300
3	C 3	M 40	N 50	O 60	P 70	Q 80	R 90	S 100	T 200	U 300	V 400	A 1	B 2	T 200	200
4	D 4	B 2	A 1	U 400	V 300	T 200	S 100	R 90	Q 80	P 70	O 60	N 50	M 40	S 100	100
5	E 5	C 3	D 4	E 5	F 6	G 7	H 8	I 9	J 10	K 20	L 30	M 40	N 50	R 90	90
6	F 6	N 50	M 40	L 30	K 20	J 10	I 9	H 8	G 7	F 6	E 5	D 4	C 3	Q 80	80
7	G 7	O 60	P 70	Q 80	R 90	S 100	T 200	U 300	V 400	A 1	B 2	C 3	D 4	P 70	70
8	H 8	D 4	C 3	B 2	A 1	U 400	V 300	T 200	S 100	R 90	Q 80	P 70	O 60	O 60	60
9	I 9	E 5	F 6	G 7	H 8	I 9	J 10	K 20	L 30	M 40	N 50	O 60	P 70	N 50	50
10	J 10	P 70	O 60	N 50	M 40	L 30	K 20	J 10	I 9	H 8	G 7	F 6	E 5	M 40	40
20	K 20	Q 80	R 90	S 100	T 200	U 300	A 1	B 2	C 3	D 4	E 5	F 6	L 30	30
30	L 30	F 6	E 5	D 4	C 3	B 2	A 1	U 400	V 300	T 200	S 100	R 90	Q 80	K 20	20
40	M 40	G 7	H 8	I 9	J 10	K 20	L 30	M 40	N 50	O 60	P 70	Q 80	R 90	J 10	10
50	N 50	R 90	Q 80	P 70	O 60	N 50	M 40	L 30	K 20	J 10	I 9	H 8	G 7	I 9	9
60	O 60	S 100	T 200	U 300	V 400	A 1	B 2	C 3	D 4	E 5	F 6	G 7	H 8	H 8	8
70	P 70	H 8	G 7	F 6	E 5	D 4	C 3	B 2	A 1	U 400	V 300	T 200	S 100	G 7	7
80	Q 80	I 9	J 10	K 20	L 30	M 40	N 50	O 60	P 70	Q 80	R 90	S 100	T 200	F 6	6
90	R 90	T 200	S 100	R 90	Q 80	P 70	O 60	N 50	M 40	L 30	K 20	J 10	I 9	E 5	5
100	S 100	V 300	U 400	A 1	B 2	C 3	D 4	E 5	F 6	G 7	H 8	I 9	J 10	D 4	4
200	T 200	J 10	I 9	H 8	G 7	F 6	E 5	D 4	C 3	B 2	A 1	U 400	V 300	C 3	3
300	V 300	K 20	L 30	M 40	N 50	O 60	P 70	Q 80	R 90	S 100	T 200	U 300	B 2	2
400	U 400	U 400	V 300	T 200	S 100	R 90	Q 80	P 70	O 60	N 50	M 40	L 30	K 20	A 1	1
	⊗	♓	♒	♑	♐	♏	♎	♍	♌	♋	♊	♉	♈	evil

The Hebrew Notes for the Same.
Which may be wrought by Numbers.

	⊗	♓	♒	♑	♐	♏	♎	♍	♌	♋	♊	♉	♈	god
400	ת	כ	׳	פ	ח	ק	ה	ה	ד	ג	ב	א	א	1
300	ט	א	ג	ד	ה	ו	ז	ח	ט	י	כ	ל	ב	2
200	ר	ב	ה	ש	ר	ק	צ	פ	ע	ס	נ	מ	ג	3
100	ק	מ	ג	ס	ע	פ	צ	ק	ר	ש	ח	א	ד	4
90	צ	נ	מ	ל	כ	י	ט	ח	ז	ו	ה	ד	ח	5
80	פ	ג	ד	ה	ו	ז	ח	ט	י	כ	ל	מ	ו	6
70	ע	ד	ג	ב	א	ח	ש	ר	ק	צ	פ	ס	ז	7
60	ס	ע	פ	צ	ק	ר	ש	ח	א	ב	ג	ד	ח	8
50	נ	ע	ס	נ	מ	ל	כ	י	ט	ז	ו	ה	ט	9
40	מ	ה	ו	ז	ח	ט	י	כ	ל	מ	נ	ס	י	10
30	ל	ו	ה	ד	ג	ב	א	ת	ש	ר	ק	צ	פ	20
20	כ	פ	צ	ק	ר	ש	ת	א	ב	ג	ד	ה	ו	ל	30
10	י	צ	פ	ע	ס	נ	מ	ל	כ	י	ט	ח	מ	40
9	ט	ז	ח	ט	י	כ	ל	מ	נ	ס	פ	צ	נ	50
8	ח	ת	ז	ו	ה	ד	ג	ב	א	ה	ו	ז	ס	60
7	ז	ק	ר	ש	ת	א	ב	ג	ד	ה	ו	ח	ע	70
6	ו	ר	ק	צ	פ	ע	ס	נ	מ	ל	כ	י	פ	80
5	ה	ש	י	ב	ל	מ	נ	ס	ע	פ	צ	ק	ר	90
4	ד	י	ת	ז	ה	ד	ג	ב	א	ת	ש	ר	ק	100
3	ג	ת	ש	ר	ז	ד	ה	ו	ז	ח	ט	י	ר	200
2	ב	ת	ש	ק	צ	פ	ע	ס	נ	מ	ל	כ	ש	300
1	א	ל	מ	נ	ס	ע	פ	צ	ק	ר	ש	ת	ת	400
	evil	♈	♉	♊	♋	♌	♍	♎	♏	♐	♑	♒	♓	⊗

91

125

Tables of Numeral Transpositions

A № 1

1 & 1 means 2 the number 1 & 2 makes 3 so on through

A				
B	AA 1·1			
C	AB 1·2			
D	AC 1·3	BB 2·2		
E	AD 1·4	BC 2·3		
F	AE 1·5	BD 2·4	CC 3·3	
G	AF 1·6	BE 2·5	CD 3·4	
H	AG 1·7	BF 2·6	CE 3·5	DD 4·4
Ic	AH 1·8	BG 2·7	CF 3·6	DE 4·5
I	AI 1·9	BH 2·8	GG 3·7	DF 4·6	EE 5·5

א	1
בא	2
גב	3
ד אג בב	4
ה אד בג	5
ו אה בד גג	6
ז או בה גד	7
ח אז בו גה דד	8
ט אח בז גו דה	9
י אט בח גז דו חה	10

Table of even Numbers — B № 2

I					
K	II 10·10				
L	IK 10·20				
M	IL 10·30	KK 20·20			
N	IM 10·40	KL 20·30			
O	IN 10·50	KM 20·40	LL 30·30		
P	IO 10·60	KN 20·50	LM 30·40		
Q	IP 10·70	KO 20·60	LN 30·50	MM 40·40	
R	IQ 10·80	KP 20·70	LO 30·60	MN 40·50	
S	IR 10·90	KQ 20·80	LP 30·70	MO 40·60	NN 50·50

י	10
ב יי	20
ל יב	30
מ יל בב	40
נ ימ בל	50
ס יב כמ לל	60
ע יס בנ למ	70
פ יע כס לנ ממ	80
צ יפ כע לס מנ	90
ק יצ כפ לע מס נג	100

Table of even Continued

S T
100-100 make 200 – 1 & 2 mean 100 & 200 which is 300
S V
1 & 3 is 100 & 300 which is 400 &c

C
N° 3

S				
T	SS 100·100			
V	ST 1·2			
U	SV 1·3	TT 2·2		
W	SU 1·4	TV 2·3		
X	SW 1·5	TU 2·4	VV 3·3	
Y	SX 1·6	TW 2·5	VU 3·4	
Z	SY 1·7	TX 2·6	VW 3·5	UU 4·4
&	SZ 1·8	TY 2·7	VX 3·6	UW 4·5
A	S& 1·9	TZ 2·8	VY 3·7	UX 4·6 ✠

ק	100
ר	200
ש	300
ת	400
ך	500
ם	600
ן	700
ף	800
ץ	900
א	1000 ✠

Table of Odd Numbers

D
N° 4

IA 10·1	IᶜB 9·2	HC 8·3	GD 7·4	FE 6·5
IB 10·2	IᶜC 9·3	HD 8·4	GE 7·5	FF 6·6
IC 10·3	IᶜD 9·4	HE 8·5	GF 7·6	
ID 10·4	IᶜE 9·5	HF 8·6	GG 7·7	
IE 10·5	IᶜF 9·6	HG 8·7		
IF 10·6	IᶜG 9·7	HH 8·8		
IG 10·7	IᶜH 9·8			
IH 10·8	IᶜIᶜ 9·9			
IIᶜ 10·9				

ה	ז	ג	ב	יא	11
ו	ז	ד	ג	יב	12
	ז	ה	ד	יג	13
		ז	ה	יד	14
		ז	ו	יה	15
		ח	ז	יו	16
			ח	יז	17
			ט	יח	18
				יט	19

94

The Table of Odd Numbers with a Cypher

S.J 1.10	R.K 9.2	Q.L 8.3	P.M 7.4	O.N 6.5
S.K 1.20	R.L 9.3	Q.M 8.4	P.N 7.5	O.O 6.6
S.L 1.30	R.M 9.4	Q.N 8.5	P.O 7.6	
S.M 1.40	R.N 9.5	Q.O 8.6	P.P 7.7	
S.N 1.50	R.O 9.6	Q.P 8.7		
S.O 1.60	R.P 9.7	Q.Q 8.8		
S.P 1.70	R.Q 9.8		T.& 2.9	V.Z 3.8	U.Y 4.7	1100
S.Q 1.80	R.R 9.9			V.& 3.9	U.Z 4.8	1200
S.R 1.90					U.& 4.9	1300

E
Nº 5

				ק'	110
				קכ	120
				קל	130
				קמ	140
				קנ	150
				קס	160
				קע	170
				קפ	180
				קצ	190

Note (with) T.&/2.9. means 1100 &c.

10	10	10	10	5
A.I 1.9	B.H 2.8	C.G 3.7	D.F 4.6	E 5
100	**100**	**100**	**100**	**50**
J.R 10.90	K.Q 20.80	L.P 30.70	M.O 40.60	N 50
1000	**1000**	**1000**	**1000**	**500**
S.& 100.900	T.Z 200.800	V.Y 300.700	U.X 400.600	W 500

5	10	10	10	10
ה	דג	זו	בח	אט
50	**100**	**100**	**100**	**100**
נ	מס	לע	כפ	יצ
500	**1000**	**1000**	**1000**	**1000**
ך	םת	ןש	ףר	קץ

The various Numerations of 10. 100. & a 1000
Example

A.I - 1.9 stands for 10 &c. J.R - 10.90 for 100 &c
S.& - 100.900. stands for 1000 &c.
observing that it is the method of calculating the above
numbers by two Letters in any Language or Nation

Explanations of the Tables of Numeral Transpositions from the Unit 1. to 1000.
Chap 13

Example A. N° 1. A being the first letter in the Alphabet signifies. a unit. and B the second letter signifies that to Compound the letter B. or the number 2 - two units must be added together. C being the third letter and the only way of compounding the number. 1 & 2 which is A & B. D being the fourth letter, it comes into double compound (v.c). A the first letter and C the third. A C makes the number four, also two B's which is the second letter makes the same number. E being the fifth letter is also a double compound and Compounded by A1..D4.. which is five and B2..C3.. which is the same number. F being the sixth letter is a Treble compound and is Compounded by A1..E5 - B2.D4 & C3..C3. each making the same number Six G being the Seventh letter it is a treble Compound also and is Compounded by A1.. F6.B2..E5.& C3..D4. H being the eight letter it is four times compounded and is compound by A1. G7. B2. F6. C3. E5. D4.D4. I being the Ninth letter it is also four times compounded and is Compounded by A1..H8.B2.G7. C3..F6.D4..E5. J Being the tenth letter it is five times compounded and is Compounded of A1..I9.B2..H8.C3..G7.D4..E6.& E5..E5. which numbers each added together. 1 & 9 is 10. 2 & 8 is 10. 3 & 7 is 10. 4 & 6 is 10. and two fives make 10. Therefore the number 10 is compounded in five ways which are the only ways it can be compounded. As such according to Numeral Transpositions the B. can be Compounded but once. The C once. The D twice. The E twice. The F thrice. The G thrice The H four times. The I four times. and the J five times. so that after the number five. each number is compounded only half the power of itself.

Example the 2nd B N°2

Which begins at the number 10 that being the revolving the unit again with the first addition of a Cyphor, on which ac--count it is revered by the Ancient Rabbies, as the Holy number which they apply to God as "Yod or Iod, and what they term the last, and the Aleph the first letter of the Hebrew Alph--abet is called the Mother of All. The first and the last Alpha & Omega i,e explain'd thus it begins with a Yod first Second thus and thirdly and lastly it finishes with a Yod thus therefore it is began and finished with a Yod the same power, being thus compounded they placed to the Earth as an emblem of the Mother of all things, and the Vau which in fact is part of its composition to the Water as an emblem of nourishment to all things. and the Yod to the fire as an emblem of invigoration of all things. for wit--hout vital heat all things must die

Now from that number being 10 the begining of the adition of Cyphers they numerate to a 100. and according to the letters of tens they class them as the former, as they are precisely compounded in the same manner. and the same number of time each Compounded as 10. 20. 30. 40. 50. 60. 70. 80. 90. 100.

Example the 3rd C N°3

which begins at the letter S, the number of which is 100. which is the Second revolution of the unit with the asis--tance of two Cyphers. as such they numerate to a Thousand as 100. 200. 300. 400. 500. 600. 700. 800. 900. 1000. which is the highest numeration requisite in this Science

Example the 4th D N°4

Are the compounds of odd numbers, as. 11. 12. 13. 14. 15. 16. 17. 18. 19. which includes one third part of the 27 letters. and shews that the number is Compounded 5 times

The number 12. 5 times The number 13. 4 times The number 14. 4 times The number 15. 3 times. The number 16. 3 times The number 17. twice The number 18. twice and the number 19. Once. So that as the compounds of the nine Digits and the even numbers of the tens increase in compounding the same so do the odd numbers decrease. as is seen by the number 19 which is the highest number yet there is only one way of Compounding it when the number 11 which is the lowest number. is compounded five different ways.

Example 5th E No 5

This is a Table of odd numbers with a Cypher added which Cypher only make a difference of the preceeding Table Marked D which plainly shews that the greater encrease in Number the less number of Compounds belongs to it — therefore as there is but one way of Compounding the number 19 in Numeral Transposition, there is no more in compounding 190 & 1300. And to make the number 100 and upwards. familiar. I shall explain the top line which is as follows. S 1. stands for 100, and J. 10 stands for 10 which added makes 110 + R 9. stands for 90, and K 2 stands for 20 which makes 110 + Q 8 stands for 80 and L 3. stands for 30 which makes 110 + P 7 stands for 70 and M 4 stands for 40 which makes 110 + O 6 Stands for 60 and N 5 stands for 50 which makes 110 + therefore the number 110 is compounded four different ways which are the only members of numeral compounds of that number. the same for the rest.

The Use made of the Tables. Every Planet according to his nature wether Good or Bad has so many offices belonging to him therefore according to what office it is there is a certian Spirit to be extracted to execute that part appointed to his power as the duties of his Office, (as a Clerk is appointed to any office under Man)

98

Example

In the tables of Trades &c Chap 8. I select under ♌. A Judge, and his office is Justice therefore I want to find the name of the Intelligence of Justice. To find which I enter the Table (for extracting Names of Angels &c Page 88 with the word JUSTICE and at the Column angels under ♌ in the line Good on the top I bring out these letters V Q R C N P H the numbers of which is 300, 80, 90, 3, 50, 70, 8. Now on looking in the square table of ♌ Page 27 I find that the number 16 is the highest as such to extract the Char-acter I cannot without <u>Numeral Transposition</u>. therefore the first letter being V and the number 300, I throw out the Cyphers and look in the Table of the Twelve Signs for extracting the Names of Angels &c Page 90. for the third letter and find it C I then look for the eight letter and find it H I then look for the 9th and find that I and so through the rest. Having now found what letters, by <u>Numeral Transposition</u>, answers to those with Cyphers I collect them together according to their numbers. C H I C E G H. adding to them EL. the
3. 8. 9. 3. 5. 7. 8
great name of God, which forms the word CHICEGHEL which is the true name of the Intelligence of Justice and must be (to gain the Character of the same) drawn out as I have before explained from the square table of ♌ Consequently if I want to Frame a Talisman to obtain Justice, thus must the Name be found and the Charact-er extracted, and in the same manner are drawn forth and Extracted all Angels Intelligences & Spirits of all the Signs, Planets, Proffesions, Trades Offices &c The Learned Rabbies advise to work from the Offices only.

As peraps all my readers may not understand the Hebrew

Notes I have placed the English letters to answer them, and as I have before advised in point of the imperfection of our Alphabet for this Science. I have only thus arranged them for the convenience of explaining the use of the Tables therefore if any wish to excel, he must follow correctly the Hebrew Language and Notes, which are correctly arranged for the purpose or he must from the same tables which I have put in english Letters into either of the Alphabets according to their Numbers at the beginning of the Work I shall say no more of this but draw a conclusion and advise that thou first seek thy Creator and serve him truly. by such means thou shalt become perfect. for in all temporal things thou ought to call upon God as a Father and pray as follows

O Lord of heaven and Earth, Creator and maker of all things Visible and invisible; I though unworthy, by thy assistance call upon thee through thy only begotten Son Jesus Christ our Lord, that thou wilt give unto me thy holy Spirit, to direct me in thy truth unto all good Works. Amen Because I earnestly desire perfectly to know the Arts of this life, for the good of my fellow Creatures, and such things as are necessary for us, which are so overwhelmed in darkness, and polluted with infinite human opinions that I of my own power can attain to no knowledge in them, unless thou teach it me: Grant me therefor O Lord one of thy Spirits, who may teach me those things which thou wouldest have me to know and learn, to thy praise and Glory, and the profit of our Neighbour, Give me also an apt and teachable heart, that I may easily understand those things which though should teach me, and hide them in my understanding, that I may bring forth as out of thy inexaustable treasures to all necessary uses, and give me grace, that I may use such thy gifts humbly, with fear and trembling, through our Lord Jesus Christ with thy holy Spirit. Amen

A Right table of Commutations.

GOOD

A	B	C	D	E	F	G	H	I	J	K	L	M	N	O	P	Q	R	S	T	V	U
1	2	3	4	5	6	7	8	9	10	20	30	40	50	60	70	80	90	100	200	300	400
B	C	D	E	F	G	H	I	J	K	L	M	N	O	P	Q	R	S	T	V	U	A
2	3	4	5	6	7	8	9	10	20	30	40	50	60	70	80	90	100	200	300	400	1
C	D	E	F	G	H	I	J	K	L	M	N	O	P	Q	R	S	T	V	U	A	B
3	4	5	6	7	8	9	10	20	30	40	50	60	70	80	90	100	200	300	400	1	2
D	E	F	G	H	I	J	K	L	M	N	O	P	Q	R	S	T	V	U	A	B	C
4	5	6	7	8	9	10	20	30	40	50	60	70	80	90	100	200	300	400	1	2	3
E	F	G	H	I	J	K	L	M	N	O	P	Q	R	S	T	V	U	A	B	C	D
5	6	7	8	9	10	20	30	40	50	60	70	80	90	100	200	300	400	1	2	3	4
F	G	H	I	J	K	L	M	N	O	P	Q	R	S	T	V	U	A	B	C	D	E
6	7	8	9	10	20	30	40	50	60	70	80	90	100	200	300	400	1	2	3	4	5
G	H	I	J	K	L	M	N	O	P	Q	R	S	T	V	U	A	B	C	D	E	F
7	8	9	10	20	30	40	50	60	70	80	90	100	200	300	400	1	2	3	4	5	6
H	I	J	K	L	M	N	O	P	Q	R	S	T	V	U	A	B	C	D	E	F	G
8	9	10	20	30	40	50	60	70	80	90	100	200	300	400	1	2	3	4	5	6	7
I	J	K	L	M	N	O	P	Q	R	S	T	V	U	A	B	C	D	E	F	G	H
9	10	20	30	40	50	60	70	80	90	100	200	300	400	1	2	3	4	5	6	7	8
J	K	L	M	N	O	P	Q	R	S	T	V	U	A	B	C	D	E	F	G	H	I
10	20	30	40	50	60	70	80	90	100	200	300	400	1	2	3	4	5	6	7	8	9
K	L	M	N	O	P	Q	R	S	T	V	U	A	B	C	D	E	F	G	H	I	J
20	30	40	50	60	70	80	90	100	200	300	400	1	2	3	4	5	6	7	8	9	10
L	M	N	O	P	Q	R	S	T	V	U	A	B	C	D	E	F	G	H	I	J	K
30	40	50	60	70	80	90	100	200	300	400	1	2	3	4	5	6	7	8	9	10	20
M	N	O	P	Q	R	S	T	V	U	A	B	C	D	E	F	G	H	I	J	K	L
40	50	60	70	80	90	100	200	300	400	1	2	3	4	5	6	7	8	9	10	20	30
N	O	P	Q	R	S	T	V	U	A	B	C	D	E	F	G	H	I	J	K	L	M
50	60	70	80	90	100	200	300	400	1	2	3	4	5	6	7	8	9	10	20	30	40
O	P	Q	R	S	T	V	U	A	B	C	D	E	F	G	H	I	J	K	L	M	N
60	70	80	90	100	200	300	400	1	2	3	4	5	6	7	8	9	10	20	30	40	50
P	Q	R	S	T	V	U	A	B	C	D	E	F	G	H	I	J	K	L	M	N	O
70	80	90	100	200	300	400	1	2	3	4	5	6	7	8	9	10	20	30	40	50	60
Q	R	S	T	V	U	A	B	C	D	E	F	G	H	I	J	K	L	M	N	O	P
80	90	100	200	300	400	1	2	3	4	5	6	7	8	9	10	20	30	40	50	60	70
R	S	T	V	U	A	B	C	D	E	F	G	H	I	J	K	L	M	N	O	P	Q
90	100	200	300	400	1	2	3	4	5	6	7	8	9	10	20	30	40	50	60	70	80
S	T	V	U	A	B	C	D	E	F	G	H	I	J	K	L	M	N	O	P	Q	R
100	200	300	400	1	2	3	4	5	6	7	8	9	10	20	30	40	50	60	70	80	90
T	V	U	A	B	C	D	E	F	G	H	I	J	K	L	M	N	O	P	Q	R	S
200	300	400	1	2	3	4	5	6	7	8	9	10	20	30	40	50	60	70	80	90	100
V	U	A	B	C	D	E	F	G	H	I	J	K	L	M	N	O	P	Q	R	S	T
300	400	1	2	3	4	5	6	7	8	9	10	20	30	40	50	60	70	80	90	100	200
U	A	B	C	D	E	F	G	H	I	J	K	L	M	N	O	P	Q	R	S	T	V
400	1	2	3	4	5	6	7	8	9	10	20	30	40	50	60	70	80	90	100	200	300

This Table is numbered according to the Hebrew Notes but the letters which are our own alphabet. are only set to explain the Nature as such the Hebrew should be made use of. to obtain truth.

A Right Table of Commutations

GOOD

ת	ש	ר	ק	צ	פ	ע	ס	נ	מ	ל	כ	י	ט	ח	ז	ו	ה	ד	ג	ב	א
א	ת	ש	ר	ק	צ	פ	ע	ס	נ	מ	ל	כ	י	ט	ח	ז	ו	ה	ד	ג	ב
ב	א	ת	ש	ר	ק	צ	פ	ע	ס	נ	מ	ל	כ	י	ט	ח	ז	ו	ה	ד	ג
ג	ב	א	ת	ש	ר	ק	צ	פ	ע	ס	נ	מ	ל	כ	י	ט	ח	ז	ו	ה	ד
ד	ג	ב	א	ת	ש	ר	ק	צ	פ	ע	ס	נ	מ	ל	כ	י	ט	ח	ז	ו	ה
ה	ד	ג	ב	א	ת	ש	ר	ק	צ	פ	ע	ס	נ	מ	ל	כ	י	ט	ח	ז	ו
ו	ה	ד	ג	ב	א	ת	ש	ר	ק	צ	פ	ע	ס	נ	מ	ל	כ	י	ט	ח	ז
ז	ו	ה	ד	ג	ב	א	ת	ש	ר	ק	צ	פ	ע	ס	נ	מ	ל	כ	י	ט	ח
ח	ז	ו	ה	ד	ג	ב	א	ת	ש	ר	ק	צ	פ	ע	ס	נ	מ	ל	כ	י	ט
ט	ח	ז	ו	ה	ד	ג	ב	א	ת	ש	ר	ק	צ	פ	ע	ס	נ	מ	ל	כ	י
י	ט	ח	ז	ו	ה	ד	ג	ב	א	ת	ש	ר	ק	צ	פ	ע	ס	נ	מ	ל	כ
כ	י	ט	ח	ז	ו	ה	ד	ג	ב	א	ת	ש	ר	ק	צ	פ	ע	ס	נ	מ	ל
ל	כ	י	ט	ח	ז	ו	ה	ד	ג	ב	א	ת	ש	ר	ק	צ	פ	ע	ס	נ	מ
מ	ל	כ	י	ט	ח	ז	ו	ה	ד	ג	ב	א	ת	ש	ר	ק	צ	פ	ע	ס	נ
נ	מ	ל	כ	י	ט	ח	ז	ו	ה	ד	ג	ב	א	ת	ש	ר	ק	צ	פ	ע	ס
ס	נ	מ	ל	כ	י	ט	ח	ז	ו	ה	ד	ג	ב	א	ת	ש	ר	ק	צ	פ	ע
ע	ס	נ	מ	ל	כ	י	ט	ח	ז	ו	ה	ד	ג	ב	א	ת	ש	ר	ק	צ	פ
פ	ע	ס	נ	מ	ל	כ	י	ט	ח	ז	ו	ה	ד	ג	ב	א	ת	ש	ר	ק	צ
צ	פ	ע	ס	נ	מ	ל	כ	י	ט	ח	ז	ו	ה	ד	ג	ב	א	ת	ש	ר	ק
ק	צ	פ	ע	ס	נ	מ	ל	כ	י	ט	ח	ז	ו	ה	ד	ג	ב	א	ת	ש	ר
ר	ק	צ	פ	ע	ס	נ	מ	ל	כ	י	ט	ח	ז	ו	ה	ד	ג	ב	א	ת	ש
ש	ר	ק	צ	פ	ע	ס	נ	מ	ל	כ	י	ט	ח	ז	ו	ה	ד	ג	ב	א	ת

This Table is used to Exchange one Name for another for Good purposes. As for the Obtaining any thing for the Benefit of Man &c

102

The Averse table of the Commutations

U	V	T	S	R	Q	P	O	N	M	L	K	J	I	H	G	F	E	D	C	B	A
400	300	200	100	90	80	70	60	50	40	30	20	10	9	8	7	6	5	4	3	2	1
V	T	S	R	Q	P	O	N	M	L	K	J	I	H	G	F	E	D	C	B	A	U
300	200	100	90	80	70	60	50	40	30	20	10	9	8	7	6	5	4	3	2	1	400
T	S	R	Q	P	O	N	M	L	K	J	I	H	G	F	E	D	C	B	A	U	V
200	100	90	80	70	60	50	40	30	20	10	9	8	7	6	5	4	3	2	1	400	300
S	R	Q	P	O	N	M	L	K	J	I	H	G	F	E	D	C	B	A	U	V	T
100	90	80	70	60	50	40	30	20	10	9	8	7	6	5	4	3	2	1	400	300	200
R	Q	P	O	N	M	L	K	J	I	H	G	F	E	D	C	B	A	U	V	T	S
90	80	70	60	50	40	30	20	10	9	8	7	6	5	4	3	2	1	400	300	200	100
Q	P	O	N	M	L	K	J	I	H	G	F	E	D	C	B	A	U	V	T	S	R
80	70	60	50	40	30	20	10	9	8	7	6	5	4	3	2	1	400	300	200	100	90
P	O	N	M	L	K	J	I	H	G	F	E	D	C	B	A	U	V	T	S	R	Q
70	60	50	40	30	20	10	9	8	7	6	5	4	3	2	1	400	300	200	100	90	80
O	N	M	L	K	J	I	H	G	F	E	D	C	B	A	U	V	T	S	R	Q	P
60	50	40	30	20	10	9	8	7	6	5	4	3	2	1	400	300	200	100	90	80	70
N	M	L	K	J	I	H	G	F	E	D	C	B	A	U	V	T	S	R	Q	P	O
50	40	30	20	10	9	8	7	6	5	4	3	2	1	400	300	200	100	90	80	70	60
M	L	K	J	I	H	G	F	E	D	C	B	A	U	V	T	S	R	Q	P	O	N
40	30	20	10	9	8	7	6	5	4	3	2	1	400	300	200	100	90	80	70	60	50
L	K	J	I	H	G	F	E	D	C	B	A	U	V	T	S	R	Q	P	O	N	M
30	20	10	9	8	7	6	5	4	3	2	1	400	300	200	100	90	80	70	60	50	40
K	J	I	H	G	F	E	D	C	B	A	U	V	T	S	R	Q	P	O	N	M	L
20	10	9	8	7	6	5	4	3	2	1	400	300	200	100	90	80	70	60	50	40	30
J	I	H	G	F	E	D	C	B	A	U	V	T	S	R	Q	P	O	N	M	L	K
10	9	8	7	6	5	4	3	2	1	400	300	200	100	90	80	70	60	50	40	30	20
I	H	G	F	E	D	C	B	A	U	V	T	S	R	Q	P	O	N	M	L	K	J
9	8	7	6	5	4	3	2	1	400	300	200	100	90	80	70	60	50	40	30	20	10
H	G	F	E	D	C	B	A	U	V	T	S	R	Q	P	O	N	M	L	K	J	I
8	7	6	5	4	3	2	1	400	300	200	100	90	80	70	60	50	40	30	20	10	9
G	F	E	D	C	B	A	U	V	T	S	R	Q	P	O	N	M	L	K	J	I	H
7	6	5	4	3	2	1	400	300	200	100	90	80	70	60	50	40	30	20	10	9	8
F	E	D	C	B	A	U	V	T	S	R	Q	P	O	N	M	L	K	J	I	H	G
6	5	4	3	2	1	400	300	200	100	90	80	70	60	50	40	30	20	10	9	8	7
E	D	C	B	A	U	V	T	S	R	Q	P	O	N	M	L	K	J	I	H	G	F
5	4	3	2	1	400	300	200	100	90	80	70	60	50	40	30	20	10	9	8	7	6
D	C	B	A	U	V	T	S	R	Q	P	O	N	M	L	K	J	I	H	G	F	E
4	3	2	1	400	300	200	100	90	80	70	60	50	40	30	20	10	9	8	7	6	5
C	B	A	U	V	T	S	R	Q	P	O	N	M	L	K	J	I	H	G	F	E	D
3	2	1	400	300	200	100	90	80	70	60	50	40	30	20	10	9	8	7	6	5	4
B	A	U	V	T	S	R	Q	P	O	N	M	L	K	J	I	H	G	F	E	D	C
2	1	400	300	200	100	90	80	70	60	50	40	30	20	10	9	8	7	6	5	4	3
A	U	V	T	S	R	Q	P	O	N	M	L	K	J	I	H	G	F	E	D	C	B
1	400	300	200	100	90	80	70	60	50	40	30	20	10	9	8	7	6	5	4	3	2

evil

This Table is as before the Numbers of the Hebrew Notes which correctly corresponds. but not the letters only to explain by

The Averse table of the Commutations

א	ב	ג	ד	ה	ו	ז	ח	ט	י	כ	ל	מ	נ	ס	ע	פ	צ	ק	ר	ש	ת
ת	א	ב	ג	ד	ה	ו	ז	ח	ט	י	כ	ל	מ	נ	ס	ע	פ	צ	ק	ר	ש
ש	ת	א	ב	ג	ד	ה	ו	ז	ח	ט	י	כ	ל	מ	נ	ס	ע	פ	צ	ק	ר
ר	ש	ת	א	ב	ג	ד	ה	ו	ז	ח	ט	י	כ	ל	מ	נ	ס	ע	פ	צ	ק
ק	ר	ש	ת	א	ב	ג	ד	ה	ו	ז	ח	ט	י	כ	ל	מ	נ	ס	ע	פ	צ
צ	ק	ר	ש	ת	א	ב	ג	ד	ה	ו	ז	ח	ט	י	כ	ל	מ	נ	ס	ע	פ
פ	צ	ק	ר	ש	ת	א	ב	ג	ד	ה	ו	ז	ח	ט	י	כ	ל	מ	נ	ס	ע
ע	פ	צ	ק	ר	ש	ת	א	ב	ג	ד	ה	ו	ז	ח	ט	י	כ	ל	מ	נ	ס
ס	ע	פ	צ	ק	ר	ש	ת	א	ב	ג	ד	ה	ו	ז	ח	ט	י	כ	ל	מ	נ
נ	ס	ע	פ	צ	ק	ר	ש	ת	א	ב	ג	ד	ה	ו	ז	ח	ט	י	כ	ל	מ
מ	נ	ס	ע	פ	צ	ק	ר	ש	ת	א	ב	ג	ד	ה	ו	ז	ח	ט	י	כ	ל
ל	מ	נ	ס	ע	פ	צ	ק	ר	ש	ת	א	ב	ג	ד	ה	ו	ז	ח	ט	י	כ
כ	ל	מ	נ	ס	ע	פ	צ	ק	ר	ש	ת	א	ב	ג	ד	ה	ו	ז	ח	ט	י
י	כ	ל	מ	נ	ס	ע	פ	צ	ק	ר	ש	ת	א	ב	ג	ד	ה	ו	ז	ח	ט
ט	י	כ	ל	מ	נ	ס	ע	פ	צ	ק	ר	ש	ת	א	ב	ג	ד	ה	ו	ז	ח
ח	ט	י	כ	ל	מ	נ	ס	ע	פ	צ	ק	ר	ש	ת	א	ב	ג	ד	ה	ו	ז
ז	ח	ט	י	כ	ל	מ	נ	ס	ע	פ	צ	ק	ר	ש	ת	א	ב	ג	ד	ה	ו
ו	ז	ח	ט	י	כ	ל	מ	נ	ס	ע	פ	צ	ק	ר	ש	ת	א	ב	ג	ד	ה
ה	ו	ז	ח	ט	י	כ	ל	מ	נ	ס	ע	פ	צ	ק	ר	ש	ת	א	ב	ג	ד
ד	ה	ו	ז	ח	ט	י	כ	ל	מ	נ	ס	ע	פ	צ	ק	ר	ש	ת	א	ב	ג
ג	ד	ה	ו	ז	ח	ט	י	כ	ל	מ	נ	ס	ע	פ	צ	ק	ר	ש	ת	א	ב
ב	ג	ד	ה	ו	ז	ח	ט	י	כ	ל	מ	נ	ס	ע	פ	צ	ק	ר	ש	ת	א

evil

This is used for Contrary effects and by a name being entered upwards produceth a Spirit of Revenge, Hatred Dislike &c

104
Example to the Table of Right Commutations

This Table is used to exchange one Name for another, as Iehovah יהדה, which I enter in the table thus, first I enter in the Iod י on the right hand line under A א from the top and opposite the angle which from Iod י on the top line from Right to left the right angle letter is ק Koph, I then enter in the same line ה He, and in the common Angle as before comes מ Mem I then enter ו Vau in the same manner. and comes כ Caph, then I enter ה He and comes מ Mem. and when collected together makes ק כ מ מ Comcam I shall now in the same manner enter the Word Saboath צבאות and these letters are drawn out מ ג ג א ם Megacash. – which is Comcam Megacash for Iehovah Saboath which means the God which produce Vegetables and the God of all vegetation. His Character is produced by the Tables of Squares, Therefore the Learned Magi made this to produce and perfect the same

Example to the Averse Table

I enter the Table of Averse Commutations as before only, instead of entering it on the right hand from the top. I enter each letter progressively from the Bottom upwards from the word, evil, finding the Common angle of the same letters from the top line to the left, the Name following is from thence extracted which is ליוי רד בלה. Railai Nudableth. This is the name of the Angel of Revenge. and a destroyer of Vegetation, whos power cannot be appeased unlefs the above name Iahovah Saboath with a Talisman appropriate is placed on the spot where the Ravages of the Evil Angel is discovered and thus In this Talismanic art is action and counter action manifested as Sympathy and Antipathy An Explanation of the Planetary table of letters which the ancients used in extracting the names of Angels of Good and Evil to work any desired effect, also of the twelve Signes,

Chap 14

Suppose any celestial effect is proposed for making a Ring Tablet or Talisman of any kind and I want to find out the name of the Angel to work the effect or the great Governor, I erect a figure of the heavens at the time proposed, by placing in order first the Signs of the Zodiac and then the planets, when the figure is completed, I then examine to what house the effect belongs, which I find in the table of Significations of the twelve houses Page 90 — for example we will say the Sixth house which is the house of sickness and disease, and disease is what I want to cure. In the first place I examine wether there is a Planet strong in the sixth if not, who or what Planet is the lord of that house. if he is the strongest the name of his Angel must be sought as follows I will suppose him to be the ☉. I enter the table on the left hand (oreen which you'll see (of Good) with S that being the first letter. I look for S in the table, then in the common angle under the Character of the ☉ which gives the letter T I then enter in the same manner U which gives S I then enter the same manner N which gives G. I then collect them together T S G having drawn forth from the table these three letters, I place them as they stand in order in the alphabet as GSTEL which is added to it EL as one of the names of God for on that depends the virtue in the Talismanic Art: having thus framed the first which is the name of the governing Angel or King. I then enter the table again with G first which produces B, and S which produces T, and T which produces E, and E which produces I, and L which produces O. having entered the table with that name I produce **BTEIO**. I now set them in order of the Alphabet which is **BEITOEL** adding to it the name of God **EL**. Therefore the Angels are said to bear the name of God according to that which is written. because my name is in him" which must be pronounced with it, for as the name of EL, means power and virtue and Iod the name of the Deity. The names of these two are used to the names of Angels, but the word EL is always used to all spirits wether good or bad, by this means you see the Second name draws forth. and in the same manner must be drawn the rest. If to find an Evil Angel or Spirit it must be entered in the same manner only on the right hand upwards from the word (of evil) for as often as is entered the names in the tables of the common angle so many different names are to be extracted and the names so extracted must be placed on the tablet &c according to their order as the first extracted first, the second third &c, in the same manner must be extracted the names of the Governing Angels and Spirits of both good and evil from the following table of the twelve Signs of the Zodiac, therefore if you want to find the name of an Angel, Good or Bad, belonging to any office, name the office you would wish him to fill. if it is to preserve Guard or protect, enter the name of the office **GUARD** &c which must be entered

107

under the good, But if to anihilate, then the offices are Destroy Destruction Main Affliction &c these must be entered on the evil side upwards, as DESTROY, these being the names of such offices, and to affix a versichle applicable, search the Bible for such as will come the nearest to the effect as by condemning and detesting the object, thing or matter, if to hinder in the same manner, following every rule as is after in the Example or Talismanic Sculpture laid down, In the same manner is drawn forth the Angel or demon of any Man either from the passions and inclinations or from the Christen name or his Profession, wether Saturnine Martial or Solary The names thus extracted may appear to the Ignorant of no use, but such as are derived from such rules are of great power and efficacy, for as the rays of the Sun collected in a Lens and thrown on any object capable of being burnt by it & is burnt or damaged by its power (though at so great a distance from the object, and at the same time by us scarce a degree of heat is felt) so these names and characters formed by Art work the effect on the object intended by the The Tables of English Letters is of no other use than to give my reader an Idea in what manner the ancients obtained the many different names of Angles Spirits &c from the diffrent parts applicable to their wishes in the holy Writ therefore whatever work is desired, must be preformed from the Hebrew tables in their letters, as the formes of their figures comes the nearest to the Celestial Harmony, for in them lies hid all the Celestial mysteries, The same is to be understood by the Table of Right Commutations i.e. to exchange one name or number for another out of the holy writ. and the general rule of these is wheresoever any

108

thing of divine essence is expressed in the scripture from that place the name of God may rightly be gathered but where that name is expressed they marked the office it his under us the office or Work of any Spirit Good or bad from thence the name of each or both Spirits may be compounded which by these verses, as by an example is manifest.

1st Let them be as dust before the face of the wind and let the Angel of the lord scatter them

2nd = Let their ways be darkness, and slippery and let the Angel of the lord persue them

Therefore it is very clear that the office of the first verse is destruction, then they enter the Table of the Cabalar Page 88. either under ♄ or ♂, with that name from which they extract the name and number of the Angel or Spirit who is to performe that office (one being a destroying Angel and the other a Spirit of Darkness to mislead and frust- erate which Spirits are found in holy writ) and they by entering their names so drawn as before, they bring out other names which names being drawn from the oth- -ers bears an affinity and by these tables any number of names they want to performe any work thus compound them — and affix them in order on the Image Talisman Tablet &c as in the course of the work will be further explained

Example. The 34 Psalm are these Words

"Thou shalt sit over him the Wicked, and Satan shall Stand at his right hand,   But in the Hebrew the 35 Psalm, and out of which they have extracted these words or names as applicable for their purpose

מידאל MIDael and מיראל Mirael these names signify them to be in the order of Warriors both instruments of mischief, (see the Spirits of ♄ & ♂ table of Angels &c)

109

They also by transposition of Letters formed a name from a name and a word from a word as follows, as Messiah. מ׳ש׳י׳ה׳ which taken thus י׳ש׳מ׳ה, the 3ᵈ letter 1ˢᵗ ׳. the 2ᵈ second or the 1ˢᵗ letter 3ᵈ ש the fouth letter 4ᵗʰ ה which transposition produce Ismah the same by Michael – מ׳י׳כ׳א׳ל׳ being transposed form Malachi מ׳ל׳א׳כ׳י׳

Now from what is laid down in showing the various meth-ods the ancients formed their (which they term Celestial Language in which are hid all their Mysteries) designs for operation, Malachi from which word is the name of that great Angel called Michael transposed from and is the reason why the Alphabet called Malachim, the writing of Angels which is used by the Cabala in all mystic Writings as it is not easy to be discovered

Michael is the Angel which always stands in the presence of God therefore he is called the Strength of God
Gabriel is called the Virtue of God
Raphael is called the Medicien of God
Baziel is called the Vision of God
Haniel is called the Glory of God

Thus the Ancient Fathers classed the Angels of the Planets &c according to their Orders and according to their Natures appointed them to performe their desires Therefore the sacred names of Good and evil Spirits deputed to each offices are drawn out of certain places in Scripture, The general rule of which is that wheresoever any thing of divine essence is expressed from that place the name of God may be gethered but in whatsoever place the name of God is expressed mark the offic, what it is under that name. For wheresoever the Scripture speaks of the office or work of any Spirit Good or Bad there may be taken the name of the Good and the name of the Bad Spirit, as for example in these verses,

Let them be as dust before the face of the Wind and let the Angel of the Lord scatter them —

Let their ways be darkness and slippery, and let the angel of the Lord pursue them

Now Mirael and Maidael being two Angels of Mischief these are chosen as the Instruments of vengence or Revenge

Chap 15

An Example or Explanation of the tables of the Seven Planets their Compass, Divine, Names, Intelligences, and Spirits set over them, with the name of the Angel of the Day his Sigil, Planet and Sign governing the Planet

---

There are seven sacred Tables endowed with innumerable vertues of the Heavens, therefore the mysterious numbers of them represent the divine order of Celestial numbers, impressed upon Celestials, by the firm Ideas of the Divine mind of Man, by means of the Soul of the World and the Harmony of the Celestial rays, receiving through great affection by the Celestial power of the Operator, a power which is the Gift of God, and which is applied through the Soul of the Universe, for as matter is fit for a form, the mediums of which, being disposed by the skill of the learned Magia

The first of them is assigned to ♄ and consists of the number Three, which multiplied by itself produce the number 9 i.e there are nine squares, the first number which is 3, is the first Holy name, the number Nine signifies the second Holy name, the number when calculated through each diameter make 15 signifies the third and fourth and fifth Holy name

Now the whole added together makes 45, this signifies the great name, the same number is the angel of the Intelligence which they use for all good purposes, and the same number is also applied to the spirit to what is Bad from out which tables and numbers, the seals and characters are drawn. their method of drawing, and forming the same, I shall show by Examples. They say that the Table &c being engraved on a plate of Lead when ♄ is fortunate, makes a man powerfull is causes success in petitions to the High Ranks, and also protects a man from harm. But if ♄ is unfortunate it hinders buildings plantations, causes a man to be cast down from his honours and dignities, it causes discords and Quarrelling, and disperses Soldiers i.e. when his Spirit for Lead is made use of with all other characters properly selected for the purpose. 2nd The Table of ♃ which consists of the number 4 that answers to the first divine name ABAB, that multiplied by itself formes superfice of 16 squares this number is ascribed to the second holy name, each deameter makes the number 34 which number is according ascribed to a great name of God, and its full number (the number of each square) collected and added, together makes the number 136 which is ascribed to his Intelligence, for good and also to the Spirit to Bad They say that if this Table &c is Engraved on a plate of Silver ♃ fortunate and powerful, it conduseth to the gain of riches, favours. Love, appease enemies confirms honours, and if Engraved on a piece of Coral, disolves enchantments. But if ♃ unfortunate it will cause all contrary effects

3rd The Table of ♂ is a square of 5 containing 25 numbers, which makes 65 in each diameter, of which being added as before makes the number 325 which numbers is ascribed to the Angel or Intilligence to Good, and likewise the number of his Spirit to Bad and out of it is drawn the Characters of both Good and Bad Which they say that if a Sword was made by Art under the proper Constelations &c and this table and characters engraved upon it when ♂ is fortun -ale and free from all evil aspects, whoever is the bearer of that sword makes him potent in war carrying all before him - making him terrible to his enemies, it may also be en- -graved on a Plate of Iron or Steel highly polished for the same effect, and if it be engraved on the Stone Correola it will stop all Hæmorrhages in Male or female - But if engraved under bad aspect of ♂ on a plate of Red Brass (the greater part of Copper) they say that it will by being buried on the spot hinder all buildings, Mills, Drive away Bees, fish, Pidgeons and Beasts from the place. It causeth contention & strife between man, it prevents procreation of Man & woman & all Animals,

4th The Table of ☉ which is the square of 6 and contains 36 numbers, wherein each Diameter produces 101 and the sum of the whole is 666, which answers to the number of the 13th chapter of Revelations from the first to 18 verse

" Here is wisdom let him that hath understanding count
" the number of the Beast, for it is the number of a man
" and his number is Six hundred, three score and six &c

This number appears to correspond in the number of that great character of France according to the Greek alphabet
B O V V Ν Π Α Τ Τ Ε
2. 70. 50. 50. 8. 80. 1. 100. 300. 5 which are the numbers of the letters composing the name, Beth, Omicron, Nu, Nu, Eta, Pi, Alpha, Ro, Tau, Epsiter, the number of Each letter added together produce 666

113

They assert that this table character &c framed by the Talismanic Art, and Engraved on a plate of pure Gold (which is the metal of the ☉) when ☉ is fortunately situated, and free from all bad aspects of evil Planets, renders the man whom it is made for and bears it fortunate in all his undertakings, to be acceptable, idolized, and looked upto by thousands to be renowned in military exploits, potent in all his works elevating him to high fortunes &c, but if a Talesman is framed under ☉ when unfortunately situated surrounded by every bad aspect possible, destroys what have been before mentioned and if secretly placed or buried near his Person or Place, the greater and more potent will be the effect of evil to him

5th The Table of ♀ consists of the square of seven drawn into itself as before, viz, 49 numbers, and through each Diameter make the number 175, the sum total of which is 1225, out of which is drawn the Characters of the Intelligences and Divine names to Good, and the Characters of the Evil Spirits to bad. They say being Engraved on a plate of Silver, ♀ being fortunate causeth concord and strife between parties, procureth the Love of all Women, it is Good against banneness, causeth ability in generation, disolves enchantment, causes peace between man & woman, Makes all kind of Animals and Cattle fruitfull and thrifty, being put in a dove house causeth a great encrease It cures all Melancholy distempers, and is fortunate to all travelers who bear it. But if on a Plate of common Brass when she is unfortunate it as a contrary effect to all what is mentioned

6th The Table of ☿ results from the square of 8 (as before) drawn into itself containing 64 numbers through each Diameter making 260 the total sum of which is 2080 with the Divine names & to what is Good and bad, and They say that if as before this is Engraved on a Plate of pure

114

Silver, Tin or good yellow Brass. ♃ being fortunate it renders the bearer fortunate in his Concerns to do what he pleases i.e. whatever is under the dominion of ♃ as his table will tell you of what he governs It bringeth gain prevents poverty — strengthens Memory understanding and creates a knowledge and understanding of occult things by dreams & otherwise But if the same as Brass made base and ♃ unfortunate it acts on all contrary

7th The Table of the ☽ The square of 9 drawn into itself as Nine times nine is eighty one — 81. squares and through the diameter each way produce the number of 369 the whole produce of the numbers contained in the 81 squares is 3321 the total with the divine names Intelligence & Characters of Good and bad Spirits. This the ancients say that if this table &c is engraved when Luna is fortunate in all degrees on a plate of pure Silver, renders the Bearer acceptable. It protects the the traveller in all journies or Voyages, increase Riches, health of body, Drives of all enemies and all evel things from what place you please. But if under evil aspect and engraved on a plate of Lead (which is the metal of ♄) wherever it is buried secretly it makes that place unfortunate, that an enemy cannot stay on the spot & if sunk in Harbours, placed in Ships, Rivers, fountains Mills &c it makes all unfortunate wherever it is, unless removed or counteracted by an opposite power It also prevents Physicians from practice also all orators by destroying the oratorical powers, and whosoever it is directly made against and corectly done it makes him fly his Country. Now these are the Assertions of the Learned Doctors of this science who have wrote upon the same Volumes or Volumns but so obstruce and in such enigma past finding out to any but the wise, but are now plainly set forth to all

I shall here by Example prove the use of these Tables and first show you how they framed the Characters of the Divine names &c

Example

Suppose I want to form a character under the Planet ♀. ie, the name and character of the Angel from the word LOVE, which is called forming a character from an office for Love is the first cause, and possesion the second, Action the third and production the fourth which from these four points a square is formed a figure so much reveranced by the Magi a figure wherein lies wonderfull mystery, but to the point, LOVE is my object therefore with the letter L I enter the Planetary table Page 88. and in the common angle under ♀ under the word of Good I find P/70 I then enter in the same manner the letter O, and I find O/60 then I enter V and I find M/40 I then enter E and I find K/20 I now collect them together as P O M K / 70. 60. 40. 20 which letters and numbers answer to the word Love. I now place them in order of the Alphabet first KMOP but finding that there is no pronounciation in them as they stand I transpose them as MOPKEL, adding to it as commanded EL being one of the Great names of God bearing a great power. by which it expresses the name Mopkel or it could be again transposed as Kompel as from the word Messeak Page 109. where the transpositions of the Magi are from the holy Writ are shewn, Now I have explained to you the art of finding or drawing forth the name of the Good Angel I shall next explain to you the manner his Character is drawn forth I place the word in the following Order

```
M O P K E L          K O M P E L
40. 60. 70. 20. 5. 30     20. 6 .40. 7. 5. 20
```

here you see them transposed, the last differing in the numbers O & P which are 60 & 70. but looking in the Table of the square of ♀ I find that her mean number is 7 and her square is

116

49. the highest number, as such I leave out the Cyphers of 60 & 70, which leaves the 6 & 7, and that bearing the true proportion I then with those numbers enters the table of squares begining with the first letter of the word which is M finding the number which it answers 40 on the top of that square to the left, (as it exactly correspondes to the Hebrew) on that point is the begining of the Character. the next letter is O and the number is 6 leaving out the cypher I then strike a strait line to the left hand to point of square containing the number 6 as fig 1. I then enter as before 7 the number of P and continue the line on the top of the square of seven. I then enter 20 the number of K and continue the line to the point of the number, I then enter the number 5 the number of E and continue the line to that point I then enter 30 the number of L and continue the line to the top point of 30. the Character is then Completed, The same rules must be kept in extracting the transposed Character Kompel there- fore to make it more easy I have laid down the two figures of transpasition to show the deffrent forms of Characters though both one Analogy.

Fig 1
M O P K E L
40. 6. 7. 20. 5. 30

22	47	16	41	10	35	4
5	23	48	17	42	11	29
30	6	24	49	18	36	12
13	31	7	25	43	19	37
38	14	32	1	26	44	20
21	39	8	33	2	27	45
46	15	40	9	34	3	28

Fig 2
K O M P E L
20. 6. 40. 7. 5. 30

22	47	16	41	10	35	4
5	23	48	17	42	11	29
30	6	24	49	18	36	12
13	31	7	25	43	19	37
38	14	32	1	26	44	20
21	39	8	33	2	27	45
46	15	40	9	34	3	28

Having now explained in what manner they obtained their Characters from both the original word and from the transposed

117

word Nopkel, I shall now explain the way they obtained the Characters of the evil Genii. I now refer to the Planetary table as before but instead of entering the name Nopkel as before. I enter it in the same manner and order on the right hand which is the evil side therefore I look for M from the bottom upwards, and in the common angle under Q I find B 2. therefor the word being entered in the same manner brings forth B J C P E L / 2. 10. 3. 70. 5. 30 which is added, now as they stand they cannot be pronounced, but I look into the table of Numeral transpositions Page 92 I find P and in the same line are the letters when joyned together makes the same number 70 and finding the word cannot be pronounced without a vowel I take O.60 and transpose them to some harmony as from BJCPEL, I transpose with the O leaving the P out the word COBJEL which is the name of the evil Genii for that Office. i.e. the first production from the word LOVE there he is the head Angel or King. and out of his name (are in the same manner) drawn forth the Character of his Spirit as often as the tables is entered as befor with this difference that instead of touching the top point of the square I take the Bottom as Example I now with the letter O enter the number belonging to it which is the number 3 and in the same manner must the whole word be entered Continueing the line to each point which is from 3 to 6 from 6 to 2 (when they run thus they must always be doubled) from 2 to 10 from 10 to 5 and from 5 to 30. which complets the full Character Example 4th. I shall now form a character from the Word Nopkel by changing it in the table of Right Communications to show the use of that Table, which is for Good, I enter the table M and take the Common angle under M in the and I find C 3 at the angle of O I find G 7. at the angle of P I find I. 9. at the angle of K I find V 300 I now collect

118

them together which is CGIV but V being beyond the compass I refere to the table of numerical transposition I look for V and find S 100, T 200 I finding in the former no pronounciation and finding that a pronounsiation can be made with either, I take the S 100, being the smallest number and transpose it for a number in the compass of the Square of Q, as such I enter S and in that line I find the two letters and numbers which when put together make the number 100, I then take the letter which is in the Compass and which will pronounce the best I there take M 40. in the place of V which forms CGIMEL adding adding the EL but still finding no pronounciciation as they stand I transpose them to CIGMEL it can be again tran-sposed to MIGCEL again GIMCEL again CIMGEL but I take the first and find his Character as before in the Good which I point on the top of the Square and the Character is produced, and if you wish to extend it by adding to it another Great name of God, I in the same manner look for the numbers of the letters and extend the lines of the Character let them fall on what point they will and appear ever so intersected it is the true Character or seal. These examples will be sufficient to enable any one to form all Characters as well as the names of Angels & Spirits and the full use of the Tables the production of so much Study and Labour

By the above Rules may be produced the Characters and seals of any Office, Sign, Star Profession trade, or Name of any Person, both their Good and evil Genii Ruling the same, with their Different Spirits attending them, likewise the Angels and spirits

119

Fig 4								Fig 3					
CIGMEL								**COBJEL**					
3, 9, 7, 40, 5, 30								3, 6, 2, 10, 5, 30					
22	47	16	41	10	35	4		22	47	16	41	10	35	4
5	23	48	17	42	11	29		5	23	48	17	42	11	29
30	6	24	49	18	36	12		30	6	24	49	18	36	12
13	31	7	25	43	19	37		13	31	7	25	43	19	37
38	14	32	1	26	44	20		38	14	32	1	26	44	20
21	39	8	33	2	27	45		21	39	8	33	2	27	45
46	15	40	9	34	3	28		46	15	40	9	34	3	28

♀

The different Characters of Good and Evil Angels drawn out from the Table of the Square of ♀ with the different Characters of the Transpositions both from the numerical & Commutation tables as Examples Fig 1 to 8.

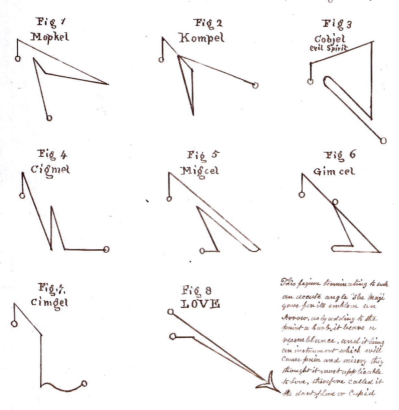

Fig 1 Mopkel

Fig 2 Kompel

Fig 3 Cobjel evil spirit

Fig 4 Cigmel

Fig 5 Migcel

Fig 6 Gimcel

Fig 7 Cimgel

Fig 8 LOVE

This figure terminating to such an acute angle The Magi gave for its emblem an Arrow, as by adding to the point a barb, it bears a resemblance, and it being an instrument which will cause pain and misery they thought it must applicable to Love, therefore called it the dart of Love or Cupid

LOVE is the word (or in this Science the office) from which all the this Character spring from. Its Character is drawn from the table without transposition only by entering the table with the numbers as they stand in the Alphabet leaving out the Cyphers of such numbers as are not in the compass of the under ♀ Sq whenever a number fall as in Fig 4. as 3 and 9 it may be found so only touch the points

Chap 16

A Table of the Essential Dignities &c of the Planets

Signs	Hou's of Planets	Exl of Plan	Trip D.N	Terms of the Planets					Faces of the Planets			Detri.	Falls
♈	♂. D	☉ ·19	☉:♃ F	♃ . 6	♀ .14	☿ .21	♂. 26	♄ .30	♂. 10	☉ .20	♀ .30	♀	♄
♉	♀.N	☽. 3	♀:☽ E	♀ . 8	☿ .15	♃ .22	♄ .26	♂ .30	☿ .10	☽ .20	♄ .30	♂	
♊	☿ ·D	☊. 3	♄:☿ A	☿ . 7	♃ .14	♀ .21	♄ .25	♂ .30	♃ .10	♂ .20	☉ .30	♃.	
♋	☽DN	♃ .13	♂:♂ W	♂ . 6	♃ .13	☿ .20	♀ .27	♄ .30	♀. 10	☿ .20	☽ .30	♄	♂
♌	☉DN	—	☉:♃ F	♃ . 6	☿ .13	♀ .19	♃ .25	♂ .30	♄ .10	♃ .20	♂ .30	♄	
♍	☿ ·N	☿ .13	♀:☽ E	☿ . 7	♀ .13	♃ .18	♄ .24	♂ .30	☉ .10	♀ .20	☿ .30	♃	♀
♎	♀ ·D	♄ ·21	♄:☿ A	♄ . 6	♀ . 11	♃ .19	☿ .24	♂ .30	☽ .10	♄ .20	♃ .30	♂	☉
♏	♂N	—	♂:♂ W	♂ . 6	♃ .14	♀ .21	☿ .27	♄ .30	♂. 10	☉ .20	♀ .30	♀	☽
♐	♃ ·D	☊ . 3	☉:♃ F	♃ . 8	♀ .14	☿ .19	♄ .25	♂ .30	☿ .10	☽ .20	♄ .30	☿	
♑	♄ ·N	♂. 28	♀ E ☽	♀ . 6	☿ .12	♃ .19	♂ .25	♄ 30	♃ .10	♂ .20	☉ .30	☽	♃
♒	♄ ·D	—	♄:☿ A	♄ 6	☿ .12	♀ .20	♃ .25	♂ .30	♀ .10	☿ .20	☽ .30	☉	
♓	♃ ·N	♀. 27	♂:♂ W	♀ . 8	♃ .14	☿ .20	♂ .26	♄ .30	♄ .10	♃ .20	♂ .30	☿	☿

The use of the above Table in the Art of Talismanic Culpture is as follows. 1st Line read from Left to Right – ♈ to ♄. i.e. aries is the Day house of Mars ☉.19 the Sun is in his Exaltation in 19° of Aries ☉F♃ means that the Sun and Jupiter governs the fiery Triplicity. ♃.6 that the first 6° of aries are the terms of Jupiter. ♀.14 that from 6° to 14° are the terms of Venus, from 14° to 21° the terms of ☿. from 21° to 26° the terms of ♂. from 26° to 30° the terms of ♄, then begins the faces of the Planets i.e –

♂.10 signifies that the first 10° of ♂ has for his face, from 10° to 20° is the face of ☉, from 20° to 30° ♀. the next two Columns are the Planets in their Detriment & fall i.e. when ♀ is in ♈ she is in her Detriment and when Saturn is in ♈ he is in his fall. Therefore the 1st column signif-ies the Signs the 2nd the Houses, the Planets belongs to, the 3d the Triplicity each Planet Governs wether Fiery Airy Wat-ery or Earthly, which the letters F,A,W,E denotes, the following 5 Columns are the degrees, each Planet claims as his terms, the next 3 Columns the Degrees each Planet claims as his face and the last 2 Columns are the Planets in their Detriments and fall, i.e. when they are most unfortunate. For a Planet in his fall is To as a Man thrown from the highest pitch of Honour to the lowest degrees of Indigence. A Planet in his Detriment is as a Man deprived of his property not able to continue his present situation being so frustrated that not knowing what to do A Planet in his Face is like A Man at his last Gasp or Shift ready to be turned out of doors having much to do to Support his Credit and reputation A Planet in his term. Is. as. a Man gaining Wealth Power and Dignity. A Planet in his Triplicity. Is as a Man meanly induced with the goods of this life and his affairs not in a very prosperous state. A Planet in his Exaltation is as a Man placed in every plenty that this life can afford and capable of performing every abstinate & Stubbon action, A Planet in his Own house is as a Man as lord and Master of his own house in a very prosperous and flourishing condition. Having now by comparison explained to you the natures of the Planets in the above situations, I must now caution you to be care-full of not missing, Day with Night and Night with Day

122

in your Works i,e when you see by the table, a Planet in his Day house at the begining of any work that you finish the same work though at different times under the different Degrees in the Day or by the light of Day – and whatever work you begin at night finish the same by night and when a Planet is in his Excaltation when you begin any work finish it under his excaltation. and if there is not time lay it carefully by till the same favourable time come round again when done. begin the same work and so go on till it is accomplished keeping strict to the time of the Planetry Hours of the planet, and strike not a stroke after his hour is up, if even you have just finished; for that would be like mixing poison with a Medicicin to cure a Disease. The same observations must be made in the terms of the Planets, and the Faces of the Planets. And when you want to make any Talisman – under the Detriment or fall of the Planets such Operations must be done at the Planetary Hour required for the work in the Night as the following Table will show you, for as Good and Evil cannot agree, so the Work done in the Night will not answer for the day, nor the work in the Day answer for the night

Note A Talisman, Pentacle Sigel Laman &c framed by Art under the Detriments fall &c will cause and carry with it every effect desired or made for, which effect cannot be removed only by the same Person who made it or by one equally or more skilled in this Art

F. A Talisman is a piece of Metal with the Characters &c engraved upon it and finished to endure &c Pentacle is a piece of virgin Parchment with the figures Characters &c of the Divine Powers to be worn by the Operator as a shield of defence which the Magi put on for the manufactoring their experiments &c

Sigel Is also a Piece of Parchment with the Characters &c of the Planets Angels Images &, by which effects are performed and brought to pass.

Lamen Is a piece of Parchment as before only the Pictures of effects to be produced and performed are painted in Colours appropriate to the Planets Signs &c Images. Are the Resemblances of Animals Vegetables, Birds, fish &c &c, which are to be effected and are made of various Compositions as Was &c or Carved out of Stone and set in fields Gardens &c

Chap 17
Demonstrating the Use Nature and Reasons of The Faces of the Planets

In this Chapter lies great secrets, therefore study well this part, for the virtues of each Planet passing through the 12 Signs of the Zodiac in their proper Faces, is very near, and therein is contained a great Mystery which every capasity cannot reach neither is it to be obtained, but by those only who are great and profound Searchers of the hidden Mysteries of Nature For as water quencheth Fire, and as Fire dryeth up water, so one Planet over ruleth another and is again counteracted by the same, A Term divides a face, a Face divides a Sign A Sign divides a Triplicity and a Triplicity the Zodiac &c. Now there are 30° in a Sign and that divided into three parts gives 10 degrees to each part which each 10° is called a Face therefor in each Sign there are 3 Faces each containing 10° and these Faces are equivalent to Signs, Forms or Shapes, by reason they shew the nature and inclination of the Planets in them as in their own houses, and as the experienced

124

Astrologers by these Faces foretold accidents, Natures Dispositions & inclinations, by the faces of each Planet-so likewise are the effects to be wrought by the Talismanic Art. To know the proper Faces then of the Planets I shall begin with ♂ and give him the first Face of ♈. i.e when ♂ enter the first degree of ♈. he then is entered in his 1st Face, and remains there till the first 10 degrees are finished, he then at the same time being in his house See the first line of the table. The second Face which is from 10° to 20° is the Face of ☉ he following in rotation to ♂ and is located under him in the heavens, the 3rd Face is from 20° to 30° that is given to ♀ as she necessarily follows the ☉. The first 10° of ♉ is given to ☿ he following the Planet ♀ the 2nd Face of ♉ is given to the ☽ The Moon following ☿ and the 3rd to ♄ being the first of the Planets which is reckoned after her, she being the last. In the same manner rotatively must the Planets be traced round the Zodiac. And by following this Method you will very soon come to the exact knowledge of every Face and the Lord thereof with their Virtues and effects capable of being produced by Talismans made under the 28 Mansions of the Moon governed by this Table

Of the Faces

♂. 10°. ♈	To a Face of Boldness, Strength Magnanimety resolution, confidence &c	
☉. 20°. ♈	Of Nobleness, Might, Majesty power, renown and Authority	
♀. 30°. ♈	Of effeminancy Mildness Joyfullness, playfullness, of Sportfullness &c	
☿. 10°. ♉	To a Face of Husbandry, Buildings, governing Laws precepts and Learning	
☽. 20°. ♉	Of Power, dignity and authority Depopulat-	

	-ing towns and Castles & Constraining People
♄. 30°. ♉	Of Misery Servitude, poverty necessity and Cruelty
♃. 10°. ♊	Is a face of Writing, Casting accounts Giving and receiving Petitions &c
♂. 20°. ♊	Of Labour, Trouble and Study in what is painfull and in dishonest Actions
☉. 30°. ♊	Of Forgetfulness, disdain, Jarring Scoffing and Baldness
♀. 10°. ♋	Is a face of Strength Understanding Wit, Power, and desiring favours of Men
☿. 20°. ♋	Of Sport, Mirth, Women, Riches fertility and Abundance
☽. 30°. ♋	Of Hunting persuing Runnaways, gain-ing strength by Arms and opposing Men
♄. 10°. ♌	Is a face of Cruelty, Mischief and Violence labour & toyl, Boldness & Lust
♃. 20°. ♌	of Quarrels Mischief causing Wars and Strife
♂. 30°. ♌	of Love and friendship causing Fear of War and Commotions and leaving a place
☉. 10°. ♍	Is a face of Ploughing, Sowing Tilling and gaining Riches by the Same
♀. 20°. ♍	Of Gaining, and growing Rich, Covetousness and obtaining the help of Man
☿. 30°. ♍	of Age Weakness, decripedness, destroying enemies and pulling up trees by the roots
☽. 10°. ♎	Is a face of Justice, Right & truth helping the weak & needy, and helping deformity
♄. 20°. ♎	of Quietness, profit and gain, and a happy Life
♃. 30°. ♎	Of Gluttony Letchery, revelling, debauchery

126

and following all ill Causes

♂. 10. ♏. Is a face of Quarrelling, Fighting, Mischief Slaughter, Robbing &c

☉. 20. ♏. Of Contentious Strife Theft Causing Mischief, debates amongst Men and deceptions

♀. 30 ♏. Of Wars, Violence, drunkeness, Rapes and Fornications

☿. 10. ♐. Is a face of Boldness Forwordness Freeness and Strength

☽. 20. ♐. Of Great trouble of Mind and Body, Fear Mistrust &c

♄. 30 ♐. Of Abstinency, Willfulness, Mischief, Quarrels and of Vile Actions

♃. 10. ♑. Is a face Of handsome Shape and Form Loving of Rambling Merriment and Sport

♂. 20. ♑. Of Causing things to be sought for and not obtained, and preventing a perfection of things

☉. 30. ♑. Of Covetousness, desire to rule and Govern or have Riches at his disposal, mistrusting himself

♀. 10. ♒. Is a face of continual trouble for Money never at rest, Labour and toil always indigent

☿. 20. ♒. Of Beauty, Understanding, Modesty, Mildness Good Behaviour &c

☽. 30. ♒. Of Contentions and Strife, repinings, causing discord, &c amongst Women

♄. 10. ♓. Is a face of Pensiveness, cogetative Unsettl'd Moving from place to place to get Riches

♃. 20. ♓. Of Haughtiness and high dispositions seeking after great and high things

♂. 30. ♓. Of Concupiscence and Lust and delighting with Women, debauching them, only in a Sly way

Now the use of this in Astrology is no more than to Judge of the inclinations and Qualities of the Native when Born when the ascendant is in any of these faces or the Planets found therein which then his Qualities and inclinations are answerable to these faces, Now the use of them in this Art is as follows

Example I want to make a Talisman under any of the Mansions of the ☽. I look for the effect desired in the table, Page 86, and finding the effect, I then refer to the Table Page 120 and see what Face it is under and finding that, I then take the Proper Metal of the Star &c under that Planet in that Face and with the Appropriate Characters &c as is fully taught in the Body of the work, and what effect it is designed to work, if made by Art, it is sure to preform let it be what it may. The same observations must be made in the table of Faces whatever the effect therein Specified will be the same produced

Chap 18
Of the Impediments of the Moon a most essential thing to be observed in this Talismanic Art

The ☽ being one of the greatest Lights of Heaven, the grand recipient of all the influences of the other Planets and she being the nearest to our Earth, and through her influence all things receive the different Virtues and powers either in facilitating good or evil, which is according to her different changes as encreasing or decreasing &c There being ten impedements she is subject to I shall here point them out

First when in combustion with ☉ to 12° before and after his Body which is that situation it is affirmed

128

she causes Lunacy to all under her influence, and the length of affliction is known by the Sign the Configuration happens in wether Movable Common or Fixed, when in the latter the Malady is lasting & dreadful

Secondly. If she is impedited in the degrees of her fall which is in the 3° of ♏

Thirdly, when she is in ☍ to ☉

Fourthly, when joined with the unfortunes or in Quartile or ☌ of them

Fifthly, when she is within 12° of the Head and Tail of the Dragon, which is the term or place of an Eclipse

Sixthly, when she is in the latter degrees of a Sign wherein there is an Unfortunate ♄ or ♂

Seventhly, when she is cadent from an Angle or in Via Combusta the burnt-way, which is the last 15° of ♎ and the first 15° of ♏ this is the worst situation for her to be in

Eighthly, when she is in detriment, i.e. in ♑ or in Quartile with her own house

Ninthly, when she is Slow in Motion i.e. when she moves twenty four hours, less than than in her mean Motion i.e. 13°. 10'. 36"

Tenthly, when she is Void of Course i.e. when she is in any sign and not beholding any Planet till she passes into another, therefore in all manner of Work for the Benefit of our fellow Creatures let the ☽ be strongly dignified and in good aspects with the fortunes The ☽ being of that nature that in whatever situation she is placed in, in the performing any work in this Science such is the effect she will produce Whether it is for Good, or for Evil. I have been as brief as passable and every thing is at thy command for consider, that the times, seasons, places &c of the Signs and planets must be known, before any work can be perfected

A Table of Elections of the ☽ Aspects To the other Six Planets

	☌	✶	□	△	☍
day ♄	Unfortunate go no Journeys Speake not to Princes nor old men avoid the Company of all Husbandmen	Converse with old men and Husbandmen Build & Plant trees graft but beware of Women in point of Connection	Converse not with old Men nor Sue to Princes take no Physic on Journey, defer thy desire for them is danger	Converse with old men and Husband men Repair what is in a Ruinous state and manure Ground	Hire no Servants Seek after no gain take in hand nothing new or continue what is begun but lay it by
day ♃	Fortunate go to Noblemen Judges & Prelates Take Counsell and sue for your Rights	Converse with Lawyers and all Ecclesiastical Persons - Read the Laws and get understand them easily	Apply to all manner of Philosophical Studies and take Counsel	Begin any Work take your Journeys to Kings & Great men, Judges Prelates &c	Go thy Journey go to all Judges Prelates and all Ecclesiastics
day ♂	Unfortunate Take no Journey avoid the Company of all Military Men &c	Buy all manner of Warlike weapons or horses Hire Champions Kindle the fire for Alchemy	A very unfortunate day to be cocheured in all things avoid contentions make no league of new friendship	Dispose of all warlike things Buy Cattle and all kind of Beasts	Very unlucky day for all Company and friendships & Beware of Women
day ☉	Begin not any thing thou wouldest have Kept a Secret for all will be Discovered	Take in hand all affairs of Kings, Princes & Royal Personages and Sue for preferment under them	A Fatal day in all things beware of Great men, or you'll be brought into Great troubles	Offer presents to Princes & all Royal Personages your suits Petitions &c will be heard	Sue for Judgments from all Great Men But avoid all dealings with Rich Men
day ♀	Seek all Pleasures, & delights Seek the Love of Women & Put on new Garments	An Amorous day seek the Love of Women and they will Yield to your wishes. Contract Marriage &c	Hire all sorts of Servants or Workmen, make Sports Sing dance and be merry a Day of Mirth	Seek the Love of Women and Put on new Clothes &c But see that the ☽ be not in ♌	Hire all Men and Maid Servants, Contract Marriage and all sorts of recreation for your health
day ☿	Begin all Writings and accompts to Trade &c Send Messengers and Carriers with Goods	Apply to Study make accompts trade, Take Charges, send Youths to School talk with Sages and all wise men	Send Embassadors Orators and all sorts of Messengers & Carriers Buy & Sell and take your Journeys	Compose Poetry and all which requires a Good invention. Send Children to School use Exercise for Health	Repair to Scribes and Chancellors Send messengers trade in all merchendize follow thy Study and take thy Journey

129

130

The use of the Table of Elections of the ☽ to the Planets is only for those who have not the time or capasity of Judging by the Rules already laid down, having met with with this table in a manuscript, have coppied the same, and of Judged according to the seperate conditions of man may be made useful, i.e. that which concerns Kings and Noble's cannot concerne the affairs of Common People, Therefore the use of this table is as follows. In the Ephemeris you'l find all the Lunar Aspects for every day in the year. As such you must look what day such aspect falls on, and then to find the signification in the table is thus Supose it is the Conjunction of ♄ it is explained in the first square, If the ✶ in the second square and so throught so that it is the ☽ to the ☌ of of ♄ ♃ ♂ ☉ ♀ and ☿ To the ☌ ✶ □ △ ☍ of ♃ To the ☌ ✶ □ △ ☍ of ♂ To the ☌ ✶ □ △ ☍ of ☉ To the ☌ ✶ □ △ ☍ of ♀ and to the ☌ ✶ □ △ and ☍ of ☿ the explanations of which is to be found at their common angles, (<u>Chap 19</u>)

A Table to find the Length of the Planetry Hour for every 10 days in each Month through the Year

		First 10 days	Second 10 days	Third 10 days
		h m	h m	h m
Jan'y	♒	0 ... 40	0 ... 42	0 ... 45
Feb'y	♓	0 ... 47	0 ... 50	0 ... 52
Mar	♈	0 ... 55	0 ... 57	1 ... 0
Apr	♉	1 ... 2	1 ... 5	1 ... 7
May	♊	1 ... 10	1 ... 12	1 ... 15
June	♋	1 ... 17	1 ... 22	1 ... 24
July	♌	1 ... 22	1 ... 19	1 ... 16
Aug	♍	1 ... 13	1 ... 10	1 ... 6
Sep	♎	1 ... 2	0 ... 59	0 ... 56
Oct	♏	0 ... 52	0 ... 49	0 ... 46
Nov	♐	0 ... 43	0 ... 40	0 ... 38
Dec	♑	0 ... 36	0 ... 37	0 ... 38

A Planetary Table shewin what hour each Planet rules every day in the Year

Sun	Mon	Tues	Wed	Thur	Frid	Sat
P * H	DAY					P * H
☉ – 1	☽ – 1	♂ – 1	☿ – 1	♃ – 1	♀ – 1	♄ – 1
♀ – 2	♄ – 2	☉ – 2	☽ – 2	♂ – 2	☿ – 2	♃ – 2
☿ – 3	♃ – 3	♀ – 3	♄ – 3	☉ – 3	☽ – 3	♂ – 3
☽ – 4	♂ – 4	☿ – 4	♃ – 4	♀ – 4	♄ – 4	☉ – 4
♄ – 5	☉ – 5	☽ – 5	♂ – 5	☿ – 5	♃ – 5	♀ – 5
♃ – 6	♀ – 6	♄ – 6	☉ – 6	☽ – 6	♂ – 6	☿ – 6
♂ – 7	☿ – 7	♃ – 7	♀ – 7	♄ – 7	☉ – 7	☽ – 7
☉ – 8	☽ – 8	♂ – 8	☿ – 8	♃ – 8	♀ – 8	♄ – 8
♀ – 9	♄ – 9	☉ – 9	☽ – 9	♂ – 9	☿ – 9	♃ – 9
☿ – 10	♃ – 10	♀ – 10	♄ – 10	☉ – 10	☽ – 10	♂ – 10
☽ – 11	♂ – 11	☿ – 11	♃ – 11	♀ – 11	♄ – 11	☉ – 11
♄ – 12	☉ – 12	☽ – 12	♂ – 12	☿ – 12	♃ – 12	♀ – 12
P * H	NIGHT					P * H
♃ – 1	♀ – 1	♄ – 1	☉ – 1	☽ – 1	♂ – 1	☿ – 1
♂ – 2	☿ – 2	♃ – 2	♀ – 2	♄ – 2	☉ – 2	☽ – 2
☉ – 3	☽ – 3	♂ – 3	☿ – 3	♃ – 3	♀ – 3	♄ – 3
♀ – 4	♄ – 4	☉ – 4	☽ – 4	♂ – 4	☿ – 4	♃ – 4
☿ – 5	♃ – 5	♀ – 5	♄ – 5	☉ – 5	☽ – 5	♂ – 5
☽ – 6	♂ – 6	☿ – 6	♃ – 6	♀ – 6	♄ – 6	☉ – 6
♄ – 7	☉ – 7	☽ – 7	♂ – 7	☿ – 7	♃ – 7	♀ – 7
♃ 8	♀ – 8	♄ – 8	☉ – 8	☽ – 8	♂ – 8	☿ – 8
♂ – 9	☿ – 9	♃ – 9	♀ – 9	♄ – 9	☉ – 9	☽ – 9
☉ – 10	☽ – 10	♂ – 10	☿ – 10	♃ – 10	♀ – 10	♄ – 10
♀ – 11	♄ – 11	☉ – 11	☽ – 11	♂ – 11	☿ – 11	♃ – 11
☿ – 12	♃ – 12	♀ – 12	♄ – 12	☉ – 12	☽ – 12	♂ – 12

132

In the Table to find the Length of Planetary Hours for every ten days in the Year, as the difference of ten days is so little it is the nearest division necessary for this Art Therefor whatever Work is began must be began on the hour intended for the purpose and the Work must not be carried on after the limited time unless the Hour following has an Affinity to the intended Work the rules of this I have noticed elsewere. As such I shall by Example make clear the use of the above Table of the lengths of the Hours, and likewise the use of the Succeeding Table of Planetary Hours by Day and Night both which must be carefully attended to have the effect desired for without the nicest discrimination of Combining both Metals, Plants, proper times for operating &c (as a Medical Prescription improperly Compounded) will loose its desired effect. So all labours will be lost in this Art

Example. Supose I want to frame a Talisman under the ☉ called a Solar one, which is as follows I first look in the Planetary table for Sunday which on the top is marked SUN under which I see ☉ – 1. that the Sun rules the first Hour of that day. and it is so called the Planetary hour, because it is the hour that the Sun rises which is the exact time that all Talismanical work must be began for in that hour must be the preparation as well as the beginning. In the same Column I look down and see ☉ – 8 i.e. on the eight hour from the first. I may begin the same work again. Now supose it is in the Month of January I wish to performe my work I want to know how long that hour is, i.e. how long I may work on the device before the Planetary hour is past. To find that I refer to the Table to the length of Planetary Hours and in the first I find Jan᷎ on the top line. First 10 days. Second 10 days Third 10 days. under which. 0. 40ⁿ ᵐ – 0. 42ⁿ ᵐ – 0 – 45ⁿ ᵐ. i.e. the first 10 days of January, the Planetary hour is 40 minuits in length

133

therefor I can work not a minnit longer than that time and must lay it carefully by (from all prying eyes) till the eight hour at which time I may resume my work again, and work 40 Minnits longer and if it is to work only a Solar effect it must be done only on the Sunday (being his day) and only in his hour after which it must always be carefully wrapt up in a piece of new white Linnen and put by till the before mentioned time comes round alternately till finished and when finished, Secrecy retaines its Virtue Now if it is a Combination of effects either under a Conjunction Trine &c the friendship of the Planets and their enmities must be looked to for instance the ☉ & ♃ they both belonging to the Fiery Triplicity is to be seen by the Table of Essential Dignities Page 120 consequently they are friends as such I shall take the hour of ☉ to work in the day of ♃ which is on a Thursday. I then look for thursday in the table of Planetary hours and in the Column under thursday I find ☉ – 3 which means that the Sun rules the third hour of Thursday in the same Column ☉ – 10. i.e. he also Rules the tenth hour that day. which is in Compass of the ten days given for the length of the Planetary hour without any alteration, as such I persue my work each of these hours for 40 Minnites and if not finished in that time I then wait till a favourable time revolves for my purpose, Choosing the calmest & finest time possible which is more suitable to all matters for the Benefit of Mankind. therefor when properly finished in its framing the Talisman must go through the other procefses as is mentioned in another part of the Work at large The same rule must be observed in the aid of other Planets I must make a few necefsary remarks, you first observe that to make a Solar Talisman of the Greatest power look in the Ephemeris. and see what sign he has his Longitude in when you wish to performe your work if he is in his own Sign ♌ he is then more powerful and if with Judgement you then work your labour will be Crowned with succefs

And as the ☉ is most powerfull in ♌ so is ♀ in ♎, ☿ in ♊, ☽ in ♋, ♄ in ♒, ♃ in ♐ and ♂ in ♈. These being the Day houses of the Planets, Therefor all Work under these Signs must be performed in the Planets hour in the Day. But when ♀ is in ♉, ☿ in ♍, ♄ in ♑, ♃ in ♓, ♂ in ♏, these being the Night Houses of the Planets and all work made under these signs must be performed in the hour of the Planet in the night. Observe the same rule by night only seek in the bottom table of Planetary hours. NIGHT, as for the Day. By this table you see that whatever the Hour looses in the Day it gains in the Night and whatever the hour looses in the Night, it gains in the Day. That when ☉ enters into the first degree of ♈ and into the first degree of ♎ the days and Nights are equal for which reason these two Signs are called Equinoctial. And when he has passed the Tropical Sign ♋ he then becomes in a state of Retrogration leaving our Earth for which reason the Days Shorten and Nights Lengthens. Also observe the friendship and enmities of the Planets for this Work ♂ is in enmity to every planet but ♀ ♂ is powerful in himself so is ♄. ♂ & ♄ are in great enmity, and when ♂ oppose ♄ ♀ or ♃ and ♄ oppose ♂ ♀ or ♃ the Ancient allow these positions to be the most inveterate amongest the Celesticals. And for whatever purpose a Talisman is framed under them to be the most powerfull. ♀ denotes Love and is called the goddess of Love ♂ is in sympathy with her, ♂ is a hot fiery planet and of the fiery Triplicity therefor by his heat rouses it to passion. Possession then follows but if disapointment steps in between Anger appears after which comes hatred who rouses the Spirit of revenge and every means is suggested to execute the same on the object as our common enemy therefor ♂ is calculated for this purpose as the executioner

The Seven Planets Called the Seven Governors of the World their names in this Art by the Magi

The Seven Planets are by the Great Philosopher Hermes called the seven Governors of the World and has applied to them many names &c according to their natures, powers times, Seasons &c

♄ is Called Coelius, Sythe Bearer and is always Pictured as an old man holding a Sythe, this planet they called the father of the Gods, and by some they put in his other hand an hour Glass, and call him the father of time, and thus Pictured him as Time with large Wings. He is also called the high Lord, the great, the wise, the author of Contemplation, impressing or depressing great in the mind and hearts of Man, capable of Preserving and destroying all things, overturning all force and power, and constituting, a keeper of secret things and of shewing them, also causing loss, and life and Death, as is further seen in the Tables of Saturn

♂ is Called Mavors powerfull in War Bloody, powerfull in Arms, a sword bearer, magnanimous, Bold untamed, like Lightening, of great power and furious haste against whom none can defend himself if he resists him capable of destroying the strong, and powerfull, deposing kings from their thrones. His Colour is Red, and is called the Lord of heat and power, and the Planet of Blood. for further research See his Table of Angels &c These two Planets being the only two capable of annihilating or touching life are called Malevolents whos power can only be resisted by the power of the ☽ and by this Art

♃ is called the king of Heaven the God of Thunder & Lightening Magnanimous and unconquered high and Mighty — great & mighty author of all Good, every way Fortunate, Sweet and Mild, of good will, honest, pure, the Lord of Honour and Joy, and in Judgment wise & true, the Judge of truth & Justice, the Lord of Riches & wisdom, & excelling in all goodness. See the Table of Jupiter

136

♀ The fruitful Lady of Love and Beauty, and the Goddess of Love Beautifull, White Fair, pleasing, Powerfull in affection, the first parent of Mankind who is the beginning of all things, joyned diversity of Sexes together with a growing Love and with an eternal affection offsprings propagates all kinds, both Men and animals, the Lady of friendship, society, always beautifull to Mortals, and Mother to the conditions of them in distress & Misery and a safeguard to Mankind always capable of doing good, and by her power overcomes all things, humbling the high to the low, the Strong to the week, and the Vile to the Noble rectifying all things, and she is found in every Sex and Mind for which reason she is called Aphrodite also Lucifera i.e. Bringing light, and when she follows the Sun i.e. her Heliocentric motion she is (in that situation) Called Hesperus and Phosperus because she leads through all things, though ever so hard. See her Table

☿ is called the Son of Iupiter the cryer and interpreter of the Gods, Stilbon the Serpent bearer or Rod bearer Pictured as a Man with wings on his head and feet, Signifying a messinger of the Gods, the notary of the Sun, the messinger of Iupiter, and also a messinger between the Supernaturall and infernal Gods, Male with Males Female with Females and most fruitful in both Sexes. The God of Learning, the great Philosopher, Lucan calls him the arbitrator of the Gods eloquence, bringer of gain & wisdom, He is also called Hermes i.e. interpriter, and he brings things to light, out of Obscurity, and by his means, are things opened which were before made secret, Therefor he is powerfull both in good and evil See his Table

☉ Is called Phoebus Deospiter Apollo Titan Pean Phanes Horus & Osiris as is Described by the oracle as follows,

The Sun Osyris, Dionysius gay
Apollo Horus King ruling the Day
Who changeth times who giveth wind and Rain
The King of Stars and the immortal flame.

He is called Ancitenem Burning fiery, golden flaming radiating. The Eye of the World Lucifer seeing all things ruling all things, the creator of Light and Lord of all good. Fortunate to all who are honest, prudent intelligent and wise, shining over the whole World, governing and vivifying all Bodies that have a Soul The Prince of the world keeping all Stars under himself, from whence all recive their luster, and by whose presence they are darkened & overcome, Giving splendor and light to all things. In the Night he is Called Dionysius but in the Day Apollo & Phœbus as by his presence all will flee Therefore the Athenians called him Alexicacen and Homer Ulion i.e. The driver away of evil things Phœbus from his beauty & brightness and Vulcan from his fiery violence, The Grand Mover of all Nature and Giver of Life See his table of Angels

☽ is called Phœbe, Diana, Lucina, Proserpina Hecate Menstruous, a horn bearer a preserver, a Night-walker giving light by night, the Queen of Heaven and Spirits the Mistress of the Elements, whom the Stars & Planets answers, Seasons returns, Elements serve and at whose nod Lightnings burst forth, Seeds, bud, plants increase, the initial Parent of fruit, the Sister of Phœbus, the Goddess of Light, conveying light from one Planet to another, the Mistress of Rain and Waters, the Giver of Riches, the Nurse of Mankind, the governess of all states, protecting Men by sea or Land, Mitigating all the tempests of fortune restraining the rage of evil spirits, of whose Majesty the

138

the Birds in the air are afraid. the Wild Beasts struggles in the Mountains, Serpents hide in the ground, Seeher Tale. and for a more curious inquiry See the Hymns of Orpheus

The Philosopher Porphyrie in his Book be Responsis says that all Talismans properly framed and made according to Art. Breath forth a power of the Gods and by these powers were recived commands how and what they were to do He also saith that Hecate commanded by such revelation how images were to be made. and how they should be constituted to her. which command properly. attended to she would appear and answer the worker by dreams the following is the Oracle of Hecate i.e. the Name of the Moon

>Mark I will teach what statue thou shalt make
>For me, boughs of the Wood and wormwood take
>Then garnish it, or paint domestic Mice
>Let ornament be fair, and of great price
>Then Frankincense, myrrh, Storax, mixt with Blood
>Of Mice then sing thou words secret and good
>As thou seest shapes of Mine, so on it lay
>As many real Mice; than take thy bay
>And out of the trunk thereof a case prepare
>To put it in; then see thou have a care
>That to the Statue thou devoutly pray
>Also thy debts, and vows take care thou pay
>If that these things that here required be,
>Thou Shalt perform, in dreams thou shalt see me

Note, according to this Oracle. a Statue or Image was formed in the hour of the ☽ where strong, of a Wood under her influence and Painted or Carved thereon Mice. as many as effects were desired. then wrapt it up in Wormwood sprigs. and,

139

perfumed it with Blood, Myrrh, Storax &c using at the same time an Imprecation (Then sing thou Words secret and good) which is framed from various parts of the Scriptures, Virgil, Ovid and the Hymns of Orpheus. the Image when finished they hold in high estimation, by lying under their head in sleep and receive whatever secret information they want by Dreams

Chap 20.

Of Imprecations, and Joining Many Words together as sentences and verses and of the Virtues and the

Astrictions of Charms

The Ancients were always very methodical in all their transactions, and were always prepared in every thing necessary for their work, and selected such Sentences, Words Names, Verses &c and combined them in form in small Books, which were always kept in their possession, some outlines of them have been in print, but the most sacred part of them are totally extinct. They say that there are much greater Virtues and power in Sentences, and Verses found in the holy Writ, as they proceed from truth, which is called the Great Seal of God, and which hath a most patent power in impressing, changing, Binding Charming Facinating &c Which Virtue is not in simple words only, but in sentences. composed by art, by which any thing is affirmed or denied, by which sort of Verses so composed are performed, Inchantments, Facinctions, Invocations Obtestations Adjurations &c. Therefore in the composing such Verses, and Orations for the Attracting the Virtue of any Spirit or Star, to work an effect, You must consider diligently the Virtue and power of that Spirit or Star and what property it containes answerable to your purpose. and if to obtain any thing we desire it must

140

be done by Supplications as David in the 57 Psalm,
" Be merciful unto me O God, be merciful unto me, for my Soul
" trusteth in thee, and under the shadow of thy Wings shall be
" my refuge, until this tyranny be over past
" I will call upon thee most High God, even unto the God
" that shall performe the cause which I have now in hand,
Therefore whatever Star this apperatiues to, the mentioning
the Star and its properties, must be attended to
David for the destruction of his enemies, has this saith
In the 35 Psalm 8th &
" Let a sudden destruction come upon him unawares
" and his net that he hath laid privatly catch himself
" that he may fall into his own Mischief
When David prays for God to defend him he says thus
" Give sentence with me O God and defend my cause against
" the ungodly people, deliver me from the deceitful & Wicked Men
For the Persecution and Confusion of his Enemies, Psalm 35 ver 6
Now it appears, that the only instrument of enchantments,
Bindings &c, is a pure Harmonicacal Spirit warm, breathing
Living, bringing in motion, affection and significations Com-
pond of its parts, endued with sense, and conceived by reason,
By the quality thereof of this Spirit, and by the Celestral simil-
-itude; besides, these things, which are already treated upon,
verses also from the opportunity of time, recive from above
most excellent virtues, Therefore the object, or things, that are
to be enchanted &c The Magi Breathed upon them the words of
the verse, or to breath in the virtue of the Spirit; so that the
whole virtue of the Soul is directed on and to the thing ench-
-anted; being so disposed by Art for receiving the said virtue,
They belive the power of Enchantments, & verses is so great that
they belive they are able by them to subvert all natures; and
Josephus testifies, that Soloman, was well skilled in these

141

kinds of Enchantments; Also that great Philosopher Celsus Africanus reports, according to the number of the faces of the Signs in the Zodiac, that each Face had a Spirit to rule over it, which in all are 36, and each undertake to defend the part of Mans Body appropriated to them, and that the Magi of Egypt called them seperate names in a peculiar voice; who being called upon, restore to health with these enchantments, the diseased parts of the Body. And that every Oration, writing, and words induce some accustomed motion by their usual order, in being pronounced, or wrote to produce common Effects; But if wrote or pronounced backwards, unusual effects and of these, Lucan says

    Thessalian Verse did into's heart so flow
    That it did make a greater heat of Love

Also Virgil in Damon
    Charms can command the Moon down from the sky
    Circes Charms changed Ulysses Company

142

Magic Circle for the first hour of Sunday the ☉ in the Spring

Magic Circle for the first hour of Monday the ☾ in the Summer

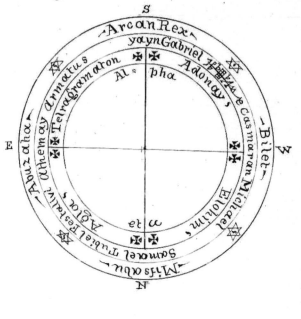

Magic Circle for the first hour of Tuesday — ♂ in the Autumn

Magic Circle for the first hour of Wednesday — ☿ in the Winter

144
Magic Circle for the first hour of Saturday ♄

In drawing the four Magic Circles, as examples for the veri=ation of each Quarter, the names being so long I cannot put them in their proper place so have framed one under ♄ with every name in its true situation as follows

First on the South point in the Out side Circle the King & following his Ministers. In the Second Circle the name of the hour under the King following in that Quarter the Angel of the day & his Sigil, on the west point the name of the Angel of that Quarter, on the South point the name of the Angel of the Quarter. On the East point the head of the Sign of the Quarter, following the name of the Earth ☉ & ☽. then in the West the Angel of the day and from the north the Second Angel, all being in proper order & so with the Rest—

The figures of Divine Letters of the Seven Planets which are used in Framing of all kinds of Talismans as Seals &c

The Characters of ♄

of ♃

of ♂

of ☉

of ♀

of ☿

of the ☽

Of the Sacred Characters of the Seven Planets and their Use in this Art
Chap 21

The Stars and Planets which God has placed in the Heavens have in them all their peculiar Natures & properties and conditions the Seals and Characters of which is produced through their Rays even in these inferiour things. i.e in the Eliments, in Stones, in Plants, in Animals, and all their Members whence every thing receives from an harmonious disposition & from its Star shining upon it some peculiar Seal, or Character, stamped upon it which is the signification of that Star or harmony, containing in a peculiar virtue differing from other virtues of the same matter, both generically specifically and numerically. Every thing therefore hath by nature its Character pressed upon it by its Star which governs it; and it is evident that these Characters, contain & retain in them the peculiar natures and virtues, and roots of the Stars and produce the like operations upon other things on which they are reflected by Stiring and helping the influence of the Planets fixed Stars figures and the Celestial Signs i.e. when a Matter is made and formed of fit Materials to and in their Due & accustomed times Which the Learned and Wise Men considering well, watching every effect and cause of nature with all the Occult properties of things setting down in writing all things, the images of Stars, their figures, Seals, Marks, Characters &c such as nature has herself described in them by the rays of the Stars in these inferiour Bodies, some in Stones, some in Plants and Joints and knots of Boughs, of Trees, and in Trees, and some in the different Joints of Animals. For Example the Sun being a Body of fire, which throws from it a great degree of heat hits Rays must Diverge from its Center into space therefor all things that resemble the same is called Solary

147

and signifies that the Sun governs the same. Take a branch of the Vine cut it in two and you'l see from a Spot in the Middle lines will diverge. the same therefore is a signature of the Sun and is called Solary. The Oak, the Bay Tree, the Lote Tree, the Marigold, by being cut will show the Same signiture, and a number of others also. The Stone Ætites. which is called the Eye of ☉. as it is like the Eye in form and the rays diverge, The same the Carbuncle Chrysol-ite, Iris, Heliotropion, Hyacinth, Pyriophilus, Pantauras, Panth-erus, or Pantochras (in the Scripture called) Evanthum; The Topaz, Ruby and the Dimond these are all Solary Stones Take the Stone Heliotropion and with the Juice of the Herb of the same Name and put them in clear Spring water. and set them in the rays of the Sun in its highest state, a phen-omenon will take place that will surprise you; The Stone Iris being held in the rays of the Sun reflecteth them in the form of the rainbow. Ætites is a Stone found in an Eagles nest and cureth the Epilepsy of falling Sickness and all poisons, these stones have various other properties see Albertus Magnus and William of Paris, and various Works of ancient Occult Phil-osophers. But for the full use of what I have here intended is sufficiently noticed

Note That according to the experiment desired, whether it be required from the power of ♄, ♃, ♂, ☉, ♀, ☿ or the ☽ the char-acters of the different Planets must be selected appropriate to the effect. wether good or evil - if for Good purposes, those must be chosen that are in appearence a kind of harmony If for evil the most aukward or ugly possible If for torment or punishment to your enemies - all sharp Angles & points, and so on according to your Judgement, keeping as near to the Resemblance of the Characters as possible in point of form. but of size length, bredth wedth &c is very immat-

immaterial, for in this Art Resemblance or Similitude is every thing Therefore the most essential point is in selecting the Characters for Combination for the ☌, ✶, and △ of the Planets, as these Aspects are the Aspects of Harmony and Concord, But the □ or Quartiles and ☍ are Aspects of Discord, Strife and Enmity

Chap 22

A Four fold Table of the names of the four Quarters, their heads the Angels and the Sun & Moon

	♈	♋	♎	♑
	Spring	Summer	Autumn	Winter
Q	Talvi	Casmaran	Adarael	Farlas
A	Caracasa	Gargatel	Tarquam	Amabael
	Core	Tariel	Guabarel	Otarari
	Amatiel	Gaviel		
	Commisoros			
H	Spugliguel	Tubiel	Torquaret	Altarib
E	Amadai	Festative	Rabinnara	Geremiah
S	Abraym	Athemay	Abragina	Commutaff
M	Agusita	Armatus	Matasignais	Affaterim

☞ Q The names of each Quarter A the names of the Angels governing each Quarter H the names of the heads of the Signs E the names of the Earth S the names of the Sun M the names of the Moon The use of this Table is explained fully by the four Examples of the four Magic Circles.

Note, the names, in the first Column will answer for any hour day, Week or Month, in the compass of the Spring Quarter The Second Column the names will answer for the same in the compass of the Summer Quarter, and the same with the Autumn & Winter Columns,

Names of the Planetry Hours Numbers and the
Angels ruling both day & Night

Sunday

Hours of the Day	Names of the Day Hours	Angels ruling each Hour	Hours of the Night	Names of the Night Hours	Angels ruling each Hour
1.. ☉	Yayn	Michael	1.. ♃	Beron	Sachiel
2.. ♀	Ianor	Anael	2.. ♂	Barol	Samael
3.. ☿	Nasnia	Raphael	3.. ☉	Thanu	Michael
4.. ☽	Salla	Gabriel	4.. ♀	Athir	Anael
5.. ♄	Sadedali	Cassiel	5.. ☿	Mathon	Raphael
6.. ♃	Thamur	Sachiel	6.. ☽	Rana	Gabriel
7.. ♂	Ourer	Samael	7.. ♄	Netos	Cassiel
8.. ☉	Tanic	Michael	8.. ♃	Tafrac	Sachiel
9.. ♀	Neron	Anael	9.. ♂	Sassur	Samael
10.. ☿	Iayan	Raphael	10.. ☉	Algo	Michael
11.. ☽	Abay	Gabriel	11.. ♀	Calerna	Anael
12.. ♄	Natalon	Cassiel	12.. ☿	Salam	Raphael

Monday

Hours of the Day	Names of the Day Hours	Angels ruling each Hour	Hours of the Night	Names of the Night Hours	Angels ruling each Hour
1.. ☽	Yayn	Gabriel	1.. ♀	Beron	Anael
2.. ♄	Ianor	Cassiel	2.. ☿	Barol	Raphael
3.. ♃	Nasnia	Sachiel	3.. ☽	Thanu	Gabriel
4.. ♂	Salla	Samael	4.. ♄	Athir	Cassiel
5.. ☉	Sadedali	Michael	5.. ♃	Mathon	Sachiel
6.. ♀	Thamur	Anael	6.. ♂	Rana	Samael
7.. ☿	Ourer	Raphael	7.. ☉	Netos	Michael
8.. ☽	Tanic	Gabriel	8.. ♀	Tafrac	Anael
9.. ♄	Neron	Cassiel	9.. ☿	Sassur	Raphael
10.. ♃	Iayan	Sachiel	10.. ☽	Aglo	Gabriel
11.. ♂	Abay	Samael	11.. ♄	Calerna	Cassiel
12.. ☉	Natalon	Michael	12.. ♃	Salam	Sachiel

Tues-day

1. ♂	Yayn	Samael	1. ♄	Beron	Cassiel
2. ☉	Janor	Michael	2. ♃	Barol	Sachiel
3. ♀	Nasnia	Anael	3. ♂	Thamu	Samael
4. ☿	Salla	Raphael	4. ☉	Athir	Michael
5. ☽	Sadadali	Gabriel	5. ♀	Mathon	Anael
6. ♄	Thamur	Cassiel	6. ☿	Rana	Raphael
7. ♃	Ourer	Sachiel	7. ☽	Netos	Gabriel
8. ♂	Tanic	Samael	8. ♄	Tafrac	Cassiel
9. ☉	Neron	Michael	9. ♃	Sassur	Sachiel
10. ♀	Jayon	Anael	10. ♂	Aglo	Samael
11. ☿	Abay	Raphael	11. ☉	Caterna	Michael
12. ☽	Natalon	Gabriel	12. ♀	Salam	Anael

Wednes-day

1. ☿	Yoyn	Raphael	1. ☉	Beron	Michael
2. ☽	Janor	Gabriel	2. ♀	Barol	Anael
3. ♄	Nasnia	Cassiel	3. ☿	Thamu	Raphael
4. ♃	Salla	Sachiel	4. ☽	Athir	Gabriel
5. ♂	Sadedali	Samael	5. ♄	Mathon	Cassiel
6. ☉	Thamur	Michael	6. ♃	Rana	Sachiel
7. ♀	Ourer	Anael	7. ♂	Netos	Samael
8. ☿	Tanic	Raphael	8. ☉	Tafrac	Michael
9. ☽	Neron	Gabriel	9. ♀	Sassur	Anael
10. ♄	Jayon	Cassiel	10. ☿	Aglo	Raphael
11. ♃	Abay	Sachiel	11. ☽	Calerno	Gabriel
12. ♂	Natalon	Samael	12. ♄	Salam	Cassiel

Thursday

1. ♃	Yayn	Sachiel	1. ☽	Beron	Gabriel
2. ♂	Janor	Samael	2. ♄	Barol	Cassiel
3. ☉	Nasnia	Michael	3. ♃	Thanu	Sachiel
4. ♀	Salla	Anael	4. ♂	Athin	Samael
5. ☿	Sadedali	Raphael	5. ☉	Mathon	Michael
6. ☽	Thamur	Gabriel	6. ♀	Rana	Anael
7. ♄	Ourer	Cassiel	7. ☿	Netos	Raphael
8. ♃	Tanic	Sachiel	8. ☽	Tafrac	Gabriel
9. ♂	Neron	Samael	9. ♄	Sassur	Cassiel
10. ☉	Jayon	Michael	10. ♃	Algo	Sachiel
11. ♀	Abay	Anael	11. ♂	Calerna	Samael
12. ☿	Natalon	Raphael	12. ☉	Salam	Michael

Friday

1. ♀	Yayn	Anael	1. ♂	Beron	Samael
2. ☿	Janor	Raphael	2. ☉	Barol	Michael
3. ☽	Nasnia	Gabriel	3. ♀	Thanu	Anael
4. ♄	Salla	Cassiel	4. ☿	Athin	Raphael
5. ♃	Sadedali	Sachiel	5. ☽	Mathon	Gabriel
6. ♂	Thamur	Samael	6. ♄	Rana	Cassiel
7. ☉	Ourer	Michael	7. ♃	Netos	Sachiel
8. ♀	Tanac	Anael	8. ♂	Tafrac	Samael
9. ☿	Neron	Raphael	9. ☉	Sassur	Michael
10. ☽	Jayon	Gabriel	10. ♀	Algo	Anael
11. ♄	Abay	Cassiel	11. ☿	Calerna	Raphael
12. ♃	Natalon	Sachiel	12. ☽	Salam	Gabriel

152

Saturday

#	Planet	Name	Angel	#	Planet	Name	Angel
1.	♄	Yayn	×Cassiel	1.	☿	Beron	Raphael
2.	♃	Ianor	×Sachiel	2.	☽	Barol	Gabriel
3.	♂	Nasnia	×Samael	3.	♄	Thanu	Cassiel
4.	☉	Salla	Michael	4.	♃	Athir	Sachiel
5.	♀	Sadedali	Anael	5.	♂	Mathon	Samael
6.	☿	Thamur	Raphael	6.	☉	Rana	Michael
7.	☽	Ouner	Gabriel	7.	♀	Netos	Anael
8.	♄	Tanic	Cassiel	8.	☿	Tafrac	Raphael
9.	♃	Neron	Sachiel	9.	☽	Sassur	Gabriel
10.	♂	Iozan	Samael	10.	♄	Aglo	Cassiel
11.	☉	Abay	Michael	11.	♃	Calerva	Sachiel
12.	♀	Natalon	Anael	12.	♂	Salam	Samael

Note ×Cassiel or Zaphiel, × Sachiel or Zadkiel, × Samael or Camael

This Table is from Peter De Abano in his Arbatel dated 1555. I shall explain the last Saturday, as it is near the eye and easy to refer to, which will serve for the rest;
Saturday. shows the day the table is made for
N°. 1 to 12 are the hours from Sun rise. ♄ to ♀ are the Planets which rules the hour of that day. ♄ in the first line means that it is the day of ♄ being Saturday and that he is lord of that day. he ruling the first hour. The second column, Yayn, Ianor &c are the Occult names of the Hours, The third column Cassiel Sachiel &c are the names of the Angels ruling each hour of the day which is the first and Eighth. The fourth Column. 1. ☿. Mercury rules the first hour of the night and is Lord of the Night, Beron is the name of that hour, and Raphael is the angel of that hour therefor the same observations must be made for the night as well as the day and to know the length of the Planetry hour &c you must refer to the Table of Planetry hours, for every day throughout the Year Page 130 and 131

Chap 23

The Angels ruling the day, the Air, the Heaven their Ministers, and to what Quarter of the World they belong, the Perfumes, their Offices and Conjurations

☉. Sunday. The Angels ruling the day Michael, Dardiel; Huratapel, ruling the Air

Varcan King

His Ministers Tus. Andas Cynabal. Angels of the 4th Heaven of the East, Samael, Baciel. Abel. Gabriel. Vionatraba; of the West. Anael Pabel. Ustael. Burchat, Suceratos, Capabili of the North Aiel. Aniel, vel Aquiel Masgabriel. Sapiel. Matuyel. of the South. Haludiel, Machasiel. Charsiel, Uriel, Naromiel

Perfume, Red Sanders

The Conjuration of ☉ day

I conjure and confirm upon you ye strong and holy Angels of God in the name, Adonay. Eye, Eye, Eya which is he who was, and is and is to come Eye, Abnay, and in the name. Saday. Cados. Cados, sitting on high upon the Cherubin; and by the Great name of God himself strong and powerful who is exalted above all heavens Eye, Saray, maker of the world, who created the world the heavens the earth the sea and all that in them is in the first day, and sealed them with his holy name, Phaa, and by the name of the holy Angels, who rule in the fourth Heaven, and serve before the most mighty, Salamia, an Angel great and honourable; and by the name of his Star, which is Sol, and by his Sign, and by the immense name of the living God, and by all the names aforesaid I conjure thee Michael, Oh' great angel, who art chief ruler of the Lord's day; and by the name Adonay, the God of Israel, who hath created the world, and

154

all that therein is, that thou labour for me, and fulfill all my petitions, according to my will and desire, in my cause and business

The Ancients Magi assert, that the Spirits of the Air on Sunday are under the North Wind and their nature is to procure wealth, to obtain favour and benevolence to dissolve the enmities of men, to raise man to honours to carry on take away infirmities &c

☽ Monday. The Angels Ruling the day Gabriel Michael; Samael ruling the Air

Arcan King

His ministers. Bilet. Missabu Abuxaha — Angels of the first Heaven, which are called from the 4 Quarters
From the East Gabriel. Gabrael Madiel Deamiel Ianack
From the west Sachiel Zaniel Habiel Bachanael Corobael
From the North. Mael, Urael, Valnum, Baliel Balay Humastran
From the South Curaniel Dabriel Darquiel Hanun Anayl. Veluel,

Perfume. Aloes

The Conjuration of ☽ day.

I Conjure and confirm upon you ye strong and good Angels, in the name. Adonay. Adonay, Adonay. Eye Eye. Eye. Cados. Cados. Cados. Achim Achim Ia. Ia. strong Ia who appeared in mount Sinai with the glorification of King. Adonay Saday Zebaoth Anak-her Ya Ya Ya. Marinata. Abim, Ieia who created the Sea and all lakes and waters in the second day, which are above the heavens and in the earth, and sealed the sea in his high name, and gave it

155

bounds, beyond which it cannot pass; and by the names of the Angels who rule in the first Legion who serve Orphaniel a great precious and honourable Angel, and by the name of his Star which is ☽. and by all the names aforesaid, I conjure thee Gabriel, who art chief ruler of Monday, the second day, that for me thou labour and fulfill

The Spirit of the air this day are subject to the West wind which is governed by the ☽ and their nature is to give Silver; to convey things from place to place, to make Horses swift and to disclose the secrets of persons both present and future

♂ Tuesday. The Angels Samael, Satael,
   Amabiel ruling the Air
Samax King, His Ministers Carmix, Ismoli, Paffran,
The Angels of the fifth Heaven
From the East: Friagne Guael, Damael, Calzas Arrugon
West: Lama Astagna Labquin Soncas Iaxel Isiael, Irel
North: Rahumel Hyniel Rayel Seraphiel Mathiel Fraciel
South: Sacriel Ianiel Galdel Osael Vianuel Zaliel
   Perfume Pepper

The Spirits of the Air this day are under the East Wind * governed by ♂ their nature is to cause wars, Mortality death and Combustions, to bring destruction on our enemies and causing either infirmities (whatever is under him) or perfect health.

* When this wind is high on the begining in the Manufacturing of any Talisman Ring Seal &c in the planetary hour of this day (which is influenced by ♂ it will be of a greater power and will have greater effect on the subject made for

The Conjuration of ♂ day

I Conjure and Call upon you ye strong and good Angels; in the name Ya Ya Ya, He He He, Va, Hy Hy, Ha Ha Ha, Va Va Va, An An Ain Aialia, Alia, El, Ay, Elibra. Eloim, Eloim, and by the names of him the high God, who hath made the Sea into dry Land and by his word hath made the Earth, and produced Trees & hath set his Seal upon the Plants of it with his precious honoured, revered, and holy name: and by the name of the Angels governing in the fifth House, who are subservient to the great Angel Acimoy, who is strong powerful, and honoured, and by the name of the Constellation, which is called Mars. And I call upon thee Samuel, and the names above mentioned thou great Angel; who presidest over the day of Mars; and by the name Adoney the living and true God, that you assist me in accomplishing my labours &c&c (as in the conjuration of Sunday)

☿ Wednesday. The Angel Ruling. Raphael, Meil.
  Saraphiel, Ruling the Air
Mediat or Modiat King. Ministers Suquinos, Sallales,
  The Angels of the Second Heaven
East: Mathlai, Tarmiel, Baraborat,
West: Ierescue Mitraton
North: Thiel, Rael, Iariahel, Venahel, Velel, Abuiori, Ucirnuel,
South: Milliel, Nelapa, Babel, Caluel, Vel, Laquel,
  Perfume Mastick

The Spirits of the Air on this day are subject to the South West wind & their Nature is to give all kinds of Metals, to reveal all earthly things past, present, and to come, to pacify Judges, to give Victory in War to re-edify, and teach experiments in all the Sciences and to change bodies mixt of elements conditionally out of one into another, to give health, and cause infirmities to our base enemies to raise the poor, to cast down the rich or high ones to bind and loose Spirits

∗ on the hour of this day when ☿ reigns your Talisman will be most powerfull if the wind (South west) is strong

The Conjuration of ☿ day

I Conjur and Call upon you ye strong, good and powerful Angel, in a strong name, of fear and praise Ia, Adoney, Eloim, Saday, Saday, Saday, Eie, Eie, Eie, Asamie, Asaraie, and in the name of Adoday the God of Israel, who hath made the great light, and distinguished day from night; and by the name of all the deserving Angels governing openly in the Second house, before the great Angel Tetra, strong and powerful; and by the name of his Star, which is ☿, and by the name of his seal which is the seal of a powerful and honoured God, and I call upon thee Raphael and the names above mentioned thou great Angel, who presidest over the fourth day; and by the holy name which is written in the front of Aaron created the most high Priest; and by the name of all the Angels who are constant in the grace of our Saviour, and by the name and place of Ammalium that you assist me in my labours &c (as in the conjuration of Sunday)

♃ Thursday, The Angels of this day, Sachiel Castiel
Asaßiel or Asaiel, Ruling the Air
Suth, King; Ministers Maguth Gutrix
Note, As there are no Angels above the fifth Heaven this prayer must be said, turning yourself to the East; O Great and most high and everlasting God, honoured be thy name world without end,

158

―facing the West; O wise, pure and just God of divine clemency I most humbly beseech thee most holy and merciful father that this day I may by thy will perfectly understand and accomplish my petition work and labour (here mentioning what you are going to performe) thou only father of our Lord and Saviour Jesus Christ and who livest and reignest world without end   Amen

Facing the North; O God strong and mighty from time everlasting.

Facing the South; O mighty and merciful God hear my petition and grant me the Arm of thy power – through the Name of our Lord Jesus Christ ~ Amen ~

Perfume Saffron

The Spirits of the Air of this day are subject to the South wind i.e. if this wind is high at the begining of any Talisman &c it will be most-powerful; Their nature is to procure the Love of all women, to pacify strife and contentions, to heal the Diseased and to cause infirmities & Disease on all which is under ♃; to procure losses, or take them away.

The Conjuration of ♃ day

I Conjure and confirm upon you Ye holy Angels, and by the name Cados, Cados, Cados, Eschereie, Eschereie, Eschereie, Hatim, ya strong founder of the worlds, Cantine, Jaym, Janie, Anic, Calbot, Sabbac, Berisay Alnaym; and by the name Adonay, who created fishes and creeping things in the waters, and birds upon the face of the earth, and flying towards heaven in the fifth day; and by the names of the Angels serving in the Sixth host before Pastor, a holy Angel and a great and powerful Prince; and by the name of his star which is ♃, and by the name of his Seal, and by the name Adonay, the Great God creator of all things, and by

the name of all stars, and by their power and virtue
and by all the names aforesaid, I conjure thee Sachiel
a great angel, who art chief ruler of Thursday, that
for me thou labour &c

♀ Friday, The Angels of the day, Anael, Rachiel, Sachiel,
    Ruling the Air;
Sarabotes; King Ministers, Amahiel, Aba, Abalidoth, Blaef,
        The Angels of the third Heaven
at the East; Setchiel, Chedusitaniel Corat Tamuel Tenaciel
West; Turiel, Coniel, Babiel, Kadie. Maltiel, Huphaltiel,
North; Peniel, Penael, Penat, Raphael, Ranie, Doremiel,
South; Porna, Sachiel, Cherniel, Samael, Santanael, Famiel
        Perfume Pepperwort
The Spirit of the Air of this day are governed by the West-
wind. Their Nature is to give silver, to excite men and
incline them to Luxury, to reconcile enemies through Luxury,
and facilitate Marriages for females, to allure Men to Love
them and bring them over to their wishes, to cause infirmities
to afflict our enemies in any part of the Body under the
dominion of ♀, likewise to take them away, and to enable
the Artist to performe all things which have motion
        The Conjuration of ♀ day
I Conjure and confirm upon You Ye strong angels holy &
powerful; in the name On, Hey, Heya, Ia, Ie, Adonay, Saday,
and in the name Saday, who created fourfooted beasts,
and creeping things, and man in the sixth day, and gave
to Adam power over all creatures wherefore blessed be
the name of the creator in his place; and by the name
of the Angels serving in the third host, before Dagiel
a great Angel, and a strong and Powerful Prince
and by the name of the Star which is ♀ and by his
Seal which is holy, and by all the names aforesaid

160

I conjure upon thee Anael, who art chief ruler of the sixth day, that thou labour for me &c

♄ Saturday. The Angels of this day Cassiel, Machatan, Uriel,
  Ruling the Air
Maymon, King. Ministers. Abumalith Assaibi Balidet
   Fumigation Sulpher

The planet ♄ being above the fifth heaven, there are no spirits ruling the Air, therefore use those orations of ♃. South wind or South west wind, and their Nature is to sow discord hatred, evil thoughts and cogitations, they give leave and readily to slay and destroy their enemies and to lame or maim every member

   The Conjuration of ♄ day

I Conjure and confirm upon you Caphriel, or Cassiel, Machaton, and Seraquel, strong and powerful Angels, and by the name Adonay, Adonay, Adonay, Eie, Eie, Eie, Acim, Acim, Acim, Cados, Cados, Ina or Ima, Ima, Sallay, Ia, Sar, Lord and maker of the world who rested on the seventh day; and by him who of his good pleasure gave the same to be observed by the children of Israel, throughout their Generations that they should keep and sanctify the same, to have a good reward in the world to come, thereby and by the names of the Angels serving in the seventh host, before Booel a great Angel and powerful Prince, and by the name of his Star which is ♄, and by his holy seal, and by the names before spoken, I conjur upon thee Caphriel, who art chief ruler of the seventh day, which is the Sabbeth day of the Ancients, that for me thou labour &c

☞ The ancients assert that if these tables &c are well understood & framed according to art have their effect in the circumferance of 100 Miles in a short time. The Conjurations or not used in Talismanic Art

161

Four Examples, for the forming four Circles for the four Quarters of the year Spring Summer, Autumn and Winter.
Called by the Rabbies Magic Circles
Chap 24

The formes of these Circles are not always the same as they changed them according to the Order of spirits desired their places, times, days, and hours as they always considered what time of the year what hour and what spirit they wanted what office they were to fill what Star and region belonged to them after all these considerations, and being prepared with every information necessary they then repaired the place proper and answerable to their purpose they then made a Circle (with Consecrated Chalk) Nine feet in Diameter and three more circles within the one, at four inches from each other, which formed three Spaces, In the 1st space from the outside Circle, They look in the Tables of Angels ☽ Page 153. ☉ Sunday and find Varcan, King which they place on the top or South point, then at the West, North and East points they place his Ministers, In the second circle under the King, the name of the Hour ruling that day, according to the Planetary table Page 131 next to that. Michael which is the angel ruling that day after which his Character or Sigil as in the tables of squares Pages 26 to 33, then take the Angels Ruling the Air of that day, which is Dardiel Huratapal, then from the Table of times places &c Page 148 take the name of the Quarter which is Talvi, the names of the angels. Caracasa Core. Amatiel. and Commissoros. following with the names of the head of the Signs. Spugliguel, the name of the Earth. Amadas, the name of the ☉. Abrayim, the name of the ☽. Agasitas, thus having finished the second Circle they Divide the same into four Quarters, and the

162

third Circle. they place the four great names of God
In the East quarter the Great name Tetragramaton
In the South Adonay. In the West Elohim and In the
North Agla, with a Cross ✠, on each side of the line
In the Very near the top divided by the pale Al-pha
and at the Bottom et-w. which signifies Alpha and
Omega, the first and the last and at the four extr-
=emeties or angls, four Pentagons as In the figure
for Sunday ☉ Spring Page 142 This is the true manner
from the Original Copy. I shall now teach you in what
manner to very and form the other three Quarters under
the ☽. ♂ and ☿

To Frame a Circle under the ☽ on Monday in the Sum-
=mer Quarter, you must enter the tables under the ☽
in the same manner as that of the ☉, first looking
for the King. which you will see is Arcan. and his
Ministers Bilet. Miss-abu and Abuzaha, which must
be placed as before, then look in the Table of the
Angels hours you will see under Monday Yayn the
hour and Gabriel the ruling angel, and her character
is in page 33 which must be placed as in the Circle for
Spring. then look in the Table of the Quarter and
under the word Summer youl see the name of the
Quarter, the Angel ruling the Quarter, the head of the
Sign the name of the Earth, the Names of the ☉ and ☽ -
all which must be placed as in the Example of Summer
in a correct manner. as in the large Circle which is
Complected according to Art. and in the same man-
-ner must the other Circles. Autumn and Winter be
Compounded, The Difference between Talismans and
these Circles are but little indeed they are proper
Talismans. For the ancient Magi. used them as a

protection to their Persons from all evil Spirits in all their Exorcisms &c which you'l see at large in the Arbatel of Magic by Peter De Abano, translated by Robert Turner 1555. also the full use of Pentacles of which I shall give a few drawings with their for= =mation and Virtues

Fig 1

The Pentacle of Solomon

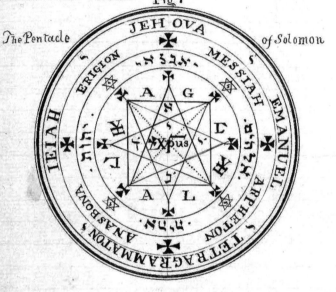

Fig 2

The Pentacle of Peter de Abano

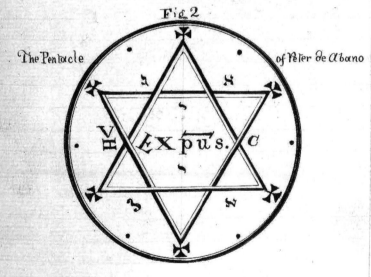

164

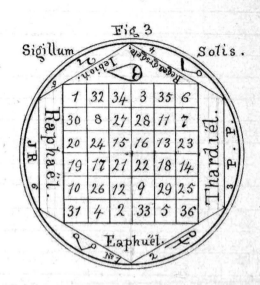

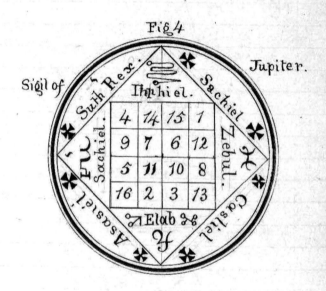

Fig 1 Is the Penticle handed down to us from tradition to be that of King Solomon, and which he always kept about him this grand Penticle was made of pure gold, and engraved thereon the same Characters as in the figure, the mysteries of which are great, and as far as this Science will permit me I will endeavour to explain, and as the framing of

these vary in point of ornament or private Character which every artist use – These I shall omit and give an outline of the most material Composition of Characters In the center Circle is framed a square, which figure is by the Learned Magi Ascribed to God as the projection of it is four points and by the Pythagorian's is called Tetractis, The reason they ascribed this four square figure to god the father is that it contains the whole mystery of the Trinity, as the divine trinity in god is always written in four letters, and termed the perpetual fountain of nature the fountain and head of the whole divinity. As it contains the four degrees in the Scale of nature. i.e. to be, to live, sensibility and understanding The four motions of nature The four Corners of heaven The four Winds of heaven The four Elements The four Triplicities, the four Qualities under heaven Cold Heat Dry and Moist The four Humours of the Body. The four Quarters of the Year The four Rivers of Paradise. The four kinds of Animals The four Consecrated Animals The four Angels ruling the four Corners of the elements The four Evangelists. The four perfect Kinds of mixt Bodies — Animals. Plants, Metals, & Stones. The four properties of Plants that answers to the Elements, Seeds, flowers Leaves & Roots. The four properties of Stones so answering, Bright and Burning, Light & Transparent, Clear & Congealed, Heavy and Dark. The four Elements of Man or Microcosm; representing the four Elements, Fire, Air, Water & Earth, i.e. The Mind, the Spirit, the Soul, the Body The four powers of the Soul Intelect Reason Planetry & Sense The four Judiciary Powers, Faith Science Opinions and Experience. The four Senses answering the Elements Sight Hearing, Taste & Touch. The Elements of Mans Body

166

Spirit, Flesh, Humours, Bones, The four fold Spirit. Animal. Vital, Generative, Natural; The four humours Blood Choller Flegm, Melancholly, The four Manners of Complexions, Violence Nimbleness, Dulness, Sloness, The four offensive Princes of Devils Samael, Azazel Azael & Makazael The four infernal Rivers Styx Phlegeton, Cocytus, Acheron, The four Princes of Spirits upon the four Angels of the world Oriens, Paymon. Egyn, & Amaymon The number comprehends all nature in its terms i.e. Substance, Quality, quantity and motion In moral philosophy the four Virtues. In Metephysics the four bounds. Necesity, being, Virtue and Action, The Number four having so great a power in mystery The Pathagorians, called it their Oath and always swear by the same as followers

" I with pure mind by the number four do swear
" That's holy, and the fountain of nature
" Eternal parent of the mind

Also the Prophet Ezekiel speaks of it, and so do Daniel. & in the Revelations of St John it is mentioned, The Hebrews not only reverence this number but the Arabians, Persians Magicians, Mahometans, Grecians, Truscans, Latins &c who all wrote the chief name of God in four letters as, Thet, Alla, Sire, Orsi Abdi, &c's, Esar, Deus, The Square is divided diagonally by dotted lines which shows four distinct trines, that being divided again, diametrically produces four more points or angles as such there is contained in the four Square twelve trines, answering the twelve signs of the Zodiac, the twelve months of the year, the twelve deities, The twelve consecrated Birds, The twelve Consecrated Beasts & the twelve Trees. The twelve Members of Man destributed to the twelve signs over which they bear great power. Eight Coupes over each paint are Emblems of forgiveness of our Sins and is com-
=memorated and esteemed by all the Learned Magi as a

figure of the greatest power containing every thing within itself. The four letters in the four Cardinal points אדני Adony signifies the God of Fore Knowledge Prophesy &c AGLA this Word means That God is the Eternal Strength ♄♃♀ signifies a conjunction of ♄♃♀ the properties of which is well known ⌐ this Character I cannot account for unless it is a compounded Chaldean character signifying the number 1010 which appears to me to be the time limited to the virtue of the Pentacle in years. In the Center Χρϛ signifies the spirit and the ϛ added to it signifies the Spirit X which the Greek apply to Ignis, Fire which must signify The Fiery Spirit which passes through every thing, is in every thing and every thing contain's which is called Vital fire without which nothing can exist. The י or Iod means God himself from whom originates the Spirit. In the first Circle are four Pentagons with י or Iod in the center is a mysterious figure of great power being a pentacle itself as youl see in Page 163 there are also four letters on the top point אגלא Agla which signifies The mighty God for ever on the right point יהוה Iehovah The most high God an emblem of the name of 72 Letters On the left point אלהים Elohim i.e. the God who produced the fruits of the Earth. The bottom point אהיה Ehieh which means the divine Essence of God. In the next Circle on the top is the Cross with three more in the Circle the emblem of which I have before explained. On the left is the Holy Name MESSIAH. the other names wether they are made names by Salomon or wether by transcription are misplaced I cannot account for only that they bear no affinity to any formed by the rules of this art. On the outer Circle are four Great names on the top JEHOVA The Godhead at the bottom TETRAGRAMMATON Joined to it י Iod the numeration

of which is Hochma i e wisdom and signifies the Divinity of
Ideas and the first begotten, and is attributed to the Son and
hath his influence by the order of Cherubims, or what the
Hebrews call Orphanim. i e the forms of wheels; from thence
to the Starry heavens where he fabricates as many figures as
he hath himself Ideas, and by which distinguish the very
Chaos, of Creatures by a particular intelligence called RAZIEL
who was the Angel which was the ruler of Adam. on the left
Ieiah. must mean Iaia. God our God is one God. On the
right Emanuel. God is with us. From the composition of this
grand Pentacle it is very evident that Solomon was well
skilled in this Sublime Science and knew well every combination of Nature as is testified by Josephus and other great writers,
there is no doubt that Solomon obtained many great & wonderfull
acquisitions from this Study

Note, the word Anpheton in the middle Circle must mean
Ephratah which is spoken of in the Psalms 132 & ver 6th.
"Lo we heard of it at Ephratah; we found it in the fields
"of the Wood; or Anephexeton, which word Aaron
heard and Spoke and was made wise,

Fig 2 Is a Pentacle made in the day and hour of ☿ the ☽
encreasing and nearly equal, but free from all combustion
or bad aspect from ♄ or ♂; and if possible in her Exhalt-
=ation; drawn on Virgin Parchment made from the Skin
of a young Kid; As the figure and finished according
to rules mentioned in this work, This Pentacle they put on
just before they began any work in this Science, Repeating
as follows; A Noor, Amacor, Amides, Theodonias, Aniter; by the
merits of the Angels O Lord I will put on the garment of Salvation,
that the thing which I desire (mentioning the effect) I may
bring to effect; thro' thee most holy Adonay whose kingdom
endureth for ever and ever – Amen

Fig 3 Is a French Sigil made under the ☉ in his day and hour with his table and appears to be a Compound one as Raphael the principle ruling angel of the day & hour of ☿ is placed therein, therefore I conclude as the ☉ & ☿ are in friendship together it must be made in the day of ☿ and Hour of ☉ also, which by the table of Planetary hours is on a Wednesday in the sixth hour; as well as on the eight and first hour on the Sunday; The Character Nº 1 is the two first Holy Names of God ו Vau and ה ה He, the numbers of which are 6, 5 & 1 making together 12, therefore the Character is taken as is seen in the square; begining at ו which is 6 from thence thence to ה which is 5 and from thence to ה which is 1 the termination & ends with ○ this is the true compounded Character Vau & He extended as in the table of ☉ under the divine names Page 24, and in the same manner are formed the other Characters, and for what use Talis= =mans of this discription are made as Nº 3, Page 153 — though this table of Numbers differ in their positions to the table Page 29 yet their numbers correspond, the first number being multiplied by 6 makes 36 which is the number of Squares, each line calculated makes 111 each way & in all 666, which is clear that the French Philosophers work on the same universal principle though differ in passition

Fig 4 Is a Pentacle made under ♃ in his day & hour In the table of Angels under ♃ Page 157 you'l see Suth Rex which is placed in the Assending angle and in the other Angles His three ministers Sachiel, Cashiel and Asasiel, with the emblem of the Cross In the four Inside Angles. In the East Sachiel with his great Character, In the oposite Angle Zebul, the name of the Heaven, with

170

his Sign ♓ (this Sign is the night house of ♃ which must be a mistake for) ♓ his Day house which signifies it must be made in the day and hour of ♃ by day. In the upper Angle is the name of the Intelligence with the Character drawn from the table of his Square in the as I have before shown, In the bottom Angle is his Divine Name in number 34 the exact sum of each line either way which is Elab or Alab the character of his Planet ♃ and the Characters of Alpha & Omega in the Celestial Characters of the Alphabet (See Celestial writing Page 21. In the Table or Square the Character of his Spirit which I have only placed there in red, that you may be familiar in drawing out these Characters, which is that of the Spirit to evil and is placed on the top angle; and Iophiel which is the name of his Intelligence to Good must be left out. (the reason why) that the Intelligence is placed over good, so must the evil Spirit be placed there as in a situation over the work designed for him to perform;

Note when the Intelligence & his Character is made use of it is to good purposes, as such the work must be performed by day, in the day & hour of the Planet requisite for the purpose when he is situated in his Sign called his House as he is then in his Greatest Power, But when his Spirit to Evil & his Character is to be used, the work must be done in the hour of the Planet by Night; which the Table Page 131 will show you; as I have before mentioned for whenever the Spirit of any Planet is called to aid the work in hand it is to answer, Anger Hatred & Revenge &c which is to Bind to hinder overthrow and Sedate or Destroy whatever that said Planet hath power over as the Table will declare. The Situation of the ☽ must be attended to as to her defferent Names she is called according to what effect you would wish her to perform for in all work Beneficial to mankind she must be strong in her own house which is ♋ or in her Exaltation as in ♉ then she takes the name of Phoebe, Diana, Lucinia, but in work to effect an opposite nature she is then Called Prosepina & Hecate (when she is under the Earth) as she is then the mother of all evil which the Table of Essential Dignities Page 120 will direct, i.e. when she is at her full she is Called Hecate, and in her last Quarter Prosepina she then being under the Earth and is Mistress of all evil, and in these passitions did the Ancient Caco Magicians performe all their Magical Enchantments Spells, Charmes, & Incantations;

Various Inscriptions to be engraved in the outside Circle of Talismans when framed applicable and according to the Rules of Art

    From an ancient manuscript

♄ For Dreams
    Cum ejsum super Fusnina Cubar asperti sunt Occuli

♄ Against Accidents which Cause Death
    Ne unquam ob dormiam in Morta me quando client inimicus: prevalni adversus cum,

♄ Against Inundations
    Rupti Sunt Amnes Sontes et cataractæ coeli apertæ sunt et facta est pluera Multa,

♄ Against the possession of evil Spirits,
    Constitue Super cum paccatum et Satanas Stet Dextris ejus.

To find hidden Treasures and Mines
♄ Obiem antan fodit in terram et abscondit pecuniam domini sui sed reversus ad Dominum,

172

♄ For increase of Fruits
Ignis grando nix Spiritus procellarum Sux faciunt verbum Domini Dei,

♀ For secret Love
Dixit elohim crescite et multiplic amini in terra,

♀ To procure the Love of the Fair
In Firmamentest magno, ere cortuum et rene,

♀ Amorous Intrigues
Dixit elohim eres cite multiplicamini replete terram,

♀ Another for the same
Pone me ut Signaentum super cor tuum Fortis ut Mons- -ests

♃ For Success in Trade &c
Gloria et honore coronasti eum enim domine super omnia onera tua,

♃ To discover hidden Treasures
Divitice Siaff Lucunt nolite eis cornestrum opponere,

♃ To be fortunate at Gaming at Hazard &c
Illumina oculas mens ne quando dicat inimicus prevalut adversus eum,

☿ To be fortunate in Gaming chance Traffic &c
Dextra Domini Fecit Virtutem dextra Domini exaltavit me

☿ To cause a person to be fortunate at Hazard,
Hartiti sunt vestimenta mea et super vestem sortiti sunt,

♂ Against fire Arms
Deus in adjutorium meum intende domini Festina

♂ Against the vexations of Enemies
Non cor Fortis sicut deus noster qui semper adest nobis,

♂ To make a person invunerable,
Dominus sit mihi adsutor et non timebo quid Faciat homo,

♂ To render a Military Life happy
Et domina Bitur a mari ad mare et Flumine ad terminos,

☽ Against danger by Sea or Land,
   Dominus sit mihi adjutus in brachio suo Fortisimo
   et patentis simo
☽ To gain a familiar Spirit,
   Obedite præpositis vestris subnacete casip sivigikant
☽ To Enchant treasures that they may not be taken
   Fundamenta montium conturbala sunt
☽ To prosper in Love Affairs
   Hoceninias de ossibus meis et caro de came mea
   et emut disouna,
☉ To make all Spirits Obedient
   Super aspidem & Basilicum ambulalis super-
   -leanem & draconam,
☉ For Honour and Riches
   Gloria et Divitice in Domo Ejus et Iustitia ejus menet
   in Sceculum,

How to make the Renowned Electrum for all
Magical and Talismanic purposes as Lamens,
Bells, Speculums, Images, Rings, Seals, Tablets, &c
which is highly esteemed for receiving the Planety influence,

Chap 25

The surprising effects which has been produced by
the following Compounds when made by Art, which
is the universal Compound of the Seven Planets
1st Take an equal Quantity of very fine Lead and Tin
and melt them in a new Crucible under the ☌ of ♄ & ♃
2nd Take an equal Quantity of very fine soft Iron & Gold
and melt them in a new Crucible under the ☌ of ♂ & ☉
3rd Take an Equal parts of fine Copper Mercury and
fine Silver. and melt the ♀ & ☽ adding the ☿ when melted
under the ☌ of ♀ ☿ & ☽. Then chuse a fair day in the
Spring when all vegetation is gitting forward The ☽.

174

encreasing, and the Planets all fair and free from bad aspects one with the other, In the day of ♃ and in the hour of ☉ put them into a new Crucible and melt all together, cast them into an ingot this don, take it to the flatting mills, and in the hour & Day of ☿ have it run through 3 times, then in the Day & hour of ♃ have it run through 4 times. In the Day & hour of ♂ run it through 5 times, In the Day & hour of ☉ 6 times In the Day and hour of ♀ 7 times, In the Day & hour of ☿ 8 times in the Day & hour of the ☽ 9 times, and if it is not thin enough finish it in the Day & hour of ♃ & ☉. when finished lay it by for use in a piece of clean linen cloth, and on the Day & hour you want to frame a Talisman — prepare a piece of it to the form required the rest observe as before; If the ♂ cannot be easily obtained the △ will do, and in melting it the last 3 may be mixed one part of Regulas of ♂ Antimony.

Some of the Learned Magi recommend the following i.e. That if they want to make a Talisman for Saturns use, when ♄ is fortunate and strong they

Melt in his day & hour   ♄ & ♂ | For ☉ or Solar use   ☉ & ♂
For ♃ his use   ♃ & ♂ | For ♀ or Venereal uses ♀ & ♂
For ♂ or Martial uses   ♂ & ♂ | For ☿ or Mercurial uses ☿ & ♂

Note the ♂ that is to be used must be the Regulas of Antimony, and in this last preperation, must be melted first and the ☿ stired in before the ♂ is congealed, The former is an approved composition of Paracelsus.

Of Holy Pentacles Sigils &c their Nature how Made and Compounded according to the Rules of Art, Also the use made of them in the Talismanic Art

Chap 26

The Learned Rabbies do affirm that these holy and Sacred Pentacles and Sigils, are Wonderfully potent and certain in their Effects desired and they used these as it were as certain holy Signs to preserve themselves from all evil charmes and events, also in Bindings, exterminating, and driving away all evil Spirits, and alluring the good Spirits of the superior Order, reconciling them and making them familiar to man. Now these Pentacles and Sigils consist either of Characters, of Good Spirits of the Superiour Order, or of Sacred Pictures of holy Letters or Revelations, with suitable Versicles which are composed either of Geometrical Figures and holy Names of God; according to the Course and manner of many of them; or they are compounded of all of them; or they are mixed according to Art; Therefore the Characters &c which are used to constitute and make these Pentacles, &c they are the Characters of the Good Spirits of the first and second Order, and sometimes of the third Order; and those Characters as being taken from out the Body of the Scriptures are called holy, therefore Whatsoever Character or Characters of this kind is to be instituted we must draw about him a Double Circle wherein we must Write the name of his Angel: and if some Divine Name is added therein congruent with his Spirit and Office, the effect desired will be more potent and it is also recommended, to draw about him some angular figure according to the manner of his Numbers, But the holy Pictures which these Pentacles consists and of which they are constituted are every where to be found in the Scriptures in both the Old & New Testament, as the Figure of the Serpent hanging on the Cross &c They also may be found and taken from the Visions of the Prophets as in Esaias, Daniel, Esdras, and many others

176

also out of the Revelations of the Apocalipse Therefore when any picture is chosen of these holy Images, let it be regul=arly drawn, then let there be a Circle drawn round it wherein let there be written some divine Name that is suitable to the effect of that Figure; and there is also written upon it some versicle from the Scripture answerable to the desired effect, As for Example. If a Sigil or Pentacle is to be made to gain a Victory, or a Revenge against ones Enemies, as well visible as invisable, i e public or Private The Figure may be taken out of the second Book of Macchabeus i e. A Hand holding a Golden Sword, Fig 2 Page 63, where is written about it a Verse out of the fifth Psalm; this also may be wrote in its stead, as the operator chooses (Take the Holy Sword the gift of God wherewith thou shall slay the adversaries of my people Israel) but either in Latin or Hebrew as (accipe gladium sanctum, muneratum a Deo, in quo con considos adversarios papuli meï Israel) and the name that should be wrote about for this purpose should be some divine Name that signifies, Fear a Sword, Wrath, the Revenge of God, or some name Congruent and agree=ing with the effect desired; Now these are two Pentacles or Sigils highly estimated by the Ancients, of the most Subtile Virtue and of great Power which they conceived very necessary to be used by the Operator in the Consecration of experiments — Implements for use &c. One of which is taken from the 1st Chap of Apocalypse. i.e. A Figure of the Majesty of God sitting upon a throne, having in his mouth a two edged Sword, as it is therein written therefore of this a Drawing is made with a Circle drawn around and therein must be written; I am Alpha and Omega, the begining and the end, which is and which was, and which is to come, the Almighty, I am the first and the last, who am living, and was dead, and behold I live for ever and ever; and I have the Keys of Death and Hell (Ego primus & novissimus vious & sui mortuus & ecce sum vivens in secula secidorum & habeo claves mortis & inferni) around in another Circle is written the ten Names of God. Elohim, El, Elohim Gibor, Eloha, Sabaoth, Elohim Sabaoth, Sadai, Adonai, Eheie, Iah. Some Rabbies leave out one of the last three & substitute the great Name Tetragrammaton. They then on the Reverse side write these Verses

1. Give Commandment O God, to thy Strength,
2. Confirm, O God, thy Strength in us
3. Let them be as dust before the face of the Wind, and let the Angel of the Lord scatter them,
   Let all their ways be darkness and uncertain,
   And let the Angel of the Lord persecute them

The other Pentacle is the Figure of A Lamb slain having seven eyes, and seven Hornes, lying on a Book sealed with seven Seals, which is taken out of the 5th chap of the Apocalypse. and round it (as before) is written this Verse, Behold the Lion hath overcome the Tribe of Judah, the Root of David. I will open the Book and unloose the seven Seals thereof, and round must be wrote (as before) the ten great Names of God, and on the reverse must be wrote this Verse, I saw Satin like Lightning fall down from Heaven. Behold I have given you power to Stand upon Serpents and Scorpions and power over all your Enemies, and nothing shall be able to hurt you; Now these Pentacles or Sigils are to be made on Virgin Parchment, and wrote with a pen made of a Quill taken from the Wing of some consecrated Bird belonging to the Planet, and the

178

Ink must be from the smoke of a Consecrated Wax taper, or from the Blood of some Bird or Animal as before, and for the other parts — the Body of this Book will explain These Pentacles or Sigils if made according to Art No Enemy hath power to hurt you either Visible or Invisible, Private or public, and the more they attempt against you the more they seek their own destruction

· Note, The First Seven Names out of the ten are belonging to the seven Planets, and if the Hebrew Names were used they will be more patent, as such I have here under placed them in their regular Order

♄ – אהים Elohim. ♃ – אל El. ♂ – גבר אהים. Elohim Gibor. ☉ – אלוה Eloha, ♀ – צבאות Sabaoth. ☿ – אהים צבאות Elohim Sabaoth, ☽ – שדי Sadai אדני Adonai, אהיה Eheie. יה Iah,

Some of the Rabbies make use of these ten names and assent they are equally of great Power if proper=ly placed. El, Elohim, Elohe, Zebaoth, Elion, Ejerchie, Adonay, Iah, Tetragrammaton, Saday. I have endeavoured to find the Origen of these names but cannot either by Rule or Art, and can only find according to the Ancient Tradition that they are Divine Names which was obtained by Revelation some of which I shall notice and to whom they were revealed and the use they were applied to, and also the Effects produced from their being pronounced. The great Name of God. Aglai. was revealed to Lot and the pronouncing of which he and his Family was saved, The Name of Ioth was revealed to Iacob by the Angel who wrestled with him, and by the pronouncing of which he was delivered from the hands of his Brother Esau, The Name Anephexeton was revealed to Aaron and by the pronouncing of which he was made wise., The Name Zabaoth was revealed to Moses the pronouncing of which when he was in Egypt all the Rivers and Waters were turned into Blood. The Name Escerchie Ariston was also revealed to Moses which he pronounced and all the rivers brought forth Frogs. The Name Elion was revealed to him and on his pronouncing it there was great Storms of hail such as never was before witnessed. and by the pronouncing the Name Adonay or Adonai which was also revealed to him all Egypt was surarmed with Locusts which eat up every thing left by the hail another Great Name was also Revealed to Moses which is Primeumaton which commands the whole host of Heaven his naming of which the Earth opened and swallowed up Corah, Dathan, and Abiram, These were the Intelligencies revealed by God to Moses and by these did he perform his Miracles, and by the power of these did he Overcome the Enemies of Truth, and by these were the Israelites freed from Bondage and Pharoah and his whole host destroyed, And by the Great and powerful Name Schemes Amithia which was revealed to Joshua and which he called on the Sun stayed his Course, The Prophet Daniel had the Name of Alpha & Omega revealed to him, which by his pronouncing the same he destroyed Bel and slew the Dragon; The three Children who were by the order of Nebuchadnezzer the King cast into the midst of the burning Fiery furnace had the name Emanuel revealed to them which they Sung and was delivered from the power of

180

the Scorching flames and saved. The Scriptures abounds with words of these kinds and each carries a meaning and power with it. It is very clear not only Moses, Recived these Revelations from God but all the Prophets, which their Books will prove, and it is very evedent that these words were not inserted as a mere matter of form. No the Rabies were men of profound Wisdom and valued the treasures of God as Divine Gifts, and handed them down to posterity in a man-
-ner that they might not be prophaned by the Wicked. The secrets of which has been lost from the depravity of the Ages.

In the Course of the Work you will see the word AGLA very often repeated in experiments of Talismans, Pentacles, Sigils, Lamens &c Therefore I shall explain it as from the manner of the Learned Rabbies, אגלא. ALGA. which signifies as follows You are Everlasting power, God. אתה You are גבור the Power לעולם everlasting - אדני God

You are Everlasting Power God

אתה-ג-בור — לעולם — אדני

א ___ ל ___ ג ___ א

A ___ L ___ G ___ A

In the same manner are all other Words explained which appears to the ignorant as Obsolete and without meaning or foundation therefore you see that the first letter is taken from each word and when compounded makes the word AGLA which is highly reverenced by the Ancient Magi, and made use of as one of the Great Names of God. the signification of which is You are the Power Everlasting God, which sentence may be transposed verious ways. Such are what is termed by the Magi, the great power of God or his attributes the number of which are ten. all of which are compounded from different parts of the Scriptures

as for Example, from the heads of these two Verses in the

Name of יׁשׁי JESU Extracted by taking the first letter from each word יביאשׁלהוּלוּ. i.e. Untill the Messiah shall come, and the other verse is שׁמריוה וּוּגוּ i.e His name abides till the end, therefore by taking the first letters of each word as you see I have dotted the letters. the word Jesu is extracted, and in the same manner is the word Amen, which is used at the end or terminations of all Prayers. This word is Extracted from the following Verse אדני מלך נאמן. i.e, The Lord the faithful King, Therefore the three heads or first letters of each word collected and compounded makes the Word אמן Amen

In the same manner is all names good or evil extracted and after which these being of the first order their agents &c are extracted by entering the Table of Good and Evil Angels, and after which their characters are extracted from out the Tables of Squares of the Planets as is fully explained

------

Verses from various parts of the Psalms approporate to the Talismanic Art

For Preservation. Psalm 86, V. 2, Psalm 121, V. 7, 8, Psalm. 150, V. 1, 4, 8, 9, 10, Psalm 16, V, 1, Psalm 35, V. 1, 2, 3, For Prosperity Psalm 118, V 25, For Wisdom Psalm 119, V, 18, 22, 27, 29, 33, 58, 66, 73 For Concord Psalm 65, V. 4, For Wealth Psalm 39 V. 15, To Heal Diseases Psalm 103, V. 1, 2, 3, For Loss of Speech, Psalm 32 V 10, Against Evil Spirits Psalm 68, V. 1, 2, To bring Curses of God on your Enemies Psalm 129 V, 5, 6, 7, 8, To Defend yourself from your Enemies Psalm 59, V, 2, 13 Psalm 43, V. 1, Psalm 40, V. 3, 4, Psalm, 71, V. 2, 4, 13, Psalm 7, V. 10, Psalm 25, V. 20, Psalm 31, V. 2, 5, Psalm 62, V, 6, 7 To find out your Enemy, Psalm 21, V. 6. To destroy him V. 10. To Gain Revenge on your Enemies and over power

182

them Psalm 109, V. 7, 8, 9, 10, 12, 13, 17, 18, 19, 29. Psalm 5 V. 10, Psalm 6 V. 10, Psalm 7, V. 6, Psalm 63, V 9, Psalm 68, V 1, 2, Psalm 69, V. 23, 24, 25, Psalm 83, V. 13, 14, 15, 16, 17, Psalm 26, V. 4, Psalm 35 V 4, 5, 6, 7, 8, 26 Psalm 15 V. 15, Psalm 41, V 8, Psalm 51 V. 6, Psalm 58 V. 7,

Now these are taken from the Psalms of David the force and power of which God heard and granted him all his petitions David was also as well as his father King Solomon Skilled in the Occult Sciences therefore his Writings were handed down from generation to generation. I shall now conclude this first book by giving you a few proofs showing the verity of this Sublime & heavenly Science, from the Scripture

Psalm 19th Ver 1 to 6th David gives a description of the Words Line and Sun, which certainly means the Zodiacal Circle, the Signs and the Sun passing through them

Isaiah, gives a reason Why the Heavens is called a Book i.e. by their being Rolled together

St. Paul, saith a Man may understand by the Heavens Therefore the most Learned Rabbies calls the heavens Sacred Books Exodus. Therein is mentioned Celestial Writing, St Luke, also makes mention of Coelestial Writing, which means the Writing of the Angels of which in this Science it is used and is fully described in the Body of this Work

The Patriarch Jacob, tells his Children on giving them his Blessing that he has read in the tables of the Heavens all that will befall them & their whole Posterity

Indeed there are so many parts in the Scriptures which proves the verity of this Study that a Man to doubt its Existence must disbelieve, holy Writ in toto, his God, his Saviour, and his own existence.

End of the First Book

The Lost Found, or the Mysteries of the Ancients Developed.

The Clouds of Enigma Dispersed,
And
The true Knowledge of that much revered,
and Heavenly Science of

TALISMANIC SCULPTURE
—— Restored ——

Displaying the Beauties, and Wonderfull Effects of Nature, the Four Elements.

FIRE. AIR. EARTH. WATER.

Planets, Stars, Signs, Intelligences, That through their Medium, & the Soul of the World, the Divine Gifts are Received by Man

Compiled and Selected
BY. W. H. IBBETT,
Book. II.

Also the two great Lights of Heaven, the twenty eight Mansions of the Moon, their Images Seals &c with the Art of Making the Same, according to the true system of the Eastern Philosophers,

Chap 1st
Of the four Elements

There are four Elements, and original grounds of all corporeal things, Fire, Earth, Water, Air, of which all elimentary inferiour bodies are compounded; not by way of heaping them together, but by transmutation and union, and when they are, destroyed, they are resolved into Elements, For there are none of the sensible Elements that is pure, but they are more or less mixed, and apt to be changed one into the other — Even as the Earth becomes dirty, and being disolved, becomes Water, and the same being made thick and hard, become Earth again; and if evaporated through heat, passeth into Air, and that Air being kindled passeth into Fire, but being extinguished returns back into Air, and being Cooled becomes Earth Stone or Sulphure, this is manifested by Electricity. Earth of itself is not changeable but is relented and mixed with other Elements which disolves it and then it returns back to itself again Now every one of these Elements hath two specificat qualities, the former retains as proper to itself in the other as a mean, it agrees with that which comes next after it, For fire is hot and dry, the Earth dry and cold, the Water cold and moist, the Air moist and hot, And so after this manner the Elements, according to two contary qualities are opposite one to the other, as fire to water, and Earth to Air The Elements are upon another account, are opposite to each other, Some are of a heavy quality as Earth & water, and others are light as Air and Fire, As such the former are called passive, and the latter actives and have assigned to each of them three peculiar qualities, viz. to Fire brightness, thinness, and motion, but to the Earth, darkness, thickness and quietness and according to these qualities the Elements of Fire and Earth are contrary. But the other Elements, Air & Water, borrow their qualities from the Elements, Fire and Earth, so that the Air receives two qualities of Fire, thinness and motion, and one of the Earth, darkness. In like manner Water receives two qualities of the Earth, darkness and thickness, and one of Fire viz motion. But Fire is twice more thin than Air, thrice more Movable and four times more bright. The Air is twice more bright, thrice more thin and four times more movable than Water. Water is twice more bright than Earth thrice more thin, and four times more movable. As therefore the Fire is to the Air so Air is to the Water, and Water to the Earth. Again as the Earth is to the Water, so the Water is to the Air, and the Air to the Fire. This is the root and foundation of all Bodies, Natures, Virtues, and Wonderful Occult Works. And he that shall persevere and study well the Mirror of Nature shall know these qualities of the Elements, and their Mixtures and shall easily bring from her Womb such things to pass as will strike the World with Wonder and astonishment.

Chap 2

A three fold consideration of the Elements

As there are four Elements, Fire, Earth, Water, and Air, without a perfect knowledge of each, no effect can be gained in the Occult Science. Now each of them are three-fold, that so the number of four, which is four times three makes the number twelve, and by passing by the number seven into the number of ten, there may be a progress to the supream Unity, upon which all virtue and wonderful opperations depends. Of the first order are the pure Elements, which are neither Compounded nor changed, nor admit of mixtion, but are incorruptible, and not of which, but through which, the virtues of all natural things are brought forth into action. No man is able to declare their virtues by reason that they can do and act all things upon all things, and He that is ignorant of these and their seperate qualities can never be able to bring to pass any wonderful matter. Of the second Order, are Elements that are compounded, changeable, and impure, yet such as may by art be reduced to their pure simplicity, whose virtue, when they are thus reduced, above all things doth perfect all Occult and common operations of Nature; and these secrets are the whole foundation of natural Magic. Of the third Order, are those Elements which originally, and of themselves are not Elements, but are twice compounded, various, and changeable they are one into the other. They, are the infallable Medium, and therefor are called the middle nature, or Soul of the same. In them is, by means of certain numbers, degrees, and orders, the perfection of every effect in what thing soever, whether Natural Celestial or super-celestial, they include innumerable wonders, and Mysteries, and are operative, in Natural Magic, so divine; For from these thr-=ough them, are performed the bindings, loosings, and transmutation of all things, and not only foreknowledge but driving forth of evil, and gaining good Spirits. Let no man therefore, without these three sorts of Elements, and the knowledge thereof, be confident that he is able to any work or thing in the Occult Sciences, but whosoever shall know how to reduce those of one Order, into that of another, impure into pure, compounded into simple, and understand distinctly the nature, virtue, and power of them in number, degrees, and order, —

without dividing the substance, shall easy attain the full knowledge, and perfect operation of all Natural things and the full beauties of Celestial secrets

Chap 3rd
The Wonderful Natures of Fire and Earth

Fire and Earth are two things, sufficient of themselves, for the operations of all wonderful things; the former being active and the latter passive. Fire is in all things, it passes through all things, it comes and goes away bright, it is in all things bright, and at the same time occult, and unknown, When it is by itself (no other matter coming to it, in which it should manifest its proper action) it is boundless and invisible, of itself, sufficient for every action that is proper to its moveable, yielding itself after a manner to all things that comes next to it, renewing, guarding nature, enlightening, not comprehended by lights that are vailed over, clear, parted, leaping back, bending upwards, quick in motion, high always raising motions, comprehending another, not comprehended itself, not standing in need of another, secretly increasing of itself, and manifesting its greatness to things, that receives it. it is Active, powerful, Invisibly, present in all things at once; it will not be affronted or opposed, but in revenge, it will reduce on a sudden things into obedience to itself, incomprehensible, impalpable, not lessoned, most rich in all its dispensations. Fire is the boundless, and mischievous part of the nature of all things, it being a question difficult to solve whether it absolutely destroys or produceth most things. Fire is of itself one, and penetrates through all things it spreads abroad in the Heavens shining but being straitened and confined it becomes tormenting. Fire therefore of itself is one, but in that which receives it manifold, and in different, obj=

objects it is distributed in a different manner. That Fire then, which we use is called Occult-philosophical fire, and is fetched out of other things, It is in stones, and is brought forth by the stroke of the steel. It is in the Earth. It is in Water. It is in the Air, and is plainly demonstrated that all Animals & living things whatsoever, as also vegetables are preserved by heat, And all things that lives, lives by reason of the Fire inclosed them. The property of Fire that is above (which I term Celestial Fire) are heat, making all things fruitfull, and light-giving life to all things. The properties of the infernal fire are a parching heat, consuming all things it comes near and making all things barren The Celestial & bright Fire drives away the spirits of Darkness, also our Fire made of woods, philosophically prepared, and under the Constellations, at certain Hours under the Planets governing such certain times drives away the same, in as much as such Woods constellations, Hours & Planets, have an Analogy therewith and is the vehiculum of that superiour light: as also of him who saith I am the Light of the World, which is the true Fire. from whom every good thing that is given, comes Sending forth the light of his fire, and communicating it first to the ☉, & the rest of the Celestial bodies, and by those as by mediating instruments conveying that light into our Fire. Now the Basis and foundation, of all the Elements is the Earth, for that is the object subject, and recepticle of all Celestial rayes, and influences, in it are contained the seeds and Seminal virtues of all things. and therefore it is said to be Animal Vegetable, and Mineral; It being made fruitfull by the assistance of the other Elements, and the Heavens. being forth all things of itself It receives the abundance of all things and is as it were the first fountain, from whence all things springs, it is the center, foundation, and mother of all things, Take as much of it as you please, seperate it, wash it depurate it Subtilize it, and if you let it lye in the Air a while it will be fully impregnated, being full, and abounding with Heavenly virtues, of itself will bring forth, Plants Worms and other living things, In it are great secrets. and if purified & reduced by Fire & Water It is the first matter of our Creation, and from it is gained a Rare Medicine to restore & preserve man

* hence it was the first institution of the ancients in burning Candles or torches in their religious ceremonies & after the discease of any person, till interred, which is observed to this Day

Chap 4
The Wonderful natures of Water, Air and Winds

Water, and Air are not less efficacatious than the former neither is nature wanting to work wonderful things in them There is so great a necessity for water and it is so essential, that without it no thing can exist. No herb nor Plant whatsoever, without water can branch forth In it are contained the Seminary virtue of all things, especially of animals whos seed is watery. The seeds also of Trees and Plants, although they are Earthy, must before they can be fruitful, be rotted in water, wether imbibed with the moister of the Earth or with dew or rain from Heaven, For the holy Writ tells us that not only Earth and Water bring forth living soul but ascribes a two fold production to the water, viz of things swimming in the waters, and of things flying in the Air, and that those productions in, and upon the Earth, are partly attributed to the Water and that Plants & Herbs did not grow, because God had not caused upon the Earth, Such is the efficiency of Water, The Ancient Magi therefore concluded that Water was the beginning of all things, and is the first and most potent of all the Elements, as being master over the rest; The necessity of it is no less than that of Fire, Infinite are the benefits and diverse are the uses thereof, as being that by virtue of which all things subsist are nourished and increased, Water swallow up the Earth, Extinguish flames, assends on high, and falling on the Earth all things are nourished, The Air is a vital spirit, passing through all Beings, binding, moving and filling all things, Hence it is that the Ancients reckoned it not amongst the Elements, but count it as a Medium or Glue, joyning things together, and as the resounding spirit of the Worlds instrument It immediately recives into itself the influences of all Celestial bodies, and then communicates them to the other Elements, as also to all mixed bodies Also it recives into itself, as it were a divine Looking Glass, the species of all things, as well natural as artificial, as also all manner of speeches, and Retains them; carrying them with it to any distance and entering into the bodies of Man and all animals through their pores making an impression upon them, and is the whole cause of dreams, From which the ancients are of an opinion, that a man passing by a place where any person has been murdered and the carkass newly hid, is moved with fear & dread, because in that place the Air becomes troubled, and being breathed in, move & troubles

8

the spirit of the man. with the like species, which cause fear, and what is still more wonderfull is that any Images artifically painted, or written Letters, in a clear Night. set against the beams of the full Moon, whose resemblance being multiplied in the Air, and caught upwards and reflected back together with the beams of the Moon, any other person who is privy to the thing at a long distance, sees reads, and knows them in the very compass and circle of the Moon, And as these resemblances are reflected back to the sight; so also, sometimes to the hearing, as is manifested in the Echo, There are more secret arts then these and such whereby any two persons may converse at a very great distance, and understand each other distinctly There are also from the Airy Element, Winds. which are but Air moved and stirred up Of those there are four that are principle, blowing from the four Corners of the Heavens. Viz. from the South or South wind is called Notus. from the North Boreas. from the West Zephyrus. from the East Eurus Notus is the South Wind, cloudy, moist warm, and sickly which is called the Butler of rains. Which Ovid beautifully describes. Boreaus is contrary to Notus. and is the Northern Wind, pierce and roaring, discussing Clouds, makes the Air severe, and binds the Water with Frost, Zephyrus, which is the Western Wind, is most soft, blowing from the west with plesent gale, it is cold, and Moist, removing the Effects of Winter, bringing forth branches from Trees and Flowers from the Earth, making every thing fruitful, To this Eurus is contrary which is the Eastern Wind, and is called Apeliotes, and is waterish. cloudy and ravenous of which Ovid Beautifully describes,

Chap 5

The various kinds of Compounds what relation they stand to the Elements & what relation there is between the Elements themselves, and the Souls, senses, and dispositions of Men

Next after the four simple Elements, follows the four kinds of perfect Bodies compounded of them by the Works of Nature and they are, Stones, Metals, Plants, and Animals, and although into the generation of each of those, all the Elements meet together in the composition, yet every one of them follows, and resembles one of the Elements, which is most predominant, For all Stones are earthly, they are naturally heavy and descend, and so hand with dryness, that they cannot be melted, But Metals are waterish, and may be melted and are generated of a viscous Water, or waterish argent vive, Plants have such an afinity with the Air, that unless they are abroad in the open Air or in an Airy place they will neither bud, shoot, nor increase, So also of all Animals; Have in their Natures a most fiery force And also spring from a Celestial Source, Fire is so natural to them, that that, being extinguished they presently die, and every one of those kinds are distinguished within itself by reason of the degrees of the Elements, For amongst Stones those which are Earthly, are dark and more heavy, Those which are waterish, are transparent, & are compacted of water congealed as Crystal, Beryll and Pearls in the shells of Oysters &c. Those which are called Airy swims on the water, and are spongious, as the sponge stone, pumice Stones &c Those which are Fiery out of which Fire can be extracted, or which can be resolved into fire, or which can be produced by fire, as Thunderbolts, Fire Stones, the Stone Asbestous &c

10

Amongst Metals, Lead and Silver are Earthy, Mercury is Water=ish, Copper, and Tin are Airy, Gold, and Iron are Fiery In Plants, the Roots resembles the Earth, by reason of their thickness, the Leaves the Water being juicy, the Flowers the Air because of their subtility, and seeds the Fire, because of their multiplying spirit, Besides they are called some hot some cold, some moist & some dry, borrowing their names from the qualities of the Elements. Amongst Animals also some are in comparison, Earthy as those that dwell in the Bowels of the Earth, as Worms, moles, and other small creeping things; others are Watery, as Fish, others Airy which cannot live out of the air, and others are Fiery, living in fire as Crickets &c (or breathing of fire or a fiery heat) as Pigeons, Sparows Wagtails &c Besides in animals the Bones resembles the Earth, flesh the Air, the vital spirit the fire, and the Humours the water, and these humours partake of the Elements, for yellow choller is of the fire, blood the Air, Flegm the Water, and Black choller is of the Earth (being Melanch--olly) and lastly in the Soul itself, the understanding represents the Fire, the Reason Air, imagination the Water and the Senses the Earth. And these senses are also divided amongst themselves by reason of the Elements, for the Sight is fiery as it cannot perceive without Fire and light, the Hearing is Airy, for the sound is produced by vibration, the Smell & Taste resembles the water, as wit-hout it the Moister there can be neither Smell nor taste, and lastly the feelings is wholy Earthy, and taketh gross bodies for its Objects. The actions also, and operations of man are governed by the Elements. The Earth, signifies a slow & firm Motion, the Water fearfulness and an amiable disposition, but Fire a fierce, quick, angry disposition. The Elements therefore are the first of all things and all are of, and according to them, they are in all things & diffuse their powers and Virtues through all things;

Chap 6
Of the Virtues of things Natural, depending immediately upon the Elements

Some Natural Virtues of things are Elementary, as to heat, to cool, to moisten, to dry, and they are called operations or first qualities, and the second act; for these qualities only do change the whole substance, which one of the other qualities can do and some are in things compounded of Elements; these are more then first qualities, and such are those that are, maturating, corroding, burning, opening, evaporating, strengthening, mitigating, conglutinating, obstructing, expeling, retaining, attracting, repercussing, stupefying, bestowing, lubrifying, and many more Elementary qualities do many things in a mixed body which they cannot do in the Elements themselves, and those operations are called secondary qualities, because they follow the nature of the Mixtion of the first virtues, as is largely treated of in the Dispensitores. Maturation is the operation of natural heat, according to a certain proportion in the substance of the Matter, — Induration is the operation of cold; so of congelation, and of the rest. Also Many things made by Art, which cause Men (not knowing them) to wonder at. As a fire used by the Greeks, and is called greek fire, it burnes in water. In like manner there is made a Fire that is extinguished with oil & kindled with Water, and a Fire which is kindled either by the Rain, Wind or the Sun, and there is made a fire which is called burning Water, which consumes nothing but itself; The Stone Asbestus and the flax called Asbestum which no fire will destroy, also by ant Wood or any other Combustible matter can be endered so that it can recive no harm by fire, A Com=position there can be made that by anointing the hands therewith May Carry Red hot Iron without danger, & many other Wonderful things may be done that will strike the mind with astonishment

Chap 7
Of the Occult Virtues of things, How Occult Virtues are infused into the several kinds of things by Ideas, through the help of the Soul of the World and rayes of the Stars; and what things abounds most with this Virtue,

There are also other virtues in things, which are not from any Element, as to expel poyson, to drive away the noxious vapours, of minerals, to attract Iron, or any thing else & these virtues are a sequal of the species, and form of this or that thing, whence also they being little in quantity, are of great efficancy; which is not to any Elementary quality For those virtues having much form, and little matter can do very much; but an Elementry virtue, because it hath more materiality, and requires much matter for its acting. And they are called occult qualities, because their Causes lie hid, and mans intellect cannot in any way reach or find out, For as in the Stomach the meat is degested by heat which we plainly know, so it is changed by a certain hidden virtue which we know not, for truly it is not changed by heat alone, if so it might as well have been changed by the fire side, then in the Stomach, Therefore it is plain that there are in things, besides the Elementary qualities which we know, other cert==ain imbred, created by nature, which we admire and are amazed at being such as we know not; and indeed seldom or ever seen, as Ovid mentions of the Bird called the Phoenix, The singing stones, The Ostrich concocting cold and most hard Iron, and digest it in its stomach, The Salamanders & crickets living in fire and seems to burn but are not hurt, All these things are the effects of Occult Virtue; Now all inferiour bodies are exemplified by the superior Ideas. An Idea is a form, above bodies, souls, minds, and is one, simple pure, immutable, indivisible, incorporeal, and eternal; and the nature of all Ideas is the same; Ideas in the first place is very goodness itself (i.e.) God by way of cause, and is the very Intelligible part itself (i.e.) in the Soul of the World — differing one from the other by absolute forms, so that all Ideas in God are but one form, but in the soul of the World, they are many, They are placed in the minds of all other things, whether they are joined to the body, or seperated from the Body, by a certain participation, and by degrees are distinguished more and more; The ancient Magi first place them in nature as certain small seeds of forms infused by the Ideas, secondly they place them in matter, as shadows, Hereunto may be sudden, that in the Soul of the World there may be so many Seminal forms, of things, as Ideas in the mind of God, by which forms she did in the Heavens above the Stars frame to herself shapes also, and stamped upon all these some properties; on these stars therefore shapes, and properties, all virtues of inferiour species as also their properties do depend; so that every species hath its Celestial shape or figure that is suitable to it, from which also proceeds a wonderful power of operation; which proper gift it receives from its own Idea, through the Seminal forms of the

Soul of the world (observe the dog star which appears in the month of July and the wonderful power it has over the Animals of its Name & various other things suitable to itself) For Ideas are not only essential causes of every species, but are also the causes of every virtue, which is in the species, and these are the properties which are in Nature; and indeed are only the opertions of the Ideas moved by certain virtues (viz) such as have a certain and sure foundation, not fortuitous nor casual, but efficacious, but powerful and sufficient, doing nothing in vain Now those virtues do not err in their actings but by reason of the impurity, or inequality of the Matter; for upon this account there are found things of the same species more or less powerful according to the purity, or indisposition of the matter; for all Celestial influences may be hindered by the indisposition and insufficiency of Matter, Which Virgil beautifully describes

"Their natures fiery are, and from above,

"And from gross bodies freed divinely move,

Wherefore those things, in which there is less of the Idea of the matter (i e) such things which have a greater resemblance of things seperated, have more powerful virtues in operation being like to the operation of a seperated Idea, We see then that the situation, and figure of Celestials are the cause of all those excelent Virtues, that are in all inferior species,

Chap 8

How it is that particular Virtues are infused into particular Individulas, even of the same Species and showing from whence Occult Virtues of things proceeds

There are in many Individuals, or particular things peculiar gifts, as wonderful as in the species, and these are from the figure, and situation of Celestial Stars, For every Individual, when it begins to be under a determined Horus-cope, and Celestial Constellation, Contracts together with its essence a certain wonderful virtue both of doing, and suffering something that is remarkable, even besides that which it receives from its species, this it doth partly by the influence of the Heavens, and partly through that obedience of matter of the things to be generated, to the Soul of the World, which obedience indeed (comparatively speaking) is such as that of our Bodies to our Souls, For we perceive that there is this in us, that according to our conceptions of things, our bodies are moved wether by chearfulness or by fear, what can effect the Body more, than what is termed lowness of Spirits; which is produced from the Intellectual part of the Mind; which without an alteration the Body would be totally destroyed, Ideas the first seminal form of the Soul, which the womb of the mind being impregnated therewith comes forward to conception, So many times when the Celestial souls conceive several things, then the matter is moved obediently to it, Also in Nature there ap= =pears divers prodigies, by reason of the imagin= =ation of superiour motions, So are conceived and imagined divers virtues, not only things natural, but things artificial, and this especially if the Soul of the operator be inclined towards the same, Whence the Ancient Magi observe that what= =soever things are done here must have been before in the motions, and conceptions of the Stars and orbs. So in things various effects, inclinations, and dispositions are occasioned not only from the matter variously disposed, as many may suppose, but from a various influences and divers form, not with a specifical difference, but peculiar & proper and the degrees of these are variously distributed by the first cause of all things God himself, who being unchangeable, distributes to every one as he pleases, with whom notwithstanding second Causes Angelical and Celestial co-operate disposing of the Coporeal matter & other things that are committed to them All virtues therefore are infused by God through the Saul of the World, yet by a perticular power of resemblance, and intelligences over-ruling them, and concourse of the rayes & aspects of the Stars, sought out in a peculiar harmonious consent wonderful things are brought to bear; It is well known to all that there is a Certian virtue in the Load Stone, by which it attracts Iron, and that a Diamond when in its presence taketh away that Virtue, The great power, and human destinies are couched in the virtues of Stones and Herbs, But to know from whence these come a higher speculation is required, The Ancients attribute these virtues to Ideas, the formes of things, and reduce=th these kind of operations to Intelligences, to the Stars, and to the specifical forms of things, For God in the first place is the end and beginning of all Virtues, he gives the seel of the Ideas to his servants the Intellegences who as faithful officers sign all thin=gs intrusted to them with an Ideal virtues the Heav=ens and Stars, as instruments, disposing the matter in the mean while for the receiving of these forms which reside in Divine Majesty, and to be conveyed by the Stars, and the giver of forms distributes them by the Ministry

of his Intelligences, which he hath set as Rulers and Controulers over his works, to whom such a power is intrusted in things committed to them, so that all Virtues of Stones Herbs Metals, and all other things may come from the Intelligences, the Governour The form therefore, and virtue of things comes first from the Idea's thenfrom the ruling and governing Intelligencies theenfrom the Aspects of the Heavens disposing, and lastly from the tempers of Elements disposed, answering the influencies of the Heavens, by which the Elements, themselves are ordered or disposed. Such dispositions, times, seasons, places,, Aspects &c The skilful Astrologer may soon know, These kinds of operations therefore are performed in these inferiour things by express forms and in the Heavens by disposing virtues, in the Intelligencies by mediating rules, in the original Cause by Ideas and examplary forms all which must of necessity agree in the execution of the effect, and virtue of every thing; There is therefore a wonderful virtue, and operation in every Herb and Stone, but much greater in a Star, beyond which, even from the Intelligencies every thing receiveth and obtaineth many things for itself especially from the Supreme, with whom all things do mutually and exactly correspond, agreeing in an harmonious consent, as it were in praising the Most High, as maker of all things –
There is therefore no other cause of the necessity of effects, then the connection of all things with the first cause, and their correspondency with those Divine patterns and eternal Idea's whence every thing hath its determinate, and particular place in the exemplary world, from whence it lives, and recives

its original being; and every virtue of Herbs, Stones, Metals, Words, Speeches, and all things that are of God is placed there

Chap 9
Of the Spirit of the World, what it is, and how by way of Medium it unites occult Virtues to their Subjects

Democritus, Orpheus, and other Philosophers having most diligently searched into the virtues of Celestial things and natures of inferiour things, Observes That all things are full of God, and not without a cause, For there is nothing of such transcending virtues which being destitute of Divine assistance, is content with the nature of itself. Therefore they called those divine powers which are diffused in things, Gods; Zoroaster, Divine allurements, others Symbolical enticements, Lives and Souls, saying that the virtues of things depends on these, because it is the property of the Soul to be from one matter to another and is extended into divers things, about which it operates, So is a man who extends his intellect into intelligible things, and his imagination into imaginable things, and this is that, which they understood when they said, That the Soul of one thing went out, and entered into that of another, altering and hindering the operations of it; as the presence of a Diamond will hinder the operations of the Load stone. Now seeing the Soul is the first thing that is moveable, and is moved of itself, but the body or matter is of itself unable, and unfit for motion, and doth much degenerate from the Soul, therefore there is need of a more excellent Medium, (viz) Such a one as it were no Soul, but a Body, (viz) by which the Soul may be joined to the Body, Now such Medium, as is here expressed is that which is called the Spirit of the World, that which is called by Philosophers the quintessence because it is not of the four Elements but a certain first thing, having its being above, and besides them There is therefore such a kind of spirit required to be, as it were a Medium, whereby Celestial Souls are joined to gross bodies, and bestow upon them wonderful gifts This Spirit is after the same manner in the body of the World as is in the body of Man, For as the powers of our Souls are communicated to the members of our body by the Spirit, so also the vertue of the Soul of the World is diffused through all things by the quintessence For there is not any thing found in the whole World, that hath not a spark of the virtue thereof, Yet it is more, and most of all infused into those things which have received, or taken in most of this spirit Now this spirit is received, or taken in by the rays of the Stars, such things as have an affinity and can be rendered conformable to them By this spirit every Occult property is conveyed by Art into Herbs, Stones, Metals, and Animals, throught the ☉. ☽. planets and fixed Stars which are higher then the planets. It is necessary that the Heavens and Celestial bodies; seeing they have a power, influence, and manifest operation upon these inferiours, should be animated, seeing an operation cannot proceed from a meer body, All famous Poets and Philosophers affirm that the World and all Celestial bodies must have a Soul, and that also an intelligent, as Virgil describes

And first the Heavens, Earth, and liquid plain

The Moons bright Globe, and Stars Titanian

> A Spirit fed within, spread through the whole
> And with the Huge heap mix'd infused a soul
> Hence Man, and Beasts, and Birds, derive their strain
> And monsters floating in the marbled main
> These seeds, have fiery vigour and a birth
> Of heavenly race, but clog'd with heavy Earth

The World, the Heavens, the Stars, and the Elements, have a soul, with which they cause a soul in these inferiour and mixed bodies. And as is observed in the former chapters, that a spirit, which by the mediating of the soul is united to the body; For as the World is a certain whole body, the parts whereof are the Bodies of all living creatures, and by how much the whole is more perfect, & noble then the parts, by so much more perfect, and noble is the body of the world, then the bodies of each living things, It would be absurd, that all imperfect bodies & parts of the World, and every base Animals, as Flies and Worms should have a life and Soul, and the whole and most noble body, should have neither life, nor Soul, It is not less absurd, that the Heavens, Stars, Elements, — which gives life to all things, and soul most largely, should themselves be without life and soul, and that every plant, or tree should be of a more noble condition then the Heavens, Stars, and Elements, which are naturally the cause of them What Man can deny that the Earth and Water, live, which even of themselves, generates, vivifies, nourishes, and encreases innumerable trees, plants, and living Creatures, as most manifestly appears in things that breeds of their own accord and those which have nor cannot have any corporeal Seed Neither could Elements generate and nourish such kinds of living creatures, if they themselves were without life or Soul, But some men will say, that such kinds of living creatures are not generated by the Soul of the Earth, or water, but by the influences of Celestial Souls, These I should answer as follows, that an Accident cannot beget a substance, unless as an instrument it be subjected to the next substance. For as an instrument in the hand of an Artificer, if not moved by his will or mind, how is it possible that any effect of the Art can be perfected; so those Celestial influences, seeing they are certain accid=ents being removed far from vital substances, or from the life itself, cannot generate a vital substance in those inferiour, Which clearly proves that all thats in the World is moved either by encrease, or decrease Now all things that moves, must needs have life; and seeing that all things move, even the Earth, especially with a gener-ative motion, consequently they must of themselves live; and he that doubt that heavens live and are animated, so that the mover thereof is not the form thereof, destroy's and denies every principle of Philosophy; The World therefore lives hath a soul, and sense; for it gives life to plants, which are not produced of seed; and it gives sense to Animals, which are not generated by coition, —

Chap 10

Of the Compositions and Harmony of the Human Soul, and of the necessary Observations of all Magical and Talismanical experiments

As the Consonance of the Body consists of a due mea=sure and proportion of the members; so the Conson=ance of the mind of a due temporament, and propor-tion of its virtues and operations which are concupis=cible, irascible, and reasonable, which are so prop-ortioned together, For Reason to concupiscence hath to themselves the proportion Diapason; but to Anger

Diatessaron: and Irascible to Concupiscible hath the proportion Diapente, When therefor the best proportionated Soul, is joined to the best proportionated body it is manifest that such a Man hath recived a most happy lot in the destribution of heavenly gifts and is able to work wonders, For as the Soul agrees with the body in the disposition of Naturals, which agreement is most hid, yet after some manner shadowed by the wise, But the Harmony of the soul must be inquired into by those Mediums by which it passeth to us, (i.e.) by Celestial Bodies and Spheres; knowing what are the powers of the Soul to which the Planets answer by studying well those things the more easy it is to know their agreements amongst themselves, For the ☽ governs the Powers of increasing and decreasing, as she increase and decrease in light and form, so the Phantasy imagination and Wits depends on ☿, the Concupiscible virtues on ♀, the vital on the ☉, the Irascible on ♂ the Natural on Jupiter; and the Receptive on ♄, and the eccentric to ♅, But the Will is the grand Primum Mobile and guide of all these powers at Pleasure, for being joined with the superior intellect always tends to good which intellect ever shew the pathway to the Will, as a lighted Candle to the Eye, and never moves of itself but is the Mistress of her own operation Whence it is called Free Will; and though it tends to good as an object of itself which I term Sympathy yet sometimes being blinded by prejudice and error the Animal power forcing it, it then chooseth evil, believing it to be good which I term Antipathy, Therfore what is commonly called the Will is defined to be the faculty of the Intellect and Will, whereby the good is chosen by the help of Grace, and Evil for want of that assisting grace, as such what is called <u>Charity</u>, or infused <u>Love</u> is in the Will, which is the <u>Idea</u>, seminal virtue, or first seed, and is the first mover; which being absent the whole consent falls into Disponancy, Therefore as it is observed by the Ancients, that the Soul answers to the <u>Earth</u> by sense, to the <u>Water</u> by Imagination, to the <u>Air</u> by Reason, to Heaven by the Intellect, and thus the soul goes out into the Harmony of them according as they are tempered in the mortal body, The Stars having an influence, and cause motion on all things here below, from whom Motion took its beginning, the same hath no doubt given to all other the power of Self Motion; as such the Motion of the heavens was the first in Nature, and whatever moves must inevitably move by the Motion of the Heavens for if that once cease both Growth and Motion would also cease in all things here below for Example the heart of Man, which is the beginning of Life, and motion to all the rest of the Members, which if once wounded not only cease in motion but all parts to of the body, and even life itself; Therefore the Spirit of the World lies hid in the four Elements as the Soul is hid in the Body, and is nothing else but an Effluence and working power proceeding from the <u>Sun</u> <u>Moon</u> and <u>Stars</u> its dwelling from whence it worketh is Spiritualy encompassed with the four Elements, therefore to know how to infuse into various compositions the propitions Influx of the Stars to obtain their full force and powers must Study well their times seasons and motions, For <u>Heaven</u>

24

Earth, and every thing lies hid in Man (which is the microcosm or little World) this is clear if we consider the materials of which we are composed of, First our Body which is of the Earth dead inert and heavy and has no feeling, Secondly but Life which is light, quickeneth moveth and giveth sense into it and the Heavens are the sole spring of this light Thirdly the Soul is the Spirit of God being the freewill or understanding, in this is power, and from which three considerations we find the Reason of this Ioining or connection found in the living Man whereby he recives into himself such great Power, therefore he deliberate, reason and determine what is to be done, Observing that his cogitations proceeds from a Divine & Celestial Essence by this means he is of assisting the Essence to bring to perfection all his Desires; Every natural Virtue work things for more wonderfull when it is not only componded Of a natural proportion but also formed by a regular observation of the Celestials (viz) when the Celestial power is most strong for the effect which we most desire for the effect, whether good or evil which is put into full force by their situations & aspects) by subjecting the inferiours to the Celestial Rays as proper females to be made fruitfull by their Males, Therefore in every Magical Work there must be observed the Situation & aspects of the Stars & Planets in their Signs, Degrees and how they in reference to the length that is longitude & Latitude of the Place that such work is to be performed in by which means the Celestial Rays will be powerfull impregnated in the thing you wish to make and to make it most patent & powerfull take care to place the Star or Planet (if for a good purpose) in its dignities, fortunate as you'l see by the table of Essential Dignities Page 120, also in the Planetary Hour ruling in the Day and the Day governed by the Planet. and in the figure of the Heaven, and as nothing can be brought to great perfection without the ☽, she must be considered whether she is friendly or not to the object of thy wishes or you will fail in thy attempt. and ☿ he being the Messenger between the higher and the infernal Gods to good he increaseth good, to evil he increaseth evil — when to the bad he hath influence upon their Malevolence It is called unfortunate when it is in ☐ or ☍ of ♂ or ♄. for these planets are Malevalent and these aspects are aspects of Enmity, but the ☌, △ or ⚹ are aspects of friendship, and if a Planet is thus received it is then accounted already Conjoyned. Observe that all the Planets are afraid of a ☌ of the ☉ but rejoiceth in the △ or ⚹ aspects, and all Planets when ruling in a House in Exaltation or Triplicity in Term or face without Combustion are most powerfull — a Planet in his own House or Exaltation is as a Man in his own Castle or Strong Hold If in ☌ with a fortune, Is as a Man in the embraces of his sincere friend but if with an unfortune is as a Man fighting with his Enemy. If in a ⚹ △ or term is as a Man having friends in the act of Coming to relive him. therefore beware that if your work is for to obtain some good purpose that the Planet you have to aid are not in the least under the rays of ♄ or ♂. and the ☽ is not in the least deprest but see that she is either in her house Exaltation. Triplicity or face and in a

26

Degree convent for thy work, on that She is in one of her twenty eight Mansions as pr Table Page 86. Book 1st. Let her not be slow in course. i.e. decreasing or past the full, let her not be Eclipsed or burned up by the ☉, unless She be in unity with him, let her not be desending in the Southern Latitude nor yet let her be hindred by ♂ or ♄ These Rules correctly observe for all Good purposes But for Evil every oppasition must be observed with the same degree of Accuracy,

Chap 11

The Divine Gifts Recived by Man from Above through the several Orders of the Intelligences of the Heavens above by the power of Mans Soul in the
Mind, reason and Imagination

All powers are diffused into Man from the great and supream fountain of good by the divine Assistance of the Planets. The Planet ♄ gives to man the most extr= =aordinary magnanimity and loftiness of Mind mixed with an uncontrollable & intense desire for pursuits, romantic searchers in the more secret sciences, ♄ an Sublime contemplation and profound understanding, a solidity of Judgement, firm speculation stability and an immovable resolution. ♃ an unshaken prud- -ence, temperance, benignity, piety, modesty, Justice, Faith, Grace, religion, Equity, Clemency and Royalty. ♂, an undaunted Courage, truth and Fortitude, a fervent desire of Animosity, the power of acting and the pra- -ctice and an inconvertible vehemency of the mind not to be terrified, from when comes this Adage. How fiery that man is, Because ♂ is a hot Planet and belongs to the fiery trigon. The ☉ gives a Nobility of mind, perspicuity of imagination, knowledge & opinion, maturity, Counsel, Zealous affection for the love of Justice, Reason and Judgement in distinguishing right from wrong, purging light from the darkness of ignorance, glorying in finding out truth from falshood and a great advocate for Charity, ♀. gives a fervent Love and affection, a sweet hope, the motion of desire, order, Concupiscence, Beauty, sweetness, and a desire of propogation of her own species, ☿ gives a firm faith and belief, clear reasoning, the rigour of interpretation & pronounciation, and a gravity of speech, acuteness of Wit, discourse of reason and swift motion of the senses, a great desire of Studying all Scientific and litery persuits; The ☽ gives to Man a consonancy in making peace between his fellow Creatures, fecundity, the power of generating and growing greater, of encreasing and decreasing, and a moderate temperance A strong faith in occult things, yielding a devotion to all (ie, a Man born under the ☽ shall easier obtain the knowledge of such things) She also gives the Art of Agriculture, But these Influences are principally drawn from the Seven Intelligences who stands before the face of God and who dispose of the Soul as the seat of these virtues therefor the Planets dispose the Body of Man for the fit reception of every good thing by giving it Complexion, Proportion and perfection to recive those heavenly intelligences into it by which means we become the instruments, of the Intelligencies, But God is the primary cause of all, and those Learned Philosophers who have sought out the virtues and different dispositions of the Soul do Judge that the divine nature are obtained by Man, by the reason of the diverse dispositions

28

of the Soul and that they are not Joined to the Bodies unless they are first proportioned by the Stars. i.e. that their opinion is that a body brought into the temperament of ♃. must have a Soul infused and tempered by him also, The same by the rest, and they further say that from the Angellical Orders Man is Strengthened with wonderfull virtues, viz from the Angels he may be made the Messenger and interpreter of the divine will of the Supreme, God gave to Man power to rule over all the Beasts of the field the fish in the Sea and the fowls of the Air, he also gave to Man a power to bruise the Serpents head, I conceive that all things may be subdued by Man he comprehending the powers of all, by so doing he draws to himself all powers by a certain force both secret and supercelestial, which enables him to subject every thing to his will Therefore all those must labour in vain who trusting only on the course of Nature and the power of inferiour things (as our Modern Philosophers who from their experiments think they can obtain every thing and treat with contempt every thing that is beyond their reach) and those who think by such things only to receive the favours from the heavens will find their Mistake, as such things can only be received from God alone, What I mean by inferiour things are Animals, Herbs, Stones, Metals &c. they certainly are subservient to the heavens. and the heavens from the Intelligencies but these are to God himself in whom all things exist in the greatest power being the greater World called the Macracosm, as in Man which is the Microcosm or lesser World in which there is not a member but what hath a correspondence with some Element, Planet & Intelligence and with some Measure and number of the Archetype, Mans Soul therefor consisteth of a Mind, Reason, and Imagination, the mind illuminates reason, reason floweth into the Imagination, and all is but one Soul, Reason unless it is illuminated by the mind is not nor can be free from error but the mind gives no light to reason unlightened from above, viz, from the first light – which is from God which light far exceeds all human understanding wherefore it cannot be called an intelligable light but when it is by divine power infused into the Mind of Man it becomes intellect--ual and can be then understood and when it is infused into reason by the power of the Mind it then becomes rational and can be both understood and considered and it is infused into the Soul it is then made both cogitable & imaginable, but yet it is not corporeal, but when it goes from hence into the celestial vehicle of the Soul, it is then made corporeal but not manifestly sensible or susceptible of the heavenly influences till it hath passed into the elemental body either simple or Ariel or compoun--ded in which the light is made visible to the Eye This progress of Light The Chaldeans and other great Philosophers declares to have a wonderfull power on the Mind which gives great strength to the imagination, and enable Man to performe such wonders by art, as exceeds belief Thus is our Soul illuminated and thus does the Body receive the Soul, and when death overtakes us the Body returnes to earth from it was compounded and the Spirit returns again to God who gave it;

What came from earth, to earth returnes again
What comes from God, returnes from whence it came

Chap 12

Of the Sun and Moon, and the Considerations of their most Potent & wonderfull Powers in Magic

The ☉ and ☽ those two great and wonderfull Powers who have the Administration or ruling of the Heavens, and all Bodies under the heavens. The ☉ is the Lord of all Elementary Virtue, and the ☽ by virtue of the ☉ is the Mistress of all Generation increase & decrease. The ☉ and the ☽ infuses life into all things and are by Orpheus called the enlivening Eyes of Heaven. The ☉ giveth light to all things of itself and gives it plentifully to all things not only in the Heavens & Air but on the Earth and in the Deep, whatsoever good we have it from the ☉ alone or from it through other things. Heraclitus calls it the fountain of Celestial Life. The Platonists placed the Soul of the World in the ☉, as it fills the whole Globe and sends forth its rays on all sides, as it were a Spirit defusing its power through all things, distributing life sense and motion through the whole Universe. It is also called the Heart of Heaven, and on that Account the Caldeans placed it in the center of the Planets. The Egyptians also placed it in the center or middle of the World; between (what they term) the two fires of the World. i.e. above the ☉ they placed five Planets, and under it the ☽ and four Elements: as it is amongst the other Stars, the Image, and Statue of the great Prince of both Worlds, viz. Terrestial & Celestial, the true Light, and the exact Image of God himself, whose Essence resembles the Father, Light the Son, and Heat the

Holy Ghost; So great is the Consonancy of it to God that Plato calls it the Conspicuous Son of God, another Philosopher calls it the Divine Image of the Divine Intelligence another, the perspicuous Statue of God. It sets as King in the middle of all other Planets excelling all in Light, greatness and Fairness, enlightening all, distributing virtue to them to dispose of to inferior bodies, regulating & disposing of their Motions so that from thence they are called, daily & Nightly, Southern & Northern, Oriental & Occidental, direct & Retrograde, and as it doth by its Light drive away all darkness of Night, so all the powers of darkness must yield to its superior power, The ☉ therefore as it possesses the Middle region of the World, and as the Heart is in animals to the Body, So is the ☉ over the Heavens, & the World ruling over the whole Universe and those things which are in it, He is the author of the seasons from whence days & years, cold & heat and all other qualities, and as Ptolemy observes that when the ☉ comes to the Body of any Star, It stirs up its power, which it naturally possesses in the Air, If to the Body of ♂ (he being a hot Malevolent Star) he cause heat, with ♄ (he being a cold Star) Cold, and by these powers he disposeth the Spirit & Mind of Man, from hence it is said by Homer & approved by Aristotle, that there are in the mind of Man such like Motions, as the ☉ the moderator of the Planets every day brings to us."

But the ☽, she is the nearest to our Earth, she is the receptacle of all the Heavenly influences, and by the swiftness of her Course through the twelve signs of the Zodiac, is Joyned with the ☉ the other Planets, and Stars, every month, receiving their beams & influences and as a conception brings them forth to the inferior World being next to itself For all the Stars have influence on it being the last reciver; which afterwords communicate the influences of all the Superiors to the inferiors, and pours them forth on the Earth. Therefore her motion must be observed before the others as she is the Parent of all conceptions, which it diversely issueth forth in these Inferiors according to the diverse complexions, situations & different aspects to the planets and other Stars, and though it receiveth powers from all the Stars yet especially from the ☉, as often as she is in ☌ with the same, she is replenished with vivifying virtue, and according to the Aspects, she borrows her complexion; For in the first Quarter, she is hot & Moist; In the second Quarter, she is hot & dry; In the third Quarter She is Cold & dry, and in the fourth Quarter she is Cold & Moist — Her Age being divided into twenty eight days — that divided in four Sevens which is the four Quarters — thus she increace till her fourteenth day & decrease the other fourteen days, gaining her strength the first the first 14 days, & loosing her strength the last 14 days, and although she is the lowest of all Planets yet she brings forth all conceptions of the superiors. That series of all things which Plato calls the Golden Chain — begins from the heavenly Bodies only by which every thing and Cause being linked together do depend on the Superior even untill it may be brought to the supreme cause of all from which all things depends Therefore this Observe that without the ☽ intermediating the power of the Superiors cannot be attracted as such her situation wether fortunate or unfortunate (her good or evil aspect)

Her Herbs, Stones, plants, Birds, fish Trees &c must be, properly selected for the purpose, whether for good or evil must be carefully attended to To bring to perfection what is intended;

Chap 13th

Of the Twenty Eight Mansions of the Moon, and their Virtues, The true motion of the heavenly Bodies to be observed in the eight Sphere, Planetary hours &c Now seeing the ☽ measureth the whole Zodiacal Circle in the space of twenty eight days, which contains twelve Signs which are divided into four triplisities each having a peculiar property to itself — as first Earth, second Air, third Water & fourth Fire, these discovers Spring Summer Autumn & Winter The ☽ passing through these properties must receive in passing the various properties For instance the tides are governed by her when she appears in the heavens surrounded by a burr, (as is commonly called) we, Judge that Rain will follow; if she is clear & Bright we then Judge of a fine day succeeding, when she is at the full we Judge of its effects on a Person bereft of their senses, termed a Lunatic because his Melady is governed by the ☽, and innumerable other wonderfull properties have been discover'd, and are well ascertained In the Animal vegetable & Mineral kingdoms; Hence it is that the learned Men of the Ancient Astrologians, have granted to the ☽ the Twenty eight Mansions, and being in the Eight Sphere from her wandering through the Signs meeting and passing the Stars & Planets, Judging of the properties she must receive from those diverse Signs & Stars which are contained in them having given those Mansions such names as is suitable to their Powers and Virtues Calculating at the same time what each

34

Mansion containes, allowing for each twelve degrees, fifty one minutes & near twenty six seconds, whose names are as follows The first is called Alnath, meaning the Hornes of ♈ he being at the first degree of that Sign, and finishes at 12 degrees 51 minutes & 26 seconds the nature & properties the Table Page 86 Book 1st, will show Therefore what is wanted to be done either by Images Seal Ring or any other thing must be begun at the exact time & if not finished must be left of when the time is expired, and began again when the ☽ comes to the same degrees again — or you must look down the Table for her in any other Sign which answers the same work, then take that time & so alternately in all other signs, till your work is finished. The Second Mansion is called Allothaim or Albochan that is the Belly of ♈, he begins at 12 degrees 15 minutes & 26 seconds and finishes his term at twenty five degrees 42 minuits 52 seconds, Third Mansion is called Alchaomazon or Athoray that is Showring down. The fourth is called Aldebaram or Aldelamen, that is the Eye or head of ♉. The fifth is called Alchatay or Albachay. The sixth is called Albanna or Alchaya, that is the little Star of great light: his beginning is after the 4 degree of ♊. 17 minutes & 10 seconds The seventh is called Adimiach or Alarzach that is the Arm of ♊. 17 degrees, 3 minutes & 36 seconds The eighth mansion is called Alnaza or Anatrachya that is misty or Cloudy. The ninth is called Archaam or Arcaph, that is the eye of the Lion. The Tenth is called Algelioche or Albgebh, that is the neck or forehead of Leo. The eleventh is called Azobra or Ardaf, that is the hair of the Lions head. The twelveth is Called Alzarpha. or Azarpha. that is the tail of Leo. The thirteenth is named Albaire. that is the Dogstars or the wings of ♍. The fourteenth is called Achureth or Arimet & by some

Azimeth, or, Alhumech, or Alcheymech, that is the spike of ♍. The 15th Mansion, name is Agrapha, or Algarpha, that is covered or conveyed flying. The 16th is Called Azubene, or Ahubene, that is the Horns of Scorpio. The 17th is called Alchil that is the Crown of ♏. The 18th is Called, Alchas or Altrob that is the Heart of ♏. The 19th is called, Allatha, or Achala, by some Hycula or Axala that is the tail of ♏. The 20th is called Abnahaya, that is a beam. The 21st is Abada or Albeldach, which is a desert. The Last Quarter begineth with The 22nd Mansion from the head of ♑ and is called Sadahacha or Zodeboluch or Zandolaena - that is a pastour. The 23rd is called Zabadola, or Zobr- -ach, that is swallowing. The 24th is called, Sadabath or Chadezoad that is the Star of fortune. The 25th is called Sadalabra or Sadalachia, that is the Butter- fly or a spreading forth. The 26th is called Alpharg, or Phragal Mocaden, that is the first drawing. The 27th is called Alcharya, or Alhalgalmoad, that is the Second drawing. The 28th and last Mansion is Called Albot- -ham or Alchaloy, that is, ♓. The ☽ having now pas- -sed through her twenty eight Mansions, wherein lies hid a great many Secrets, the wisdom of the Ancients; by which, when properly understood wonders may be wrought under her circuit through all the Signs of the Zodiac; attributing to every Mansion his resemblances, Images, Seals & his President intelligences, Whenever you wish to work according to the Celestial opportunity, observe the notions of the Stars, & their times, when they are in their dignities or dejections Apetial or Occidental their days & hours distributed to them in their dominions, or the Celestial Images, Rings, Seals, &c will not have the desired effect; So great is the extent, power and efficiency of the Celestial Bodies that not only natural things but also artificial things when they are accurately exposed to those above very soon feel the effects & suffer by that most potent agent, and obtains that Wonderfull life which gives them an admirable Celestial Virtue. That famous Doctor St Thomas Aquinas, in his Book de-fato declares, that even garments Buildings & all other artificial things receive certain qualifications from the Stars The Magicians in all ages affirm that not only by the mixture & application of natural things but also Images, Seals, Rings, Glasses, &c being accurately composed, & framed under any certain Constellation, a Celestial Illustration may be taken & wonderful things be performed; for the beams of the celestial bodies being animated, living, sensual, brings along with them admirable gifts and a most potent power, do even in a moment, imprint wonderfull powers in Images &c (though their matter be less capable) But if that Image &c is composed by art and every before mentioned observation be regarded by keeping to every matter naturally congruous to the operation & Celestial Influence, Its figure being Comparative to the Heavenly One & regularly framed. It instently receives into itself the Heavenly gift desired by the Operator then as a Magnet to Steel by communicating or impregnating it with its own property, so will this Image Ring, Seal &c. on any other Matter desired act, So wonderfully powerfull are the Celesticals that all inferiors must obey them & not only them but their Images, For instance, when the ☉ is in ♍ the earthly Scorpion are effected by it, as the Dogs are effected by the appearance of the dog star. So that an

Image of a Scorpion Made under the Ascent of the heavenly sign ♏, and his Dominion, not only the Earthly Scorpions obey their Celestial – but the Image either by attracting or tormenting them doth destroy them, & so it is with all things in the Heavens, On the Earth below, in the Waters, & in the Waters under the Earth, By the permission of the Great Almighty Power, Man all things is in the Compass of thy power

Chap 14

The Composition of fumes appropriated to each Planet to be used as occasion may require, as is Recommended by the Ancient Magi, for perfecting work in the Talismanic Art

For the ☉. Take of Saffron, Amber-grease, Musk, Lignum Aloes, Lignum Balsam, Laurel Berries, Cloves, Myrrh & frankensense, any given quantity & bruise them well in a morter, then put in the Brain of an Eagle or any Bird which represents it, & with the Blood of a white Cock, make it up into Pills of half a dram each then place them in a situation so that they may gradually dry without loosing their perfume & when dry put them in a stopered bottle, for use

For the ☽. Take the Head of a frog dried, the Eyes of a Bull, the seed of white poppy, Frankincense and Champhor, Menstrous Blood, or the Blood of a Goose and make it up as before

For ♄. Take the seed of Black Henbane, the root of a Mandrake, the powder of Load Stone, Myrrh, small quantity of Black Lead, the Blood of a black Cat and a Bat, & make them up as before

For ♃. Take the Seed of Ash, Lignum Aloes, Storax, Gum Benzoan, the dust of Lazule Stone, the tops

38

of the feathers of a Peacock, incorporate them together with the Blood of a Stork or some Bird of magnatude under ♃. a Swallow & the Brains of a Hart mix and make up as before

For ♂. Take Euphorbium, Bdellium, Gum Ammon-iac, the roots of both Hellebors, the dust of Load Stone, a small quantity of Sulpher, fine Steel filings, the Brain of a Hart, Human Blood & the blood of a Black Cat incorporate and make them up as before

For ♀. Take Musk, Amber grease, Lignum Aloes, Red Roses, Red Corral powder & make it up as before with the Brains of Sparrows, wagtails & Pidgeons,

For ☿. Take Mastic, Frankincense, Cloves, and the Herb Cinque-foil and the powder of the Stone Achates, incorporate them with the Brain of a Fox-Weesel and the Blood of a Pie

☞ Great care must be taken that when these compositions are made up it must be at a time when the Planets are fortunate, & at the day and hour, for good purpose (See the Table Page 131 Book 1st) also — whatever compositions you make let them be of the finest & most Beautiful, and if for the opposite purpose, pick for your Com-positions the Contrary & make them in their Planets night and hour, The Ancient Magi were very particular in Selecting their ingredients — for the various experiments in this Science, For all matters agreeable & fit for the benefit of Mankind as good will concord, affection, Love &c, they selected all Odoriferous & precious perfumes, and in all opposite matters as Hatred, Anger, Misery, hinderances, Bindings &c, they selec-ted all venomous, poisonous ugly, nauseous vile & stinking things, and made them up as before

when the Planets were unfortunate & kept them apart in a secret dry Place for use, The great Philosopher Hermes, recomends a perfume the most powerfull of all for every good purpose which is compounded of the seven Aromatics, i.e, Peperwort, Nutmegs, Lignum Aloes, Mastic, Saffron, Cinnamons and Myrtle, which are according to the powers of the seven Planets as, ♄, ♃, ♂, ☉, ♀, ☿, ☽, They also alotted to the 12 Signs of the Zodiac their proper perfumes as to ♈ Myrrh, ♉ Pepperwort, ♊ Mastic, ♋ Camph-hor, ♌ Frankincense to ♍ Red Sanders to ♎ Galbanum, ♏ Opponax, ♐ Lignum Aloes, to ♑ Gum Benzoin, ♒ Euphorbium & to ♓ Red Storax, these Perfumes made use of when the Sign was assending, with the observations of being aspec--ted either Good or Evil, these Perfumes are to be burnt in the Thuribalum. Page 47 Book 1st. and the wood or material for the Fire must be the fuel from some Shrub &c belonging to the Planet or Sign that you would wish the effect from
I have been as explisit as possible to my reader but if he should wish for more, I shall refere him to, Ramseys Astrology, and in that valuble work he will see not only classically arranged every thing belonging to the Signs Planets &c But rules for Elections for all manner of Work To which Talismans, made Conformidable will work every effect there noticed

A Prayer to be used on the Begining of the or
    Making any Talisman
O Wise, pure and Just God of divine Clemency, I most humbly beseech most holy and most

40

merciful Father that this day I may by thy will perfect understand and accomplish this my Work and Labour, In making this Talisman of —— and Grant O Lord in it the Arm of thy Power to defend me, from and punish — — — my persecuting Enemy with (naming the punishment wished for) Therefore in thy Name thou Great Jehovah, and in the Name of thy only Son our Saviour Jesus Christ at whose name all wicked Sinners are made to tremble and all powers obey, and in the —— (mansion of the ☽ ♆c) Called —— in which I make it under and by the Sign —— the Planet —— and his Angels of the day hour and the Air —— —— and —— thee Powerfull Angels and by the Spirit of (chastisement) —— his Character, and all the other of the (☽) at whose presence all powers Nod, to assist in the above (punishment) of my (persecution) —— —— and to continue the same till he comes to a Due sense and acknowledge his error. And thou O God grant me thy power to remove and assuage the Affliction and always grant me the Arm of thy Power over him, All this I thy unworthy Servant most humbly beg In the Name of our Lord and Saviour Jesus Christ who Livest and Reignest for ever world without end, Amen ——

Note. This is the form of the Prayer but it must be varied according to the Planet Characters & effect desired or Object to be acted on

The Consecration and Benediction

First of a Circle when perfected according to Art Sprinkle with Holy Water and Say, Thou shalt purge me with hysop, O Lord and I shall be clean.

Thou shall wash me and I shall be whiter than Snow

The Benediction of Perfume

The God of Abraham, God of Isac, God of Jacob Bless here the Creatures of these kinds, that they may fill up the power & virtue of this odours; so that neither the Enemy nor any false Imaginations, may be able to enter into them to mislead or delude thy Servant, but render them powerfull & effectual to my purpose (name what you wish to have performd) Through our Blessed Lord and Saviour Jesus Christ the only Beloved & begotten Son of God;

The Exorcise of Fire

~ Upon which the Perfumes are to be put on ~

I Exorcise thee!! O thou Creature of fire by him, by whom all things were made in the Heavens Earth and Waters, that forthwith thou cast away every phantasm from thee that shall delude or deceive me or that shall be able to do hurt to any One or any thing (pause) then say Bless O Lord this element of fire and sanctify it that it may be blessed to to set forth the praise of thy Holy Name, that it may Burn & shine forth — and that no hurt may come to Me but strengthen me in my contemplating the Works of Occult Nature Throught Jesus Christ our Lord, Amen —

Chap 15th

Of the Images in the Zodiac What virtues, they receive from the Stars, obeying the will of the
  Operator (when Engraved on proper material)

In Chapter 13 I have given the Twenty eight Mansions of the ☽ and the names they are called when their proper places But we now come to the Celestial Signs of the Zodiac and their Images which are many, But I shall notice only a few & those so clear that by close attention all the rest come easy to your comprehension. The Images of this kind are framed some visible & Conspicuous and others only imaginable conceived & pictured by the Egyptians, Indians & Chaldeans, the Visible or Conspicuous are the twelve in the Zodiac (viz) ♈ the Ram, ♉ the Bull, ♊ the twins, ♋ the Crab &. These they divide into four Triplicities. Fiery. Airy. Watery & Earthy. To the Fiery Triplicity they constitute ♈ ♌ & ♐ they being Oriental are effectual Remedies against, Fevers, Palsies, Dropsies, Gouts, and all Cold phlegmatic diseases. i.e, to expel the above diseases. Take a piece of metal belonging to the Star or Sign, & Engrave upon the face of it in the Hour of the ☉ when fortunately situated free from all bad aspects the Correct Image of A Lion Passive when the first degree of ♌ ascends likewise such Characters & words suitable to the Work, Keeping your whole mind & Soul absorbed on the intent of your object-suffering no kind of interruption whatever, and particularly observe that you are not beyond your time Now the Zodiacal Image if accurately made will produce a wonderfull effect to the wearer who is afflicted with the before mentioned diseases. It is an Image of honour, eloquence, & Ingenuity. To make an Image against the Stone, diseases in the Reins, and the hurts of wild Beasts, The same figure must be Engraved, when ☉ is in the heart of ♌ obtained in the midst of the heavens, That is in the 21 degree of ♌ his Character youl see in the first Book. ♊ ♎ & ♒ constituting the Aerial & Occidental Triplicity and being the Houses of ☿ ♀ & ♄. Images framed under this Triplicity put toflight such Diseases as is under their Dominion, as you will see in the Tables of Diseases under each Sign; ♋, ♏ & ♓ Constitute the watery & Northern Triplicity which prevails against hot dry feavers &c which is to be found as before mentioned; but observe that ♏ commands the part of Generation consequently provokes lust, and if an Image is to be made for the purpose it must be formed under his third Face because it belongs to ♀ as she rules the parts of Generation as by looking into her table of claims you will discover. Now to frame an Image against Serpents, Scorpions, Poysons, evil Spirits &c you must take her second face Asscending that being the face of the ☉, and the Decanate of ♃, another most efficacious Image framed of ♋ against Serpents, Poysons &c when ☉ & ☽ are in ♂ in it and assending the first & third face, the first face being the face of ♀ and the Decanate of ☽ but the third is the face of ☽ & Decanate of ♃. It has been always observed by all Learned Professors of this Art that when the ☉ is in ♋ that Serpents are violently tormented; ♉, ♍ & ♑ Constitute the Earthly & Southern Triplicity, and Images framed under this are good for all hot infirmities as their tables shows, they are the Houses of ♀, ☿ & ♄ as ♂ having his Exaltion in 28 degrees of ♑, an Image thus framed not only protect Man but keep places in Security wherever it is Buried or hid; The Characters of the united Planets & the Characters of the four Triplicities necessary will be found in Chap 4 Book 1st

Chap 16
Of the Images of the Faces of the Signs and of Images without the Zodiac, Called fixed Stars

There are in the Zodiac 36 Images which Ascends in

44

the faces – which is, that each Sign contains 30 degrees, which 30 degrees are dived into 3 parts, i.e. 3 tens and each 10 is called a face therefore to accomplish your object you must begin your Image Tablet or Talisman exact on the first Ascension of the face i.e. as soon as the 10 degree of ♈ ascends that is called the face of ♂, then you may work or make any Image &c suitable to his Power. The 20 degree of ♈ is the face of ☉ The moment that ascends begin such work as appertains to ☉ The 30 degree is the face of ♀ which is called the 3rd face therefore you must frame your Image &c for what purpose she gives or signify as Love, friendship Beauty &c All the other faces must be observed in the same manner & as it would be needless to go through the whole of the emblematic figures that belong to each face according to the Ancient Magi I shall only give a few both in their description & properties, & for the others refere you to a Book called, <u>A New Guide to Astrology</u> or <u>Astrology Brought to light</u> by <u>Samuel Penseyre</u>, there youl find an Emblematical discription of all the Images of Degrees, Signs, faces &c

An Image made under the 2nd face of ♈ which is the face of ☉ and it being the face of Nobility, Highness, Rule, Power and Dominion must be engraven on a Plate of Gold (which is under ☉) A Beautifull formed female elegantly clothed in a White Garment, flowing to her feet, & over her shoulders a red drapery, This Image whoever its made for & bear it about him may aspire to Nobility the height of a kingdom greatness power & dominions

An Image made under the 2nd face of ♉ which is the face of ☽ and being then in her Triplicity, by Engraving the figure of a Naked man holding in his Right hand a large Key, whoever it is made for & bear it It giveth great power Nobility and dominion over People Ion the 1st face of ♋ must be engraven the figure of a Virgin richly attired with a Crown on her head, This giveth acuteness of sense subtility of wit and the Love of Men (this is a french Talisman) In the 2nd face of ♋ must be engraven the figure of a fine handsome young man handsomely clothed, This is a Talisman of Riches, mirth Gladness, and will procure the Love of Women, The first face of ♌ must be engraven on a piece of Lead (that face belonging to ♄) A Man ill-formed riding on a Lion, This is a Talisman of Violance cruelty & whatever the Operator absorbe in his thoughts to be done to his enemy such will happen very soon ♄ being one of the Molevonent Planets, The 3rd face face of ♍ must be engraven an Old decrip-ed Man leaning on a Staff, whoever it is made for accor-ding to the art laid down, it will cause weakness infirmity lop of Members & if Buried in any spot you wish to destroy nothing can resist its power of destroying all near it, The third face of ♐ is the face of ♄ therefore on a Piece of Lead must be engraved a figure of an Idle Man playing with a Staff, This is a talisman of obtaining our own Wills be what they may that is under ♄ dominion, The 2nd face of ♑ which belongs to ♂ must be engraven on a Piece of Iron or Steel, the figure of two Women & a Man looking towards a Bird flying in the Air This Talis--man Assists in requiring those things which appears impossible to be done & searching after those things, which cannot easily be known. In the first face of ♓ that belonging to ♄ must be engraven on a piece of Lead the figure of a Man well cloathed but heavily pressed

46

down with a Burthen on his Sholders. by burying it on his premises the nearer his Person the better, your enemy cannot stay in the place nor house, but will wander having no rest. untill it is taken away, In the 3rd face of ♓ which is the face of ♓. Must be engraven on a piece of Bright Polished Steel, The figures of A Naked Youth close by the Side of A Beautifull Virgin with a wreath of flowers on her head, This is a Talisman of great power in the field of Love & will easily comply to your wishes

☞ Every thing must be correctly prepared in point of time Metal, force of Mind - with Language suitable to the object you desire & your whole attention devoted to the full desire of the accomplishing your work & wishes, suffering no kind of interruption whatever or all will be fruitless,

Having now finished the Emblematical figures of the Faces, the others I have not noticed well by perseverence easily come to your mind, I shall now make a few Observations on those without the Zodiac as follows Peg asus the flying horse, An Image made under the Ascension of this Star preserves & cures all diseases in Horses. Likewise preserves all Horseman in Battle, Andromache. encreaseth Love betwixt man & Wife by reconciling. adulterors, Cassiopeia. restoreth weak bodies & Strengthens members, Serpentarius. chaseth away Poysons & cures the Bitings of venomous Beasts, Hercules, gives Victory in War, The Dragon with Both the little & Great Bear, gives craftiness ingenuity & maketh a man valient, Hydra. gives Wisdom, Riches. & resists Poysons. Centaurus. Bestowes Health, Ara conserveth Chastity. Cetus. gives prudence & happiness. by sea & land. The Ship affords. security in the waters. The Hare protects against Deceits & Madness. The Dog cureth the Dropsie resisteth the Plague

and protects you from Wild Beasts & all fierce Creatures
Orion, giveth Victory. The Eagle gives honours & preserveth
age. The Swan, cures the Palsie & Quartain ague. Perseus,
protects you against Envy and Witchcrafts. The Heart,
protects all Phrenetical & Mad People. These must be under-
-stood to be Constellations and at their Ascensions must be
made the various Images, with the same observations, as on
the Faces. and said by the Magi to produce all the effects stated.
I must now mention a few of the most wonderfull,
Talismans which have been made by the Ancient and
Learned Magi, the which are recorded,
In a Martial Stone they engraved a figure of a Man
Armed riding on a Lion in his right hand a naked
sword erect, & in his left hand (holding by the Hair)
the head of a Man. this must be done In the hour of ♂,
ascending in the second face of ♈. They possitively
declare that whoever this Image is made for & bear the
same it rendereth him powerfull in both good & evil
so that all Men shall be in fear of him it will also
give him the power of enchantment so that he shall
terrify all persons he intends by his very looks that
they will become stupefied. They made another at
the Hour of ♂ in the first Face of ♏ ascending. The
figure of a Soldier with a Crown on his head girt
by his side a large sword & carrying in his right
hand a lance, This Talisman they also declare that
whoever it is made for & bear it. can see no fear.
want for no Courage. fortunate in Battles & sure to
over throw all strife & Contentions. They observe that
these Emblems must be engraven on the Stone belonging
to ♂. but I conceive that as Iron or Steel are Metals
of ♂ they will (when highly polished) answer the same purpose,

48

In a Solar Stone as a Diamond Conelian &c they engraved an Image of a Woman standing (in a chariot drawn by four Horses) in a dancing attitude in her right hand holding a looking Glass, & in her left a staff, leaning on her Breast carrying a fleame on her head. This Talisman must be made in the hour of the ☉ in the first face of ♌. & if accurately they declare it to cure all Lunatic Passions, which always proceed from the combustion of the ☽

In a Stone belonging to ♀ they engraved the figure of a Beautifull Virgin Naked with a chain about her neck & a looking Glass in her hand, & her hair dishevelled, by her a young man holding her by the chain in his left hand & with his right holding up her hair both looking at each other lovingly. & flying round them a Cupid with his dart pointed at the heart of the Woman This Talisman must be made in the hour of ♀ when she first Ascends into ♓. & they also declare that if it is made with Judgment whoever it is made for & bear it, all women will yield to his wishes

In a Stone of ☿ or on a Mercurial Composition In the hour of ☿ ascending in the first degree of ♊ they engraved the figure of handsom young Man bearded, in his left hand a rod with a serpent twined around it & in his right hand a Dart & wings on his feet This they declare accurately framed according to art, whoever it is made for and bear it conferreth great knowledge makes him eloquent & gives great gain in Merchandise also enable him to make peace between parties. And cures all fevers.

Another of ☿ in his hour Ascending in the first degree of ♍. The figure of a Man riding on a Peacock, having Eagles feet & on his Head a Crest & in his left

hand holding a Cock or a fire This Talisman is of
great Virtue for whoever it is made for & bear it
will gain good will of all & will always be ready
in both wits and memory.
In a Stone or Composition under the ☽ they engraved
(in the hour of the ☽ ascending in the first degree of the
face of ☽) The figure of a Women with Horns riding
on a Bull or a Dragon with seven heads in her right
a Dart & in her left a looking glass, two serpants twining
around her head & horns and the same round her feet
This Talisman hath wonderfull properties, if it is Buried
in the ground in an Orchard the Trees will bear in
abundance it repels all Poisons & cures all infirmities
in Children, Having given these few wonderfull Tal-
-ismans so highly spoken of by the Ancient Magic, These
Talismans are made under the Planets only in their true
passitions for the purpose, which to performe must be
strictly observed, be constant. Ask & you shall have,
seek, and you shall find, persevere, & the Beauties of
Occult Philosophy will open to your view, & you will
soon find yourself in the Orchard of Nature where
you may choose in abundance what fruit you most
prefer, rest asured when once obtained it is a Choice
fruit, of which you must be careful & not lavish it
away. for when once gorne it is not easy to be obtain-
-ed a Second time Secrecy will enclose & Secrecy
will retain it for your use for life, feed not
the eyes of the Vulgar nor the eyes of the
unbeliver for they and they only will destroy
all Power

50

Chap 17

Images or Talismans made under the Head & Tail of the Dragon or ☽s Nodes

The ☽ has two points belonging to her called Nodes, which is commonly termed the Dragons head & tail which in Astrology & Astronomy are marked thus ☊ the head, thus ☋ the tail, the head denotes every thing good, & the tail every thing that is bad, the ancient Magic from experience knowing their Natures & properties have made them useful to their wishes in the Magical & Talismanic art as forming Images as follows,

Of the ☊, they Formed a Dragon with the Head of a Hawk between two Circles at a time when it was most powerful. i.e. when ♃ is with it in the Midheaven this they affirm to be a good Genius, as a Serpent by the Egyptians is extolled to be a divine Creature & hath a divine Nature for in it is a more acute spirit and a greater degree of natural fire than any other & contains many more properties, the length of life was yet never ascertained, nor was there a dead one ever found. Therefore the emblem of a Serpent with the tail in its mouth, is called the emblem of Wisdom and Eternity

Of the Tail they made the same figure only one of the Circles as a Moon Eclipsed in the tail & took the opportunity of performing their work when afflicted by ♄ or ♂ or by both the more afflicted the better for their purpose of Revenge, This Talisman is a dreadful one They call it an Evil Genius, as it have the power of anihilating an enveterate Enemy bringing on him every infirmity & Misfortune and driving him from his habitation, & while its force is against him he will become a vagabond and wonderer

A certain Hebrew Doctor made this Talisman & fixed in a Belt which was filled with Jewels by order of Blanch

daughter of the Duke of Bourbon which she willingly or ign-
orantly (not knowing the power of the Talisman) presented
to her Husband Peter the first king of Spain with which
when he was girt with it around his Body he instantly
seemed to himself to be encompassed with a hughed
Serpent; But he afterward discovering it to be the
Magical power of the Belt, he forsook his Wife and
could not bear either her Name or presence,

The true Forms & Figures
of the Talismans
Dragons
Tail ☋ and Head ☊

Chap 18
Of the Images or Talismans made under
the Mansions of the Moon, and their won-
-derfull properties & Effects

The Labour & perseverence of the East is astonishing to
the human mind, for by their Writings you see that
there is nothing unsought, nor no intricate path of the
heavens unnoticed by these Learned Magi for as the
Terrestial traveler seeks in all parts of the Earth for
the knowledge of Geography, so have they accomplished
the true knowledge of the Heavens & all that is therein
The ☉ ☽ and Stars their true motions natures & properties

52

and what effect they produce on the animal vegetable and Mineral Kingdoms, showing the Antipathy & Sympathy there is between them & what power Man posess if he will but be wise, do not Scripture tell us "that the heel of Man shall bruise the Serpents head" In the first Mansion of the ☽. to seek the destruction of their enemys They engraved on a plate of Iron or Iron Ring the figure of a Black Man in a loose Hairy Garment — with a girdle tight around his waist in his right hand a long lance in the act of revengefully casting it and then seal it up with Black wax, & perfumed it with Stor-ax. and while in the act of Making as well as perfuming it wishing such evil to come upon him as they desire shoud fall on him, The first Mansion of the ☽ is the first degree of ♈ that is day house of ♂. he is a Malevolent turbulent destroying Planet. therefore he is strong & powerfull & the Metal is his own & black wax for the seal is shone because Black is the Colour of ♄ and he in ♈ is in his fall. & to make it more patent it is perfumed with Liqu--id Storax because that perfume belongs to ♂ which is most gratefull to him. The imprecation to be used is suited to their own mind which many parts of the Bible will furnish as the Curses of Jobe and others,

The second Mansion which belongs to the ☉ he being in his face they engraved on a plate of Gold the figure of a King crowned & sealed it with White Wax & Mastic and perfumed it with Lignum & alvea This Talismun is against the Wrath of a Prince & to reconcile him In the Third Mansion is a Silver Ring with a square table. A Woman elegantly clothed sitting in a chair her right hand lifted to her head & sealed as before and perfumed it with Musk Camphire & Calamus Arimait

Aromaticus. They affirm, it confirms all happiness in fortune and every thing Good

In the Fourth Mansion, A Soldier sitting on a horse holding in his right hand A Serpent, & perfumed it with red Myrrhe & Storax, & sealed it with Red Wax, this Talisman they made for revenge seperation & ill will

In the fifth Mansion, for the favour of Kings Princes Officers of State &c they made in silver the Head of a Man, i.e. A Kings head either engraved, or as a Seal and perfumed it with Red Sanders. They affirm that a letter sealed with this seal will always promote good from such persons

In the Sixth Mansion, To procure Love betwixt two they made two figures in the act of embracing each other — Sealed with virgin or white Wax & perfumed it with Lignum Aloes & Amber

In the 7th Mansion to procure every thing good If there having his terms from 13 degrees to 2☋. They made an Image of a Man well clothed in a supplicant posture to heaven Sealed it in Silom & perfumed it with the perfume of Jupiter

In the 8th Mansion, for Victory in war they made an Image of an Eagle with Wings expanded & the face of a Man on a plate of Tin, & perfumed it with what belongs to ♃ which is Sulphure

In the 9th Mansion, To cause Infirmities they made a Seal of Lead, bearing the Image of A Man wanting his privy parts with his hand before his eyes and perfumed it with Rosin and Pine

In the 10th Mansion, to facilitate Child bearing & to cure the sick, they made a Seal of Gold bearing the Head of a Lion & perfumed it with Amber

In the 11th Mansion, for fear, reverance & worship they made a seal of Gold bearing the Image of a

54

Man. riding on a Lion holding its ear with his left hand & in his right a gold Bracelet. & perfumed it with Safron and all good Odours

In the 12th Mansion, To Seperate Lovers & disolve all conjugal effections they made a Seal in Black Lead bearing the Image of a Dragon fighting with a Man and perfumed it with the hairs of a Lion

In the 13th Mansion, to cause agreements between a Married Couple, who have seperated. & for the disolving all charms against Copulation, they made the Image of a man in Red Wax, & the Image of the Woman in white wax, & put them together in the act of embracing. & perfumed them with Lignum Aloes & Amber, using an Oration suitable for the purpose

In the 14th Mansion, To Cause Divorce & Seperation of Man & Woman they Made a Seal of Red Copper, bearing the Image of a Dog biting his tail & perfumed it with the Hairs of a black Dog & a black Cat

In the 15th Mansion, to obtain friendship & good will they made an Image of a Man sitting as if writing a letter, & perfumed it with Frankinsence & Nutmegs

In the 16th Mansion, for gain in Merchandize they made a Seal in Silver, bearing the Image of a Man Setting in a Chair holding in his left hand a Balance and perfumed it with all fine smelling Spices

In the 17th Mansion, to protect a place from Robbers or Thieves. on an Iron Seal or Plate they made an Image of an Ape & perfumed it with the hairs of an Ape

In the 18th Mansion, to Cure fevers & pains in the Belly. They Made on a Seal or Plate of Copper the Image of a Serpent holding its tail above its head and perfumed it with hartshorn, they do affirm that whenever this is buried no Snakes Serpents or any venomous creature can live, but will be driven away & while this Image remains they will never return

The 19th Mansion, for facilitating Child Birth and provoking the Menstrual discharge, they made a Seal on plate of Copper, bearing the Image of a Woman holding her face with her hands and perfumed it with Liquid Storax

In the 20th Mansion, for gaining Success in hunting they made in a seal on Plate of Tin the Image of a Sagittarius, half a Man & half a horse & perfumed it with the head of a Wolf

In the 21st Mansion, for the Destruction of an En-emy, they made an Image with a double face in the form of a Man, & perfumed it with Sulphure & let this thy made on Lead or Iron & kept it in a Brass box closed up with Sulphure & let, when they wanted to make their enemy feel their power, perfumed it as before under an unfortunate aspect, with the hair of him they would hurt,

In the 22nd Mansion, to secure a Person from runn-ing away, they made a Seal of Iron bearing the Ima-ge of a man with rings on his feet & a helmet on his head, & perfumed it with Argent vive

In the 23rd Mansion, for Destroying & wasting your Enemy & his property, they made on a plate or Seal of Iron, the Image of a Cat, with a Dogs head & perfum-ed it with the heirs of a savage Dog & Cat, & buried it in the place which they wished to hurt,

In the 24th Mansion. To increase & multiply Heards of Cattle, They took the horn of a Ram Bull or Goat, according to what they wished for & sealed on it with an Iron seal made on purpose (by the Talismanic art) and made it red hot, & burnt in the impression on the horn, the said Seal, whereon is engraven the Image of a Woman Giving suck to a Boy, when done hang the Horn round the neck of the leader of the flock, or Burnt it on his horn

In the 25th Mansion, for the preservation of Trees, Harvests &c they cut in a piece of fig tree Wood, The Image of a Man planting, & perfumed it with the flowers of the fig tree – and then hang it on a tree

In the 26th Mansion, To gain the Love & favour of Women they engraved on a plate of high polished ☽, the Image of a Beautifull female washing & Combing her hair, and perfumed with every sweet smelling odour under ♀

In the 27th Mansion, To destroy Fountains, Pits, Medicinal Waters & Baths, They made of red Earth the Image of a Man Winged holding in his hand an empty vessel perforated and burnt it & then perfumed it with Liquid Storax, and Apofetitæ, & bury it in the Fountain &c they wished to destroy

In the 28th Mansion, To gether together fish, they made on a Seal or plate of Copper, The Image of a Fish, & perfumed it with the Skins of fish & cast it in the water where they would wish them to be gethered

Now these Images are not to be brought to perfection, without a due observation, in making & representing their proper Characters of the Mansions, Signs Planets, Words effects &c and their proper Metals Compositions must be observed

The divine Plato commandeth us to reverence the name of God more than Images or statues of the gods – for he observes there is a more express Image & power of God reserved in the faculty of the mind of Man (especially if it be inspired from above) than in the Works of Mans hands. Therefore sacred Words have not their power in Magical operations from themselves as they are but words but from the Occult Divine Powers working working by them in the minds of those, who by faith adhere to them, by which words the secret power of God as it were through conduct pipes) is transmitted into such things so selected for our use & by this means are impregnated (being chosen by ant as proper recipients) with the divine influences, by which are obtained & have been done many wonderfull things - as we read in Media.

// Most pleasent sleep she caused, words thrice she speak
// The Seas appeased and soon their fury broke

The Ancient Hebrew Doctors have observed that many wonderfull things have been performed by Words only the Pythagorians have performed many surprising cures in the diseases of both the Body & Mind of Man, & affirm that if a Piece of Parchment be made according to the figure in Page 53 Chap 11 first book. & hanged round the Neck of a Diseased person, Repeating the letters backwards as. a. r. b. & then begin at r. b. a. then at b. a. r & till the whole is repeated it will cure all feavers. As all divine Words and Names of Antiquity have first proceeded from the Gods & appear to the ignorant short sighted to be of little use — But Zoroastes the Great Philosopher forbids changing them or even altering a character of them, let them appear ever so uncouth or Barbarous, for he says they breath forth the harmony of the Godhead & therein contains the divine Essence that all creatures above fear them, those below tremble at them, The Angles reverence, the Wicked Spirits are affrighted at them every Creature doth honour, and every Religion adore them and therefore ought to be used without corruption in their own Characters,

Chap 19
Of the Virtue of places, and what place are suitable to every Star or Constellation

In the different Books of Astrology you will se that there are various places appropriated to various Signs & stars, but they they do not give an account of their meaning, as such, I shall refer you to Samuel Pensogers, Astrology. the work being but small. or Mr Williams Astrologers Magazine now Publishing, and explain the meanings of them, as follow's Whatever Seal Talisman Ring, Tablet &c by being made in such place belo=nging to the Planet or Sign will add greatly to its Virtue, by hiding or burying such Talisman for a length of time encreases its Virtue, for example If I make a Talisman Ring &c under ♄ for any purp-ose, I must or ought, hide or bury it for a time, in some stinking place, dark, underground, Religious and Mournfull place, as Church Yards, tombs & houses not inhabited by men, & old tottering obscure dre--adfull Houses, Solitary Dens. Caves & pits, fish ponds, & standing Pools, and such like, these being the Pla--ces, appointed for ♄, the Same observations. of the Rest, NB. Not only Talismans &c being buried in such places but all instruments made for the Art, will be made of greater power & of more efficancy in performing any Mag--ical or Talismanic Experiment. As a piece of Steel when heated in the fire and plung'd in water, recives its virtue or hardness, enabling the Artificer. to work on any metal or stone with it even its own, So does the above instruments. by being so disposed of. receive a certain Occult Virtue requisite

Chap 20
Celestial Observations particularly to be observed in the Manufacturing of some kind of Images Rings, Talismans Tablets &c

The reason why the ancient Magi, performed such wonderful experiments in the Occult Philosophy was that they were so very correct & adhered to every minutia contained in the various Tables Labouriously composed for the sole purpose of this Beautiful & Sublime Science, I shall now explain Astrologically (which any student may very clearly understand)

I now wish to make a fortunate Talisman, that is to make a person fortunate in their Undertakings, I make an Election & erect a figure of the heavens for the Person desired affix the Signs & Planets according to their order, I then endeavour to make the Significator of life, the Ascendent, the Midheaven & their Lords fortunate, also the Place of the ☉ & ☽, and part of fortune & ☋, indeed I wish to say that when the figure is made the happiest possible, make the Talisman or Image, engraving or writing on virgin parchment or vellum in due order, the Angels Spirits, Characters &c proper according to the before mentioned rules, and let the Person for it is made keep it secretly under his Care

But if to make a Talisman to procure Misery & every misfortune all what was fortunate before must be now made unfortunate, by raising every malignant Star & make the figure the most unfortunate by these Observations, the ancient Magi asserts, that either Place, Region, City, or Buildings, from the highest to the lowest may be made fortunate or unfort-

unfortunate, whenever such Talismans is Buried or hid

Example, 1st Suppose I wish to chase away a certain Animal that no generation may be seen of them. I make an Image (according to the rules before laid down) under the Ascension of that Animal I wist to destroy or chase away. for example under ♏︎. at the first degree of the Sign ♏︎ Ascending, which belongs to ♂. I take a Piece of Iron or Steel plate, which is the Metal of ♂. & engrave thereon the Image of the Animal, but before, I begin my work. I must see that the Sign ♏︎ is Ascending with the ☾. the Ascendant & the Lord must be both unfortunate. likewise the Lord of the house of ♂. & if possible let the Lord of the Ascendant be in the eight house joined with a Malignant Aspect; as an ☍ or □ of ♄. after these observations are compleated, I engrave the Image & on the same face (or on the Image if large enough. I put the Character of the Ascendant as ♏︎ the Lord thereof as ♂. the ☾. & the lord of the Day and hour it shoud happen to fall on (which the Ephemeris will show) when it is thus compleated, I dig a pit or hole of such size as is proper at the time when ♂ is in his fall or Detriment (as in the Table page 120 B. 1st) I then take from the four Corners, East West, N & S of the same place some Earth & Bury the Image with the head downwards Saying. In the name of God the Creator of all things in the the heavens. the Earth & all things in the waters under the Earth, and by whose permission all things live & die I bury this Image. and let it the burying place of all (naming the animal) that they may no more infest this place; (naming the town house field or Place) The Ancient Magi passitively assent that this experiment

being accurately adhered to that no more of these reptiles will ever infest that place while the Image is there.
The same Rule must be observed on all other animals Insects & Reptiles, which belongs or governed by the same Planets.
Example 2nd If you would wish to destroy, dislodge or prejudice, & defeat the Machinations of a vile emisary or enemy, you must erect a figure as before. & make unfortunate his Ascendant & ☽, the lord of the house of the ☽. Lord of Life & Lord of the Ascendant, the tenth house, & its Lord, when this is completed, engrave on a piece of metal belonging to the lord of his Ascendant, under the Sign Ascending the figure of your enemy, with the Signs Characters &c on the face of the Talisman, as observed in first example. and what intend it for then take from the Bible a suitable verse for the purpose. I shall in another part of the work select a few suitable for the purpose — simular to that in the Tables of the Angels &c on the day of ♃ which is Thursday.
Example 3rd A Talisman for gain or prosperity in any place or Busnefs or Profession let an Image be made under the Nativity of a Man, i.e. under the Assendant or Celestial sign Ascending, that belongs to or the Place to which you would direct that gain or would make fortunate, wether House, land, Water &c which the tables (Chap 8 Book 1st will direct you) Now having erected a Horoscope compleat — suitable to your purpose as it is for gain you make the lord of the Second house (which is the house of Substance & Riches) fortunate by joining with him the Lord of the Ascendant in a △ or ✶ & if possible let there be a reception of the fortunes. Make fortunate the eleventh & its Lord, and the Eight. and if

62

you can place the part of fortune in the second, or first, it will be more powerfull. When you have thus completed your figure while the is Ascending you must (having prepared every thing in rediness) Engrave the Image or Talisman, when done Bury it in the desired place in the day, & hour belonging to the Planet to which it is subject. If it is made for a Man or Woman, let them keep it in their own possession, not only secret but sacred as exposition will destroy the effect. If this Talisman is for a contrary purpose every thing which was fortunaate must be made unfortunate, by the planets being in Ius, □, Detriment & falls, as the Table, Page 120 B 1st will show,

Example 4th. A Talisman for Concord Love or reconciliation. Make an Election as before for the Person, according to his Nature, in the Day of ♃, make an Image under his Assendant, whom you would have beloved, but first make fortunate the Assendant & the tenth, by keeping away all evil aspects of the infortunes as ♂ & ♄, take care to have the Lord of the tenth & eleventh, fortunate, & Joined to the Ascendant by △ or ✶ or with reception, then make another Image or Talisman for whom you will reconcile, or stir up to Love, first considering wether he is a friend, or companion, of him you would have Beloved, & if so let the Image &c be Framed under the Ascension of the Eleventh house, from the Ascension of the first Image. But if it should be for a Wife or Husband (as the 11th is the house of friends) it must be made under the Ascension of the seventh, that being the house of Marriage. If for a Brother or Sister or Cousin It must be made under the Ascension of the third, that being the house of Kindred &c, and the same with the rest, put the significator of the

63

first, & endeavour to let there be a reception, & all fortunate, as in the first Image (observing all the before mentioned rules) afterwards, when both are completed, Unite them both together Saying, <u>In the Name of the Father Son & holy Ghost</u> naming what you wish to have performed, mentioning the names of Both parties, & wrap them up in a Piece of fine new White Linen, & to be kept in secret by the first party, frequent fixing his mind on the same & the effect he would have produced & whenever he expects to see the opposite take care to have it about him, But for the contrary effect every thing must be reverse to the former & instead of putting them face to face, put them Back to Back & cast them into any place belonging to ♄ or ♂, using all the same time such imprecations necessarily as you will find in the Bible or Virgil,

Example 5th A Talisman for Nightly thought or Dreams which being placed under the head of the Person made for he will discover in his sleep what he would wish to know when awake, Take a Plate of Gold, & Engrave upon it the figure of a Man, sleeping in the Bosom of an Angel, when ☽ is Ascending & the ☉ in the ninth house in ♈ put on the Breast of the Man the effect desired & in the hand of the Angel the name of the intelligence of the ☉ (see table page 29) when finished & all the Characters selected thereon, wrap it up in fine linen, and place it under the pillow & such effect you desire which is under the dominion of the ☉ will be obtain'd which could not by any other means,

Example 6th Let the same Image be made when ♍ Ascends & being fortunate in the ninth house in ♈ or ♊ ascending & ☿ being fortunate in the Ninth in ♒ and received from ♄ in a fortunate Aspect & as free from

64

impediment as possible, the more correct the better, write on the Breast of the Man, the name of the effect desired, and place in the right hand of the Angel the Spirit of ☿ ♆. This must be Engraved on a Compound of Quick Silver & Lead Refined

Example 7th Let the Same Image be made when ♎ is Ascending & ♀ recived from ☿ in ♊ in the ninth house every fortunate Aspects before observed, Write on the Breast of the Man the effect desired, i.e. what belongs to her. & place in the right hand of the Angel the Intelligence of ♀ ♆. This must be engraved on a Plate of Copper mixed with a small quantity & washed with Liquid Silver produced from Mercury after finished

Example 8th Let the Same Image be made when ♒ is Ascending & ♄ fortunately possessing the ninth house by exaltation, which is in ♎, & write upon the Breast of the Man the name of the effect desired, & in the right hand of the Angel the name of the Angel of ♄. This must be Engraved on a Composition Refined Lead with a small portion of Copper, Lead being the Metal of ♄ Copper that of ♀, ♎ being her house.

Example 9th Let the Same Image be made when ♋ is Ascending, & the ☽ recived by ♃ & ♀ in the Sign ♓ fortunately placed in the ninth house and write on the Breast of the Man the name of the effect desired & in the Right hand of the Angel the Spirit of the ☽. also all the Characters requisite as is before mentioned, This must be engraved on Silver with a small quantity of Copper & Tin, After the above Talismans are properly finished (To make them most powerfull) they should be perfumed with such perfumes as belong to the Planets & Signs in the Planetary hour requisit. & while the Perfume is Burning

the Benediction should be said by the Operator (see Page 41)
These 9 Examples are laid down according to the Rules of the
Celestial Science of Astrology.

Chap 21

Talismanic Rings their Metals Composition and Manner of Making them according to the Ancient Custom

Rings when properly framed & made by art where highly esteemed by the Ancients, & no kind was worn by them but what possessed some power to answer their purpose. These Rings they possitively assent that whoever they are made for, & wear them, are fortified, against Diseases, Poysons, Machinations of enemies, evil Spirits, & all hurtfull Animals &c, & cured of the same, Whenever you wish to make a Ring, you must determine what Star or Planet you would make it under, & for what purpose it is designed for, when your determination is fixed, you must observe the Ascencion of that Star, that it is fortunately Situated, In a fortunate aspect with such other as are desired for the work or in ☌ with the ☽. you must then take a Stone, Herb &c belonging to that Star, & make what is called a Box Ring, of the Metal, appropriate to the Star, & in it fasten the Stone placing underneath it the Herb, Root &c, engraving on the Stone the proper inscriptions of Images, names, Characters, &c as is before mentioned, not omitting fumigations &c. The Talismanic Rings, their surface being so small, the emblems may be omitted & framed with the Characters &c only, engraving the name of the effect desired round inside the hoop they may also be made with characters, & concealed under, Black or other Glass or Chrystals, only observing with the accuracy as before mentioned in the 9 examples

Example. To make a Ring of the ☉ you must take care that he is in his Exaltation, i,a, in ♌ Ascending & the house which the effect desired is well fortified by good Aspect also the ☉ himself free from evil rays. & take care to Joyn the ☽ in good Aspect with ☉ and the house where the effect is to be taking from, as the First, signifies Life &c, Second, fate, Riches, poverty &c, Third, Brethen Kindred &c, Fourth, Houses Lands &c. Fifth Children Joy, Pleasures &c and so on with the rest. If it is made for Dreams the Ninth House must be observed as bef -ore & the Intelligences of the Planets must be carefully attended to

Chap 22

Of Certain Images whose likeness resemble no kind of Celestial figure, but only the likeness of that which the imaginative fancy of the Worker Desires.

These Images were very commonly made in different Countries near the East, & are even to this present time, The Ancients well knew the property of every thing in the Animal, Vegetable & Mineral Kingdoms, & of what use could be made of them, to their Advantage, all of wh- -ich are regularly classed under the Different Stars, Planets and Signs, that governes them. And as in Medicines many things are compounded together, By the Physicion to help or cure the Disease, So is compounded such various things by Art, to receive the Influences of the Heavens, to work the desired effect. And to make these Images they Mixed Clay with the dust of Some metal Belon- -ging to the Star, to work the effect; also some Ashes of Burnt wood under the Same. the Brains & Blood of different Animals in similitude to the effect, with different Insects & reptiles, this Compound they well mixed together, in the Planety Hour either by Day or by Night repeating all the time what it is for & what effect it is to work, naming the Person or thing it is for or against, (But when these sort of Images were invented the Inventors & workers might have been ignorant of Calculating but knowing that when the ☉ rose that was an hour of effect & that 12 Oclock at night was also an hour of importance towards their wishes, therefore from frequent practice, they became well acquainted with their effects, & what could be produced from them. They therefore manufactured their Compounds, in these hours, & in these hours made & formed their Images, by Moulding & forming the Compound into the form or likeness of the Person or thing they intended to work upon, as thereby forming the figure, or Image, perfect, or imperfect, deficient or distorted. They then used the Images thus made according to their several virtues, some they hang on a tree, sometimes with the head downwards, Sometimes they Bury them in the Earth, or sink them to the Bottom of some river or pond, Sometimes they hang them up the Chimney, over the Smoke, or near enough to feel the heat of the fire, & so near sometimes as to roast them, Sometimes they put them into hot water, or into the fire, Which they declare that the Images thus made, do effect the real Image itself & cause the Passions &c on those to whom, or to what thing it was, ascribed, as the mind of the Operator dictated them They made their Images also of Wax mixing therewith the same ingredients, & melted them slowly before a fire which they say as it melted, so was the Animal or thing destroyed, All these things they performed at the Hour of 12 at Night, knowing it to be an hour suitable to their purpose. & were very particular in their Composing their Seven different Clays. for that which belongs to the ☉ they mixed Gold dust & all solar things. For the ☽ they mixt Silver dust & all Lunar things, For ♂, Iron or Stal dust & all Martial things. & so for the rest always mixing the things & dust of the metal under each Planet, And if they could not accomplish their Design the first hour, they waited till the same hour came round the next week & so on till their work was ended They also watched the ☽ to see wether she was encreasing or decreasing. For Expedition they performed their work under the first & second Quarters. & to procrastinate or prevent the issue of any thing. or to encrease misery & pain they performed their work under the last two Quarters, To account for their being so perticular in regard to the Quarters of the ☽. Let any Person take a quantity of Common peas & divide the same into four parts keeping them in four different papers till the seasons comes for sowing them, Then sow the contents of the first parcel the first or second day of the new ☽. The second near the same spot on the first or second day of the second quarter of the ☽. the Third on the Second or third day before the full ☽. & the fourth on the Second or third day before the ☽ is out. The first will grow very fast Blossom most beautifull. but will not bear fruit. The second will Blosom & bear very little, The third sown three days before the full of the ☽ will not only Blosom beautifully but bear fruit in abundance. & the fourth & last will scarce rise from the Ground, The same observation stands

in pruning & seting fruit Trees & in every thing –
wether Animal, Vegetable or Mineral, therefore
to get the most beautiful flowers only sow your
seeds on the new of the ☽. As such I conceive that
(as a receiver from the Chemists Still, Recives the
spirits after Made to be conveyed away for the
service of the Chemist) The ☽ is the greatest receiver
of all the influences of the Stars & Planets. & by her
the properties of such influences, are conveyed
to the Earth which the Ancients by their intense Labour
& study have discovered, those properties & regularly –
Classed them into various tables which tables enable them to
perform such wonders as tradition has handed down
to us, which are well authenticated by the first Rabbi doctors &c
The first hour of the ☉ rising on the Sunday is called the
Planetary hour of the ☉. and at 12 of the Clock the same
Night ♄ ruses which is called the planetry hour of ♄. as
you will find in the Table Book 1st page 131, Therefore
for all good purposes they make their Images in the
Planetry hours of the day & for evil the Planetary hour
of the night. These species of Images I conceive to be the
first Origen of Talismanic Sculpture & improved upon by
the Learned as Images are mentioned in various parts of
the Scriptures of which I shall refere to at the end of this
book. These Images were compounded as Follows
To procure the Love of a Favorite Fair they take Common
Clay & mix with it the blood of Sparrows wagtails & Doves
the dust of the Metal under ♀ with the Ashes of Plants
peculiar to her all of which properly mixed in modelled
an Image as near a similitude of the female as their
Imagination would permit them in the hour of ♀ when
completed, they then under the hour of ♃ take a Clay
Compounded as before only with the metal under ♃

70

which are most applicable for the purpose while they are manufacturing these Images they repeat some verses applicable first to the female mentioning her name, the mans name & the effect desired when finished, they then in the hour of ♀ unite them together in the form & naming the effect with the names of the parties & keep about them or put them in some secret place. let this suffice as they made these Images for evil I refer to Albartus Magnus in his book (called Spirits) Now it appears to me from what I can learn that these Images were in use amongst the vile & un skilled in this most sublime Science, But the Magi being well learned in the Power of Talismans Erected them not only in the woods fields & Plains in Towns & Cities but in their Temples & on the Prow of their Ships to preserve them from evel or wreck, seeing that a Figure under ♓ & had the effect of Preserving the Ship from Storm, they also Placed at the poop of the Ship the stature of some Deity as Mars, Venus, Mecury. Jupiter Apollo &c which gives me every reason to believe that these were Talismans whence Virgil says

— Aurato fulgebat Apolline puppis and Persins

— Iacet ipse in littore, & un á Ingentes de puppe dei

This gave rise to a fable That Jupiter stole away Europa, & carried her of in the shape of a Bull, which was thus. The Cretians who stole her away put her on board of one of their Ships, who had for its Talisman, at the Prow a figure of a bull, & for its Deity the stature of Jupiter. There is another fable of the Beautifull youth Ganimed who is said to have been carried away by an Eagle, an Emblem of which has been found in the ancient ruins of a Roman Bath which was discovered at Bognor, Now the Eagle is one of the twelve Consecrated Birds. & is the Bird belonging to Jupiter in which Character Jupiter (as an emblem) is represented & youth

being the emblem of Beauty. This emblem of the Beautifull youth Ganimed conveyed away by an Eagle- was placed there as a Talisman of Purifycation, & no doubt from the virtues of Talismans which was then so well known that they placed this Image there as a Talisman of Purifycation made under ♃, he being called the Purifying King, As Orpheus sings
" Source of abundance, purifying King,
" Of various form'd from whom all nature springs;
" Propitious hear my prayer give blameless health,
" With peace divine, and necessary Wealth (Hymn 14th Ver. 15)
From this, it appears that the Magi, who placed the above Talisman there, made it as a priserver of Health, & firmly believed that whoever bathed in that Bath, would be restored to perfect health, in consequence of which Beauty must follow
The Custom of Setting Talismans or Images in Ships, is very ancient, for Tradition tells us that among those that came with Aneas from Troy there was one that had the figure of two Lions, that the Gudavenes had one with the Image of a Horse, & the ship of Alexandria, which St Paul sailed in had the Image of Castor & Pollux, or according to the Arabians the sign ♊. & that which carried Hippocrates, when he took his Journey to Abdara to cure Dinocritus bore the figure of the ☉ which practice is followed now in our own way being totaly Ignorant of the art of Making them & their properties

Chap 23

An Account of Some Wonderfull Talismans which has been found in the Eastern Countries and their Natures & power accounted for by Some Learned Philosophers

First, In the History of France, One Gregorius Turonesis, gives an account that on digging up the foundation of a Bridge at Parris, there was found a piece of Copper, whereon was engraved the figure of a Rat a Serpant & a Fire

72

which at that time was not considered important was neglected or by some means destroyed, after which it was observed in a short time a Great number of Serpents & Rats infested the City, at which time tearable to relate, the very great loss that City sustained by Fire, which till this strange piece of Copper was disturbed there never was witnessed any such distress,

It is also remarked, That in Constantinople before the time of Mahomet the Second, There was erected a figure of a Brazen Serpent, but when the disturbances broke out & Mahomet the second possessed himself of the place, the Tower Jaw of this Brazen Serpent was broke of. & in a very short time the whole place was infested with Serpents, therefore it is clear it was made by this art & placed there by a Magician.

John Tzetzen a famous Greek author in 1160 reports that Apollonius, a noted man in the art made a Talisman the figure of a Stork, the power of which was so potent that it Drove all those troublesome Birds out of the Place, he also made another of a Gnat by which all those insects were destroyed. Therefore it is a general opinion of the Philosophers that the first Gods of the Latines which they Call Averrunci or Dij Intelanes, were no other than these Talismans — which they called their Tutelar Gods, made under certain Constellations, but the poison of Idolatry, which infects the best Sciences was the cause of these Images being taken by the Ignorent to be Gods, & these were the Images they placed at the prows of their Ships

In a Plain & open Field in Mecha there is a Stone about four foot long & two foot broad, which is a choice piece of Ancient Antiquity. & the Turks call it Bractan, & as Suidas reports to be one of these Talismans. but the fable of the Turks, who highly esteem it & that it served as a Bed to Abraham when he made his Maid Hagar a Woman which is a general opinion. which is not much likely, as by that, the Turks must acknowledge themselves Bastards having descended from a servant-Maid therefore they never would acknowledge only that they sprung from Sarah. And this is the reason why they call them Sarasins others are of opinion that why the Turks hold this Stone in such veneration is, because Abraham tied his Camels to it when he went up on the Mountain top to sacrifice his Son Isaac. & some that it was erected in memory of a Certain Holy Woman, who was taken up to heaven & afterwards honoured as a Goddess for entertaining the angels Arot & Marot. Now what gave rise to this last opinion was that there was engraved on it the figure of venus with a Crescent. & from this was the opinion formed of it being A Talisman for some purpose made under that Planet & as Mr Selden, observes it was anciently taken through all Asia for the Moon & is the sole reason why the day of ♀ which is Friday is held in such high veneration with them. & in memory of this Star which is Worshiped the ridges of their Houses are adorned with Crescents, There was an Image made by Achmed Ben Tolon Caliph of Egypt the power of which drove away all Crocodiles out of that part.

Another Wonderfull Talisman as been seen by Mr Le Breves the great Cosmographier. I shall give his own words
" That in Tripolia, a City of Syria within a wall that
" reacheth from the sea side, to the gate of the City, there is
" a certain inchanted Stone, on which is figured in relif
" on by way of embosment the figure of a Scorpion which
" was placed there by a Magician, for to drive away

74

"all venomous Beasts, which infested this Province as the
"Serpent of Brass, in the Hippodromus at Constantinople,
"died, and a little above the City there is a Cave which is
"full of the Carkases & Bodies of Serpents which died at that
"time

Sultan Mahomet, when he possessed himself of the Place
caused a Beautiful figure of a Brazen horse without his
rider to be demolished which is certainly reported to have
preserved the City from Pestelence & all Contagions of the
Air; which ever since that time, this Disease has raged
so fircely that in the space of four or five months after
Many thousands of the Natives fell a sacrifice, which
mortallity every July or August has been ever since fatal
to thousands; Indeed according to very authentic
accounts All Asia was full of these Images or Talismans,
The use thereof was at length known in part to the Europeans
For the Druids made these Talismans with great success
& so did many other Men in various Countries

Having Now produced several Testimonies of the real Existance
of these Talismans, from the Tradition of the Ancients It is
now to prove that they are both Certain and Natural, and
not in the least respect above the Power of Nature, and
the means I intend to use to prove their Effects & Virtues, is
by the Power and virtue of Resemblance & Imagination,
first that betwixt the Scorpion, and the Image & the Constellation
that bears the name of that Living Creature. I shall then
prove this Virtue, by an Indiction of that which Resemblance
alone produceth throughout All Arts and Sciences as
Divinity, Philosophy, Physic, Astrology, Physiognomy,
Divination of Dreams, Painting, Sculpture, Music, &c

Chap 24
De Divnatione per Crystallum
Containing

The Treatise upon Divination by the Crystal or Berill Glass Extracted from an Antient MS. Intituled, Opera Salamonis Regis, in the Library of the late Queen Charlotte at Buckingham Palace

the Almadel

whereunto is added The Divine Call or Celestial Invocation

Here beginneth the book of Solomon called Almadel

All the Altitudes or four quarters of the world are divided into twelve parts, i.e, each quarter into three, and the angel of every altitude have their peculiar Power and virtue as will be shown in the following treatise but first is to be shown the manner of and form of the Almadel.

The almadel must be made of pure wax colored suitable to the Altitude, it must be six inches square and in each corner a hole and between each hole must be written with a new pen these words and names of **God** in the day and hour of ☉. upon the part towards the East **Adonai Helomi Pine** and on the west **Jod Hod Agla** and on the South **Helion Heloi Heli** and on the North **Tetragrammaton Shadai Jah** and betwixt the west and the other quarters make the pent= =acle of Solomon and between them write **Anabona** and in the midst of that a triangle wherein must be written,

El
Elion
Adonai

and the last name round the six angled figure as is shewn in the Example All of the same wax let there be made four Candles. i.e. divide your wax into three parts one to

Make the Almadel and the other two for the candles, and let there come forth from each a foot of the said wax to support the Almadel, and this being done, make a seal of pure Gold or Silver whereon is to be Engraven **El·Elion·Adonai**, and when you operate put the four candles upon the candlesticks, but do not set light to your candles or begin to operate untill every thing is ready, and have your Envocation ready written on virgin parchment, then lay the Alm=adel between the candlesticks upon the foot that pro=jects from the Candles, and laying the Gold seal upon the Almadel, repeat the Envocation with faith fervour and devoutness, and when the spirit appears have ready an earthen vessel of the proper color in the form of a bason, and put therein a few charcoal ashes, and put therein 3 little grains of Mastic in powder so that it may fume and the scent go up thro the holes of the Almadel, and as soon as the Spirit preceiveth the Odour, he speaketh in a low voice asking your desire and for what you have called the princes of his Altitude, then you must say

I desire that all my requests may be granted and what I pray for may be accomplished your office makes appear and declares that such is to be done by the Spirits of your order if it please **God** then add the particulars of your request with humility for what is lawful & just, and that you shall obtain of him but if he does not appear presently take the Gold seal and make with it 3 or 4 marks upon the can==dles by which marks the angel will appear quickly and when they depart they will fill the whole place with a most pleasant smell which will last a long time

The Gold Seal will serve and is to be used in all the Altitudes, but whenever you wish to Invoke these Spirits do it in the day & hour of ☉, but do not pray for any thing contrary to their office or against God and his laws but what God giveth according to the course of nature that you may ask for and obtain

The dress & the Almadel, the earthen vessel the tablecloth & the furniture of the room be all of the same Colour as the Choar or Altitude in which you work

There are twelve princes besides those ruling in the four Altitudes, and they distribute their offices among themselves every one ruling thirty days or there abouts according to the Sign the ☉ is in thus if I would call the two first of the five that belongs to the first Chord then chose the first Sunday after the ☉ enters ♈ to make the Experiment & repeat it again if you will the first Sunday, & if you will call the second that belongs to the first Chord you'l take the first Sunday after the ☉ enters ♉ but if you would call the last of the five then take the Sundays after the ☉ enters into ♊

In your Experiments of the other altitudes do the like for they have all one method of working, but it is to be obser= =ved that the Heavens have a Name formed severally in the substance of Heaven even as a character for when Spirits hear the name of God that is attributed to them they hear it by virtue of that character, therefore it is in vain to call any Spirit unless you know the name of God to call him by & be careful you do not call any angel but those belonging to the Chord or Altitude suitable to the time of the year

78

Here followeth the names, offices, and appearances of the Spirits of the four Choras or Altitudes with the Conjurations for calling them to visible apparition

The First Chora. The Angels of the First or East Chora or Altitude are named.
Almiel. Gabriel. Borachiel. Lebes. Hillison.
Their power and office is to make all things fruitfull & increase and multiply both animals and vegetables in Creation and generation advancing the births of Children and making barren women fruitful. They appear in the form of an Angel Carrying a flag having the form of a White Cross upon it. His body is wrapt about with a white cloud & is very fair & bright and a crown of roses upon his head he desends upon the Almadel as it were a fog or mist

The Color is Lillywhite

The Second Chora. The Angels of the Second Chora are named
Alphariza. Ginon. Armon. Goreimon.
The Spirits of the Second, Third & fourth Choras with their signs and princes have power over goods & riches, and can make any one either rich or poor and as the first Chora giveth increase &c these decrease and make barren. The Angels of the Second Choir appear as a young Child with Satin Clothes of a Red rose Color, having a Crown of Red gilliflowers upon his head, his face loketh upwards towards Heaven & is also of a red rose color He is Surrounded with

A bright splendor as the beams of the Sun which illuminates the room and before he departeth he speaks unto the Exorcist saying I am your Friend and Brother, and leaveth a pleasant Smell.

The Color of the 2nd Chora is **Red Rose Color**.

Third Chora. The Angels of the third Chora or Altitude are named, **Najasaj, Gelomiras, Gedobenai, Saranava, Elomnia**, They appear in the likeness of Children or as little women dressed in Green & Silver very beautiful and delightful to behold, and upon their heads a Crown of bays beset with White & Green Colors, They seem to look a little downwards, Their power & office are the same as the angels of the Second Chora,

The Color of the 3rd Altitude is **Green** mixed with **Silver**.

The Fourth Chora, The Angels of the fourth Altitude or Chora are named **Barchiel, Gediel, Gobiel, Deliel, Captiel,** Their Office is described in the Second Chora They appear in the form of little men or boys with cloathes of a black color mixed with dark green, and in their hands they hold a bird, which is naked, and their heads are compass'd with a bright shining of divers Colors, they leave a sweet Scent but very different from the rest

The Color of the 4th Altitude is **Green** mixed with **black**.

Conjuration

Thou great blessed and glorious Spirit of God. -N- who ruleth and art the first chief governing angel of the first Chora of the East I W.H.I. the poor Servant of the same Your most true and holy God. Adonai. Elome. Pine. whom you obey and who is the distributor and the disposer of all things in Heaven Earth & Hell do invocate and Conjure thee -N- that thou forth with appear by the power and virtue of the Same God: Adonai. Elome. Pine. And I command you by him who is set over you as King by the divine power of God, that you forthwith ascend from your place or order, and come unto me & shew thyself plainly & visibly unto me in this Chrystal Stone, in thy own proper Shape and glory, speaking with a voice intelligeble unto my understanding O Thou Mighty and powerful angel -N- who art by the power of God, to Govern all Animals Vegetables & minerals and to cause them and all creatures of God to Spring increase and bring forth according to their kinds & nature and I W.H.I. the Servant of the most High God. whom you obey do in his name most humbly bes= =eech thee to come from thy Celestial mansion and Shew unto all those things I shall desire of thee,

So far as in office thou may or can or art capable of performing if permit the Same

O Thou Mighty and Greacious Servant of Mercy -N- I do humbly beseech the in and by the Holy names of your **God·Adonai· Helome·Pine**, and I do also constrain you in and by this powerful name **Ana·Bona** that you fouthwith appear visibly & plainly in your own proper shape & glory in and through this Chrystal Stone that I may plainly see you and Audibly hear you, speak unto me & that I may by thy blessed Angelical and Glorious Ass-istance formiliar friendship and Constant Society both & at all other times to inform & rightly instruct me in my ignorent & depraved Judgment & unders-tanding and to assist me both herein & in all truth else, The Almighty **Adonai** King of Kings the giver of all good gifts shall in his bountiful & fatherly mercy be graciously pleased to bestow upon me therefore O thou blessed and glorious Angel -N- be friendly unto me, and do for me so far as **God** shall give you power in office to perform whereunto I move you in power & presence to app-ear unto me that I may Sing with his Holy Angels **O·Mappa la man Hallelujah**

Amen   Amen
      Amen

Appearance

When the Angel doth appear give him a kind reception and then ask what is just & lawful and that which is also suitable to his nature office & you shall obtain your desires;

I humbly desire thee O Lord God my merciful and most loving God the Giver of all graces and of all Sciences to permit an Angel of thine to Manifest unto me so much glory in this Chrystal (or glass) Consecrated & Charged as I thy unworthy Servant may be allowed free access to see into it all those things of which I am desirous of having a perfect and previous Knowledge. O' Most strong and mighty God without beginning or end, by thy Clemency & Knowledge in

All things I humbly desire thee to allow a blessed Ministering Spirit make manifest unto me in this Chrystal or Glass all the desires of my heart so as that I may be answered to my satisfaction clearly & fully throughout thy worthiness Good Lord who liveth and reigneth ever one God world without end, Amen, Amen,

O Holy patient and Merciful great God and to be worshipped the Lord of All wisdom dear and just I most humbly and heartily desire thy Clemency and Holiness to be extended unto me in permitting a blessed Angel ever before thy throne to shew me all that I require to see in this Chrystle Stone, which I hold in my hand that I by looking into it now may be enabled to ascertain the answers to my questions as alluded to above but not enumerated I do now therefor at this time most humbly request (here state your desires) To these most humble Inquiries thus made known unto thee by thine unworthy Servant do thou oh Lord God permit them to be answered & to my Comprehension I humbly implore of thee that by thy aid I may be enabled to bring this work to perfection.
   Amen   Amen
     Amen.

After having satisfied yourself in these matters with the glass for that time you are to discontinue looking into it for a few minutes and then repeat the following prayer

Almighty

AND Everlasting God who art blessed for ever more I thy unworthy servant in being satisfied in what thou hast condescended to manifest unto me at this time, I do give thee humble and hearty thanks and implore thee to open my understanding more and more in those divine things the Mysteries of Revelations that I may ask of thee in future, that I may praise & glorify thy holy and most blessed name, Amen, Amen, Amen,

The Spirit Vassago
How to obtain him & to call him in a Glass or Chrystal Sphere & to be
Retained by the Person so requesting.

FIRST provide yourself with a Laman or Plate of fine Silver and Engrave on it the seal as is hereafter shown, Then provide yourself with a Spatula made of hard wood as Pear tree, Ash or any Solid Wood let it be made very neat and in the fowling proportion. & to the form here after shown the Square part three inches each way & the third part of an inch thick, the Stem or Handle nine inches long & afterwards covered with gold or well gilt with pure gold and the Characters written thereon, When finished furnish yourself with a Glass or what is best a Chrystal Beautifully Spherical & highly polished. Repair to thy Chamber or place appointed for practice which must be very Clean & pure in the Center a Table must be placed due North, East, South & West. Coverd with a new Linen Cloth. The Chrystal or

TI.a.SS. must be placed in the Center, a Was conse=
=crated taper on each side Then being seated facing
the west Begin to Invocate as follows

Invocation

I W.H.I. Exorcise call upon and Command
Thee Spirit of Vassago, by and in the name
of the Immense and Everlasting God,
Jehovah, Adonay, Elohim, Agla, Ell, On,
Tetragrammaton, and by and in the Name of Our
Lord Jesus Christ, the only begotten Son of the eternal
and true God Creator of Heaven & Earth, and all that
is in them Wipins, Sother, Emanuel, Paimogenitus, Hom=
=onsion, Bomes, Via, Veritas, Sapientia, Virtus, Leof, Media-
tor, Agnus, Rex, Pastor, Prophetas, Sacerdos, Athanetos, Parac-
-letos, Alpha & Omega, by all these high Great and
Glorious Royal and Effible Names of the Omnipotent
God and of his only Son Our Lord and Saviour
Jesus Christ, the second Essence in the Glorious
Trenfty I.W.H.I. Exorcise command call upon &
Conjure thee Spirit Vassago. Wheresover thou art
(East, West, North or South) or being bound to any
one under the Compass of the Heavens; that you come
immediately from the place of your abode or resid=
=ence however private and appear to me Visibly in
fair and Decent form In the Body of this Chrystle
Sphere, & show to me the Characters that I may
hereafter at any time command thee by it, to

Give me every information I may hereafter at any time want. — Here pause a time and if he do not appear in the Chrystal or Glass. Then Proceed as follows

W.H.I. do again Exorcise and Powerfully Command thee Spirit **Vassago** to come and appear visible to me in this Chrystal or Glass Sphere in a decent form and show the Character by which I may command thy appearance, to give me any information I may in future, at any time want. and I do again strongly bind and command thee Spirit **Vassago** to appear visibly in that Chrystal (pointing to it) as I have before requested By the Virtue & Power of these Great and Powerfull Names by which I can bind all rebellious Obstinate and refractory Spirits, **Alla. Carital, Marilal, Carion, Urion, Spylon, Lorean, Stabea, Corian (or Coriam) Mormas Argaion, Cados. Son, Catalor, yron, Astron, Gordeong, Caldabrie, Bear, Tetragramaton, Strally, Spigros, Sother, Iah, On, El, Elohim,** By all the before mentioned Great & powerfull Names I charge and Command the Spirit **Vassago** to make hast and come away and appear vissibly in this Chrystal as I have before mentioned witho= =ut any further tarrying or delay, but instantly come in the Name of him who shall come to Judge the Quick & the Dead. and the World by fire, **Amen,**

☞ The Invocant must be patient & constant in his perseverance not disheartend nor dismayed but firm & resolute, for after all he will appear at last, Then Bind him with the Bond of Spirits & you may ask what you will & it will be granted, & if you choose he will be in fellowship with you, Observe & dont keep him longer than an hour, that is the Planetary hour of the day in the time you wish to perform your work

The Bond or Obligation of the Spirit made to one Invocant.

I Vassago, under **Baro**, the King of the West not compelled by command or fear but on my own accord and free will especialy oblige myself by these presents firmly and faithfully, and without any kind of Art or deception to ⸺ to obey at any time and at any place wheresoever or whensoever he shall call upon me personally to appear in the Body of this Glass or Chrystal and to fulfill all his commands & give him foresight and insight into all and every thing that he ⸺ commands truly, wherein I can by the virtue of all the great & powerfull Names of God Especially by these words most powerfull in the Magical Art, Lay, Abryea, Mura, Syron, Walgava, Ryshin, Layagannum, Layo, Arasin, Laysai, And by the virtue wherewith the Sun and Moon were Darkened & my own Planet, Seal & Character, and by all the Celestial Characters thereof & Primarily by his Seal binding most Solidly;

In Witness of which guilty person he commanding I have Signed this present Obligation with mine own Seal to which I always stick close & most solemnly swear to adhere protecting ⸺ from all inguries or hurts whatsoever

Charge for the Chrystal, by the Horroscope.

Take the Sign Assending and charge your Chrystal by the Spirit of that Sign or one who Rules at that time or when the (for the 12 signs See Book 1 P. 44) for the Angel of the Planet & sign, See Book 1st Page 26 & 33)

88

Question is Asked, with the Name of the Heaven the Spirit Rules, the Twelve Signs of the Zodiac, and the Angel Ruling the day & hour (see tables Book 1st page from 149 to 152) Which are the Seven Spirits that always stand before the face of God, to whom is intrusted the disposing of the whole Celestial & Terrestial Kingdom which is under the Moon & are called the Seven Governors of the World, who by the Heavens as by Instruments distribute the influences of all the Stars and Signs upon these inferences in this world Now each of these Governs the World 354 Years and 4 Months, and the Government begins from the Intelegence of ♄ afterwards in order the Intelegence of ♀ ♃ ☿ ♂ the ☽ & ☉ reigns, and then the government returns again to the Spirit of ♄. There are 4 Princes of the Angels which are set over the 4 parts of the World, whereof **Michael** is set over the E. **Raphael** W. **Gabriel** N. **Uriel** S, now every one of these Spirits is a great Prince and hath much Power & freedom in the dominion of his own Planet and Sign, & in the times Years, months, days & hours and in their elements & parts of the world & winds, And every one of them rule over many Legions of Spirits & often which as most potent Kings are set over the rest according to the four parts of the World whos names in some old works are these **Uriel** King of the East **Armaymon**, King of the South **Parymon**, King of the West, **Egin** King of the North; To Charge the Chrystal for the day (viz) in the morning to last untill night, You must take the Spirit ruling the day (see Book 1st page 149 to 152) and under the Conjurations of each day in Chapter 23 Book 1st) are the proper Charges for the same Do not neglect to dismiss your Spirit when you have done with him, for the Honour and Glory of God, Amen, Keeping yourself and the Chrystal pure and clean be watchful and keep your own counsel or no good will befall you,

A Pray to GOD to be said every morning.
Befor. raising the Chrystal

Almighty and most merciful God we thy Servant approach with fear and trembling before thee, and in all humility do most heartily beseech thee to Pardon our manifold and blind transgressions by us committed at any time, and **Oh** most merciful Father for his sake, who died upon the Cross, that our minds might be enlightened with the divine Radious of the Holy Wisdom, for seing Oh Lord of Might, Power, Majesty and dominion, that by reason of Our gross and material bodies, we are Scarce apt to recive those Spiritual instructions that we so earnestly & heartily desire Open Oh blessed Spirit, the spiritual Eye of our Soul, that we may be released from this darkness overspreding us, by the delusion of the outward Senses, and may perceive and understand these things which are spiritual, we pray the Oh Lord above all things to strengthen our souls & bodies against our enemies by the blood & righteous-=ness of our blessed Redeemer thy Son Jesus Christ and the dark understanding of thy Creatures, so that we may see with our eyes, and Comprehensively hear with our ears, & understand with our hearts, And rem-=ove far from us all hypocrisy, deceitful dealings prop-=haneness inconstancy & levity, so that we may in word and deed become thy faithful servants, and stand firm & unshaken against all the attacks of bodily enemies & likewise be proof against all illusions of evil spirits with whom we desire no communications or interest, but that we may be instructed in the knowledge of things natural & Celestial

AND as it pleased thee to bestow on Solomon all wisdom both human & devine in the desire of which knowledge he did so please thy Divine Majesty that in a dream of one night, thou didst inspire him with all wisdom and knowledge, which he did wisely prefer before the riches of this Life, So may our desires & Prayers be graciously excepted by thee, so that by a firm depen= =dance on thy word we may not be led away by the vain & ridiculous persuits of worldly pleasure & delights, they not being desirable nor of any account to our immortal happiness. Grant us Oh Lord power and strength of intellect to carry on this work for the honour & glory of thy Holy name & to comfort our neighbours, & without design of hurt or deteriment to any we may Proceed in our labours through Jesus Christ, our Redeemer **A** men.

CALL for the CHRYSTAL by the HOROSCOPE

Omnipotent and Eternal God, who has ordained the whole Creation for for thy Praise and glory, I beseech thee O Lord to send thy Holy Angel (mention the name) who will inform & teach us, and moreover show the person in this Chrystal (here mention what you desire to see) for the honour and glory of him who is called Tetragrammaton, the Holy God, the Father who says I am that I am Alpha & Omega the first and the last, Permit it Oh God thy bright & glorious angel to

Answer our demands for the honour and glory of thy holy name   Amen.

General CALL by the 4 Angels

Oh Thou Omnipotent, Omniscience and Omnipresent God who made all things in in Heaven and on Earth I humbly beseech thee to send thy holy Angellical Spirits Michael, Gabriel, Raphael, Uriel, all or one of them, who will inform and make appear unto us (here mention what you desire to see) in the Names Adonia, Elohim, Saboath, Tetragrammaton. The holy God. of Israel that you make it appear in this Chrystal this thing I desire to be seen as was showen to Abiather the Priest in the stone of the Ephod & in the miraculous Urim & Thummin for the Glorification of King Adonia to whom be all honour and Glory both now and forever.   Amen.

THE DISCHARGE FOR THE SPIRIT FROM THE CHRYSTAL.

Thou Great and Almighty Spirit inasmuch as thou comest in peace, and in the name of the ever blessed and righteous Trinity. So in this name thou mayest depart, and return to us when we call thee in his name, to whom every knee doth bow down. Fare thee well (state the Spirits name) and peace be between us through our blessed Lord Jesus Christ Amen, (then will the Spirit depart (and say) to God the Father, Eternal Spirit Fountain of Light. the

92

Son and Holy Ghost be all honour and Glory World without end. Amen.

Here followeth the form of the Chrystal, which must be set in pure gold or the frame next the Chrystal well gilt with the names Characters &c with the Circle, Almadel &c.

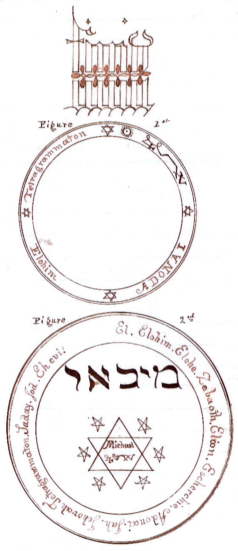

Fig. 1st The Circle of a simple construction, in which the operator must sit when he uses the Chrystal

Fig. 2nd The Lamen of Gold or Holy Table of Michael (on a large scale)

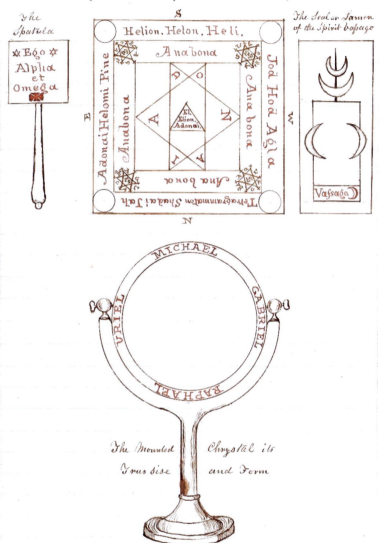

The Crystal and its Stand, which must have a band of pure gold let there be engraved inside the band next the Crystal ✡, ✶ ✤, afterwards the name, "Tetragrammaton". On the Outside of the frame let there be engraven Michael, Gabriel, Uriel, Raphael, which are the four principal angels Ruling over the Sun, Moon, Venus, & Mercury; But on the Table, on

94

which the crystal stands the following names, characters &c. must be drawn in order

First. The names of the seven planets and angels ruling them, with their seals or characters. The names of the four kings of the four corners of the earth. Let them be all written within a double circle, with a triangle on a table, on which place the Crystal

Chap 25
The Power and Virtue of Resemblance and Imagination throughout the Arts and Sciences

Divinity. Those then who are skilled in the Secrets of the Theology of the Ancients, assures us that those who first set up Images in the temples resembling the shapes of Angels, that is said to have appeared upon Earth, had no other design in so doing than from a conception by them that the Resemblance might invite down more easily the Spirits of the Blessed; which Images to this day all our Churches abounds with. And by the very same Virtue of Resemblance which is found betwixt God and Man Religion teaches us that Our Saviour is always in the midst of those who speaks with faith of his name therefore the more fervent we are and the more strong in faith we are in him, the sooner he appears to our imagination & his Image is immediately presented to us. Religion teaches us also to call on him in all our troubles, if no good can come from it, of what use is Religion? of what use is our faith, of what use is the Church & the Clergy. But so true it is that by the power of Resemblance wonders are to be worked & appearent Miracles wrought, even upon him that hath dependance upon no other, and is not under any power or Law. But such conceptions as, these are to be entertained, with all Piety and Humility being a subject which must be treated with the greatest reverence;

Philosophy. Now let us see the Virtue of Resemblance in this science, in the power of Imagination, take a female in the state of Pregnancy, How strong does Resemblance work upon her, in point of Imagination on any Object, in the Act of Copulation; for the Child will certainly, bear the very Image of the same, be what it may – or imbibe any of the Passions of the Mother whatever possest her at the Crisis, as experience daily shews, where is it more clearly demonstrated then by the strong Desires & Longings of Women in that state, by which the Child for ever bear the mark of their Mothers folly, And thus it is that a Child produced from a Married Woman though not from the loins of her Husband, shall be like him, i.e. that as in the act of copulation her mind is fixed on her husband through fear, which is by the strength of her Imagination, For further information see the works of, Paracelsus, Marcitius, Ficinus, Pius, Medina, Tostatus, Valesius, & Mirandula,

Physic,. The Resemblances of Herbs & Plants to the Human Body, which are well known to assuage the griefs and Maladies of the different parts of the Body they Resemble or seem to have some affinity with, they operate on that they represent, Baptista Porta, observes that the Citrull Cucumber, represents the Head of man by its form, & he affirms that against the Diseases of the Head it is a sovereign Remedy, The Poppy also resembles the Head & the powerful effects, of the same is well known, So with the Herb's Argemon, Seris, Beloculus, &c which represents the Eye of Man and will cure all diseases of the same, Dentaria which represents the teeth, cures the tooth Ach, Palma, Christa, &.

Ischæmon which grows in the shape of the hand, are cures for all defects in the same; as the Herb Genanopodium is, for the feet. Now Crollius proceeds more Methodically in treating on the wonderfull effects of Resemblance between the Several plan=ts & the parts of Mans Body, & the Order he observes, is this,

The Head saith he is represented by the root of the Squils, which is of the same figure & if properly applied to the same will cure all diseases thereof

The Hair, is represented by a Moss, which is called, hair Moss, it grows on the Oake & its name is Pili Quercini; also the down of Thistles, the Juices of-which obtained by Art will cause the Hair to grow very quick,

The Ears, are represented by the herb Asarum or Asarabacca, which also prepared by Art will Cure all Deafnesses,

The Eyes, are represented by the flowers of the Wild Tansie or Potentilla, the water made according to Art, wonderfully restores Sight

The Nose, is represented by the herb Water Mint, the water made by Art wonderfully recovers, the lost smell,

The Teeth, are represented by the herb Dentaria, which if properly prepared will cure the Tooth Ach instantly,

The Hands, are represented by the herb Hertrodactis, which if prepared by Art cures all diseases that are natural to the Hands

The Heart, Is represented by the Citron & the herb called Alleluja, which if prepared as before, is a Sovering Remedy for the same,

The Lungs, by the herb Lungwort, & that prepared as before is a Sovering Remedy for all Complaints incident to them

The Liver, Is represented by the herb called Hepatica or Liver Wort, which prepared as before is good against all Diseases in the same, And the same Author speaks largely on all other Simples which are in Resemblance with every Part of Mans Body, he further observes that even Colours of

97

Plants are wonderfull efficacious in medicine, for Rhubarb being yellow is a remeday for the yellow Choler or Bile. Lentiles & Rape seed are good for the Small pox & will cure the same. Why! because they resembles the Spots of the disease in their figure; Indeed take the whole veget= =able Kingdom, & according to their Natures (Plants Roots fruits &c) acts upon the Animal Kingdom according to their Signatures, & Resemblance. As those Plants which are Naturally Barren, causes Barreness, those which are fruitfull cause fruitfulness. Fair makes fair, Deformed cause Deformity, Imperfect causes imperfections. &c For which is the reason that in eating those creatures, which have no Blood wastes ours and the same in all other parts Leprosy is a Disorder of France, where they feed so much on Hogs flesh that their Bodies become in a state similar;

Astrology. This Science also shews the Virtue of Resem= =blance Judging the Qualities of the Stars & the natural affinities upon those Persons born under their influences For example ♄ who is by nature Pale & faint in colour, makes the native who is under his Influence pale & wan. ♃ & ♀ which are by nature Bright & casteth forth bright clear & pleasent Beams makes the Native under their influences both beautiful & pleasent, ♂ who is by Nature hot and fiery casts forth a glittering red light, makes the Native of a red Colour &c The same is observed by the Signs the Planets are posited in if the Signs are high & in their Apogeum, the Native in this case is great in Stature & Tall, and if they are Low, the Native is low also & of Small Stature; Now concerning Motion ♄ being slow & sluggish in motion, the Native is the same. The ☽ having a swift motion makes those under her influence Light and Inconsiderate, the same with the rest (see Sibly's astrology)

98

Physiognomy, Likewise shews us most prodigious effects of Resemblance, we see by experience, that a Man with a very round forehead, is naturally subject to folly Lightness and very unstaple &c (like a round figure as being more apt for Motion) so is a man of this discription easy moved, the reason is because that the Spirits being light, assends & meeting with a Place of a Spherical form are very easy moved every way It is also a Rule that a Person having a sharp Chin that stands forward & a little forehead are very Brutish and stupid In fact they are like the Hog whose image they in a measure bear, for further instances see Levanter's Physiognomy,

Divination of Dreams, is also grounded on Resemblance as plainly appears in Holy Writ, Joseph foretold the Cupbearer, that within three days he should be restored to his office again, But how was it; it was by Resemblance for he dreamed that he pressed three bunches of grapes into the Cup of Pharoah, and he also foretold that the Baker, after three days should be hanged & that his flesh should be devoured by the birds of the Air, Because he dreamed that he bear three Baskets full & that the Birds eat up all that they contained, He foretold also the Seven years of Plenty & the seven years Dearth by the seven Fat kine, & the seven lean ones; and by the Seven full Ears of Corn, & the seven Thin ones; which was according to the Dream of Pharoah. History also affords many Examples of this kind proving the power of Similitudes, For Heuba being advanced in pregnancy dreamed that she delivered of a firebrand which burnt up her Kingdom, & this her Child was Paris, who afterwards was the cause of the burning of Troy But for those who wish to see this subject treated more at large I would refer him to Solomon Judeas, Plato, Cicero, Valerius, Maximus, Apomazar, the

Arabian & Seinnachen the Indian writer & a number of other Authors

Painting & Sculpture, do wonderfully confirm the powerfull effects of Resemblance for Pictures highly finished on Tragical Subjects touches our feelings & rouzes the Passions according to the Subject those of a sad nature causes Melancholy & sometimes draws forth tears, When Merry & Cheerpull Pieces, makes us Joyfull & causes us to laugh. Which is the reason that in places of Divine Worship, the more serious subjects are chosen to add to the Solemnity & to act on the minds of the Congregation, As this is absolutely the effects of Similitude or Resemblance the Pictures, of Christ Crucified, also his Rising from the Dead on Sitting at the right hand of his Father, puts us in mind both of our Redemption & of his Love towards us

Music, The secret virtues of Resemblance in this Science is great, and so wonderfull is its power that it appeaseth the mind raiseth the Spirits, refresheth the weary, moderates the Rage & passions of man, The Arabians cheer & refresh their Camels under their heavy Burdens by singing soft melodys, & By the power of Music did Orpheus, charm the Birds of the Air & Beasts of the fields, David with his harp moderated the rage of Saul, Pythagoras recalled a luxurious young man from immoderate lust. Timotheus, stirred up Alexander to a rage & again repressed him All History will furnish us with most wonderfull things performed by Music. There is a Sympathy in sounds, which can be heard by sounding a Note from a flute (on any other Instrument,) over an harp or stringed instrument, & you'l hear the Chords of that Note will sound & no other. For instance Sound D, & the regular Chords will sound as the thirds, fifths & Eights, and although the sound given be ever so faint, the motion will be clearly visible by laying on the Strings a feather. How admirable then is this Power of Resemblance which doth every where produce such wonderfull Effects, we may safely conclude that it can have no lys effect in that of Talismanic Figures, which Experience will prove

Having clearly demonstrated the Powerfull effects & wonderfull virtues of Resemblance by the Sciences, & having very largely explained by Examples the true principles of Manufacturing these Talismans by art according to the System of the Ancients It now remains to prove their power to be Natural & by virtue of the Stars &c, The effects they produce & their manner and Cause of Action, which has puzzled numbers who have endeavoured to obtain this secret and being disapointed, abhors all whatsoever that bears but the name of Figure, Image or Talisman But I shall endeavour to prove their real existance, their power virtue & Innocency, By answering three Doubts of the efficancy & exixtance, First wether the Stars have any influence upon things here or not; Secondly, wether they have any Resemblance with them. Thirdly wether in Artificial Figures can be obtained & Retained their Influences and afterwards operate by them

Chap 26

The three Doubts, of the Existance Efficancy & Virtues of Talismans obtained & Retained by the Influences of the Stars Answered

The First, The Great Omnipotence from whom Motion first Originated, which hath given to all things the Power of Self motion, Now without doubt the motion of the Heavens was the first in Nature, Therefore, whatsoever Moves by the motion of the Heavens is directed & governed by that Celestial Power, Which if that motion once Ceased, Both Growth and Motion would also cease in all things, As the Heart of Man which in him is the begining of Life & Motion which communicates that Life & Motion to all the members of the Body. And if once wonded, life & motion ceases, So evidently strong are the truths of Celestial

Influences That man is able to fortell Changes of all discriptions on this our Globe, In all Diseases incident to the Human Body are told the various changes of Disease the Judicial & Critical days &c ruled by the ☽ (a knowledge requisite for every Medical man which would prevent a great many Blunders often made by them to the great danger of their Patient) which has been observed from the first beginning of Astronomy that the rising & setting of the Planets & fixed Stars have been the cause of great changes on this Earth, for who will deni that the Hyades & Plaides are not watery & cloudy Constellations i.e. that when they are in our Latitude they cause Rainy Cloudy & Dark weather. And Leo & the dog Star brings heat which are commonly called Dog Days, as that Specie feels its fatal influence. While Orion brings Wet tempestuous Weather and the same of the rest, again in flowers of a certain Nature as the Sun flower, which follows the Sun in all his directions so in many other flowers of the same nature, also there is a flower that grows in the Water, which Rise & sinks as the Sun Rises & sets, What is this but Solar influences, which influences are not confined to plants alone but Stones do so exactly act according to the Stars they are under, The Stone called Lunaria. which changes with the ☽'s changes, Indeed do not the Humours of our Bodies increase & decrease with with the ☽, But should my answer not be sufficient I must refer to Ptolomy, where the truth of Planety influences is too clear to be called in Question,

The Second, According to the Judgement of the most Learned Astrologers (to whom we are indebted for a great part of our knowledge) the Constellation of the Ram ♈ they formed that figure because when the Sun enters that sign, it hath a great influence over that Specie, which is about the 21st of March at which time procreation takes place, and that a Child Born

102

under that Constellation naturally Pious & Gentle, that he resembles in all things the Innocent Lamb, which may substitute another reason why this Constellation was so called So it is with Taurus ♉ the Sun in making his Circuit and entering into this sign as the same on Bulls as before observed on Sheep. Now Aries is one of the equinoctial Signs and why so called is that when the sun enters therein it is then equal days and Nights of 12 hours each Libra ♎ is the sign opposite & is also an equinoctial sign, which is the reason the ancients gave the Emblem of a Balance as ⚖ or more modern a Pair of Scales when the days & Nights are also equal, When the Sun enters the Sign Cancer ♋ the Crab, it is then he becomes Retrograde & leaves our earth as such time is the longest days, which is the time that Creature leaves the sea to bury their Spawn in the Sands, & as Crabs always crawls in a Retrograde manner was the cause of the emblem attributed to that Sign which is a Tropicall sign, Now Capricorn ♑ which is direc-tly opposite is called also Tropicall, for when the Sun enters that sign it is the shortest days & the sun is then approaching our Earth when Vegetation begins Motion, & a time of rejoicings & Meriment as such the ancients gave it the emblem of a Goat, which creature at that time is playful &c, and feels the pleasing influence of the Sun in this sign. so it is with Respect to the rest as the Sun passes through them which also affects the various parts of the human Body the sign represents or signifies. & as such the Herbs &c so signifying are good against such Diseases & at which times they are in their perf-ection, & ought to be gathered for Medecinal purposes

The Planets, Stars and Signs do therefore visibly work their Influ-ences on all things, and on Creatures by whos names they are called & whos Image they Bear, as such Dogs run Mad in the dog days, Lions are furious when Sol enters Leo &c. which was the only reason, on a mature consideration that moved our first Phil-osophers to name these Constellations after these Creatures

The Third and Last, which is answered in few words, Every one must know the Sun to be the Cause of Light and Heat, which

103

must by its nature warm the Artificial Image of a man as the Man himself. Now if this Planet works indifferently upon both why not the rest do the same, whose rays are increased by this proponderating Luminary. Why not the Stars Operate as well on all Artificial things as on Natural things, Which in their Essences are all natural; Should Gold be excluded as a Solar metal, because it is made into a Ring. Are Stones less natural when formed into various Shapes. If it should be Objected that by their situations they should not acquire thereby any more power or virtue than they had before. I answer that the contrary is proved by two Reasons. First that Figure renders it more apt to operate according to the intent it is designed, Form renders the Material fit & Capable of use according to the Will of the Operator. As wood or Stone is not capable of holding water without being fashion'd Hollow, A Solid Piece of Iron let fall into Water Sinks, which otherwise formed by Man Swims Therefore the great dependence on Action is in figure; Second. is that those things which we call Talismans, are wrought under certain Constellations; which communicates such Influences and Qualities to them, as they never were before possessed of as Steel heated Red hot & plunged into water is hardened & made to work upon its own body. but if again put in the fire becomes soft, again flour Eggs &c made up as for a Cake One half Baked one time is fit for Eating, when the other half Baked a short time will be bad subject to worms & soon become corruption, I shall here conclude that if Figures or Talismans are prepared with all those circumstances observed which is before laid down in the Body of this Work & engraved upon substance proper for Receiving the Influences of the Stars, they can naturally retain them, and Work all those wonderfull effects which is before asserted

Having answered three of the most principle Doubts of the Validity of the Wonderfull effects & passibility of this

Science, there may be yet in sum minds some others to be answered before we can clear this subject from the prejudices already formed against it, & the doubts and difficulties of its Real existence. Therefore I shall propose the following Objections and answer them as relatively.

First, Seeing that making one of these Talismanical Images we are to engrave only the Celestial Figure or Character we want and the rest which should occur in the Operation not finding their Image then, cannot operate at all.

Second, What a Ridiculous thing it is to engrave the Figure of a Ram, a Lion, Crab, or Scorpion &c seeing that the Constellations whose Names those are, do not at all performe the effects which we see in Nature, But rather the Sun passing through those parts of the Heavens.

Third, The Virtue of other Stars must invixtably be communicated to the Image as well as those which we chiefly desire to make use of, As the one as well as the other continually sends forth their influences; therefore those of contrary Qualities will & must certainly hinder the Operation of the other.

Fourth, That these Figures must be Superstitious, and no way Natural Seeing that the Figure of a Scorpion Engraved in a Stone can not only have the power of curing the Stinging of that reptile but is able to communicate that power to another figure, the reverse.

Fifth & Last, That in this Science there are two effects to be produced from each planet; i.e, One Good and the other Evil, and both powers equally to be brought into action.

An Answer to the First objection, A Man may if he Please engrave Divers Images according to the Diversity of the Signs that he would observe. The Influences of many Stars may be communicated to one Sole Figure If there is an affinity in their Nature, i.e. being in friendship with eachother by which may be made to act on more than one object. As the Virtue of many heurbs which proceedeth from the same stars may be reduced into one Medicine. But there is no necessity of more than one Constellation with all suitable Characters belonging to it, to be engraved upon one plate As such it need not have more than what you want to operate the most effectually & though the other stars, meet not on the Plate a resemblance of figure to their Operations, yet they in some degree operate As they continually shed their influences upon all indifferently, and communicates their Virtue to the Metal or Stone, whatever is the matter chosen to some more power, & to some less, according to the different Aspects, under which they are wrought

An Answer to the Second; It matters not whether it is the twelve Constellations of the Zodiac or the Sun in them that sheds forth these Influences so that We can be assured by our Experience that they come from such a part of the Heavens as is requisite for the effect desired which in this case will follow to a certainty. We are always therefore to make this observation, i.e, to procure a Plate of Metal or Stone agreeable to the nature, & engrave thereon such figure & characters, as is correspondent to this effect, wether it proceeds from the Sun or from the other Stars; And yet it is Manifest, that it proceeds not principally from the Sun; there being forty eight Constellations without the Zodiac through which the Sun never pass yet they in some degree Operate also, But the twelve Signs of the Zodiac being divided into four parts, & each part bearing a different nature, The Sun when he enters that Part or Triplicity Rouses and increase its Nature, as Fiery he causes an intense heat. Therefore if he enters in either, Hot & Dry, Hot & Moist, Cold & Dry or Cold & Moist, he encreases its power, & the Property

106

be what it may is conveyed through the medium of the Different Planets, upon this our Globe, & all those things which are congenial to their Nature are as recipients, receiving & retaining the same, & disposing the same to those that Nature & the art of man requires.

An Answer to the Third, As those Constellations which are of a contrary Nature to effect which we desire though they may be said to Operate yet for Want of a proper recipient: i.e. (a recipient agreeable to their nature) Operate but faintly & of very small force for we observe the time when the Planets (which we want not their aid) are not in our Hemisphere or if they are when their Aspect is the Weakest & likewise when a fortunate Star accompanies them. And as the Celestial fire cannot be extracted from the Sun by any thing but Glass & not even that unless formed into an appropriate figure, so It is with a Talisman,

An Answer to the Fourth; Is indeed the most difficult as the virtue which we find imprinted in a Talisman seems to surpass the Power of Nature yet upon the full investigation of the Wonderfull Properties & the innumerable numbers there are in Nature we are able to make it appear that there is Nothing in it But Nature & Art, i.e. Nature assisted by Art. What is the Magnet. It is a Talisman, a piece of Stale wrought by man into form or figure, which of itself (in that state has no power) but as it is a proper recipient to receive into itself the properties of Nature. That being therefore touched by a Loadstone which is the sole production of Nature It becomes then a powerfull Magnet, and is Capable of communicating the same power to any other Matter which has an affinity & also of Depriving the same of its power at will which power is invisible even to the greatest anerlitide Chemists and yet that power is visible in its action, which positively tells which is the North point or pole I say it is a direct Talisman

107

How many beautifull & wonderfull experiments are there to be shown by this power or invisible agency, which had it not been for the researches & art of man might have laid hid in obscurity. In the like manner is the nature of a Talisman or Figure. It communicates its virtue to another figure, which, have received an Impression from it as the Magnet time increases its power to work the same effects on other subjects of its own affinity. The only Difference is that of this latter power we can account, but of the former we cannot. Therefore comparatively speaking, The Talisman is as a Brick when heated by the fire & made very hot It is then able to communicate the heat to another Brick though not with so much force as that from the fire itself & the same is to be said of the Print or impression of the Piece of Clay taken from the Talisman of the Scorpion to cure the Stinging of that Reptile, though it cannot be so powerfull as the Original Talisman itself, which is heated, or prep- -ared, by the Beams of the Stars

An Answer to the Fifth & last Objection; Take a Linen cloth which is of its own nature Dry, But that dipped in water is changed in its nature to that of Cold & Moist. which if placed before the Fire its temperature is changed to that of Hot & Moist, and if left, is again changed to that of Hot and Dry, and in that state. Is capable of being in part destroyed (or its elements seperated) by that which has been the cause of its Changes. Now there two opositions which are totally inimical to nature which is Hot & Dry and Cold & Dry these two Qual- -lities. it is well known by experience that was they to last to for any length of time all Natures produce would be des- -troyed, therefore the same that produces Harmony prod- -uces discord. & out of evil, good is produced & visa versi so it is with the different Aspects of the Planets. a ☌ ✶ & △ produces Harmony and a ☐ & ☍ produce discord

Therefore all recipients which is chose by the Operator with Judgment will receive retain and communicate their influencies, as also by the same means may be obtained, retained and communicated the Evil Rays or Influencies of the Evil Aspects. And as the Serpent carries with him by Nature Poison, so does he carrie with him an Antedote, against the powerfull effects of that Poison.

Chap 27

A Few Useful Remarks to the Reader who are desirous of becoming Adepts in this Sublime Science shewing them how to find out & examine the virtues of things by way of Similitude, that a general & proper Judgement may be assertained through the whole System of Nature

It is now manifest that the wonderfull Occult properties are not from the Nature of the Elements themselves, but are infused from above, and hid from our Senses & is scarce known to us only by our Reason which we are invested with by the great Omnipotence from whence all Intelligence springs. And is the Life and real Spirit or Soul of the World, conveyed to us through the Rays of the Stars, & no otherwise than by experience & conjecture be inquired into by us Wherefore he who is desirous and wishes to enter into this Study must consider that every thing moves, & approaches that which has the nearest affinity to itself, and inclines that to itself with all its strength as well in property (which is the Occult virtue, as in quality) i.e. Elementary virtue which is sometimes to be observed in the Substance itself as we see in salt: for whatever is kept long in Salt, becomes Salt: for every Agent when it has began its action upon another Object it never causes that object to be inferiour to itself. Which is

109

Manifestly seen in all Sensible Animals in which the Nutritive Virtue doth not Change the meat into the Herb or Plant it has fed on, but changes it into solid Flesh. In what things therefore there is an excess of any Quality, or property, as heat, cold, Boldness, Fear, sadness, Anger, hatred, Love, or any other Passion or Virtue. Wether it be implanted in them by Nature or Ant; as Modesty in a Virgin, Boldness in a harlot, Savageness or Forosity in a Tiger, Laciviousness in a Monkey, Gentleness in a Lamb &c These things doth move & provoke to such a Quality Passion or Virtue So Fire moves to Fire, Water to Water, and She that is naturally Bold moves to Boldness, and is well known that the Human Body receives strength by taking into it strengthening things, & that Bloodless Animals dries up ours, and weak Animals weakens our system Therefore under these considerations the Ancients from their experience in the Occult properties of Nature, that to help the Brain of man, they applied by Ant the brains of an Animal the nearest in affinity, and the same by the Lungs to the Lungs &c and they assent that the foot of a Tortoise will cure the Gout by being applied in the following manner; The Right foot to the Right & the Left to the Left, by way of rubbing & binding thereto. They also say the same of the Right & Left Eye of a Frog, by rubbing first and then suspended in a piece of Cloth & Ribbon of its Colour: After this manner & under the same consideration they assent that any Animal that is Barren will cause another to be barren also especially the Testicles, Matrix or Urine (that these being the parts and production of generation) they act upon the parts of generation, being of their same Nature. Therefore they assent that if a Woman drinks every month the Urine of a Mule she will become barren & not capable of conception

If therefore we wish to obtain any desired effect or possess ourselves with any peculiar property or Virtue, Let us seek for such Animals, or such other things, in which such a property or Virtue is most predominant; And in these Animals &c, let us follow the before mentioned Rules, and take for our use that part in which such property or Virtue most abounds. For Example if we wish to promote Love of which ♀ Venus is the Mother, let us seek for somethink under her which is naturally of a Lascivious Nature & hot as Pidgeons, Turtles, Sparrows, Swallows, Wagtails &c and in these for our use make choice of those parts from which the effects of generation proceeds as the Heart Matrix &c. These to work any effect must be taken at the time when these Animals effections are most Intence; which according to the Laws of Nature are powerpull Provokatives. To encrease Boldness, let us examine A Lion A Cock &c Now of these we must take The Heart, the Eyes, & forepart of the Head. To conduce to Watchifullness, consider what Animal are of that Nature as the Dog, Crows & Cocks, the Nightingale, the Bat & horned Owl of these must the heart, head, & Eyes be taken. And they say that if any one carry the heart of a Crow or a Bat about them they shall not sleep, The Male for the Male & Female for the Female, likewise the Head of a Bat dried & Bound to the Right arm of a person while awake will have the same effect, But if it is thus placed when the person is asleep he will not wake till it is removed After the same manner doth the Tongue & heart or head of a Frog make A Man talk & tell his affairs when asleep by Night if laid under his head, and the heart & Tongue of the Screach Owl laid on the left Breast of a Female when asleep she will tell all her secrets & answer any Questions, the Same Also of the horned Owl, and they say that many of the talkative Birds will produce the same effects. & Animals which are natur

711

naturally long lived will conduce to the same, & whatsoever animals there are which renew themselves Conduce to the restoration & renovation of the Body of Man, the same property is well known to some, to be the case in the nature of the Snake & Viper. Therefore every thing acts by analogy of Signiture & Resemblance. & in that point only lies Affinity which in all Nature & Natures productions, there is a regular Chain so linked together (by the latter) that every thing in existance has dependance upon another; and also contains two properties, Good and Evil. The Affinities of Sexes must be considered in the Animal & Vegetable Kingdom (but more particular in the Animal. And if what is herein disclosed is well investigated by the Student. he has it in his power to use if not Command all Natures Forces,

Bibliography

Manuscript

    Wellcome GB 133 Eng MS 44

Books

Boudet, J.-P. *Entre science et nigromance: Astrologie, divination et magie et magie dans l'Occident médiéval (XII-XV siècle)*, Paris: Sorbonne, 2006.

Boudet J.-P., 'Theurgic Magic, Angelology and the Beatific Vision in the *Liber sacratus sive juratus* attributed to Honorius of Thebes,' in *Mélanges #39*, École Française de Rome: Moyen-Âge, 114, 2, 2002, pp. 851-890.

Chave-Mahir, Florence & Véronèse, Julien. *Rituel d'exorcisme ou Manuel de Magie?* Firenze: SISMEL, Edizioni del Galluzzo, 2015. (CLM 10085)

Rankine, David. *Grimoire Encyclopaedia,* Keighley: Hadean, 2 Vols. 2024.

Skinner, Stephen. *Ars Notoria* – Vol. 1 (with Daniel Clark) – Singapore: Golden Hoard, 2019.

Skinner, Stephen. *Ars Notoria – the Method,* Vol. 2 (with Daniel Clark) – Singapore: Golden Hoard, 2021.

Skinner, Stephen. *The Complete Magician's Tables.* Singapore: Golden Hoard, 2006, 2015.

Skinner, Stephen. *Techniques of Solomonic Magic.* Singapore: Golden Hoard, 2015.

Skinner, Stephen & David Rankine. *The Veritable Key of Solomon.* Singapore: Golden Hoard, 2017.

Skinner, Stephen. *Dr John Dee's Spiritual Diaries:* the fully revised and corrected edition, with full Latin translation – Singapore: Golden Hoard, 2019.

Skinner, Stephen. *Sepher Raziel: Liber Salomonis* (with Don Karr) – Singapore: Golden Hoard, 2011, 2017.

Skinner, Stephen & Daniel Clark. *Trithemius' Secret Bookshelf – the Antipalus Maleficarum,* Singapore: Golden Hoard, 2024.

Skinner, Stephen & Daniel Clark. *Summa Sacre Magice,* Books 1 & 2,

Singapore: Golden Hoard, 2024.

Veenstra, Jan. "Honorius and the Sigil of God: the *Liber Iuratus* in Berengario Ganell's *Summa Sacre Magice*" in Fanger, Claire, *Invoking Angels: Theurgic Ideas and Practices, Thirteenth to Sixteenth Centuries*, University Park: Pennsylvania State University Press, 2012, p. 151-191.

Véronèse, Julien. " God's Names and their uses in the Books of Magic attributed to King Solomon" in *Magic, Ritual, and Witchcraft*, Vol. 5, Number 1, Summer 2010, University of Pennsylvania Press, p. 30-50.

Véronèse, Julien. *L'Almandal et l'Almadel latins au Moyen Age: introduction et éditions critiques*, Firenze: SISMEL, Edizioni del Galluzzo, 2012.

Index

Almadel, 291-299

Alphabet, Latin, 55

Alphabets, table of, 37

Amorous intrigues, 98, 206

Anael, seal of, 64

Angels of the planets, 77

Angels of the Zodiacal signs, 78

Antiochus, 92

Araritha, 92

Arcan, king, 188

Aspects, planetary, 54

Astrictions of charms, 173

Barzabel, 71

Behenian fixed stars, 83

Camael, seal of, 62

Celestial characters, Hebrew, 55

Chaldean characters, 56

Characters, planetary, 179

Charles 5th of Germany, 93-94

Choras, four, 296-297

Chrystal, 306-309

Cigmel table, 153

Circles, magic, 176-178

Cobjel table, 153

Colours of the Signs, 78

Commutations, Averse table, 102-137

Commutations, Right table, 134-135

Cures, talismanic, 49

Days, conjurations of, 187-194

De Abano, Peter, 186, 197

Diana, 171

Divine Names & numbers, Planetary, 58, 59

Dragon, Head and Tail, 268-269

Dream divination, 205, 316

Elections of the Moon, 163, 164

Essential Dignities of the planets, 154

Faces of the planets, 157-158

Faces of the Signs, 158-160

Firearms, against, 206

Fixed Stars, 84-87

Gabriel, seal of, 67

Gaming, 206

Gout, talisman against, 106

Hours, planetary rulership, 165

Images of the Fixed Stars, 84-87

Impediments of the Moon, 161-162

Incenses, 255-257

Inundations, against, 205

Jupiter sigil, 198

Jupiter, Table of, 61

Kompel table, 149-150

Lamps & candles, 79

Love, secret, 206

Lucan, 170

Man, astrological parts, 44-47

Mansions of the Moon, 120-121, 251-255

Mars, Table of, 62

Maymon Rex, 178

Medea, 95

Mediat Rex, 177

Melachim angelic characters, 57

Mercury, Table of, 65

Michael talisman, 310

Michael, seal of, 63

Moon Nodes, see Dragon, Head and Tail

Moon, Table of, 66

Mopkel table, 149-150

Muriel, angel, 92-93

Name extraction, Hebrew, 125

Names & numbers, Planetary, 58-59

Names, extraction of good & evil, 122-124

Notariacon [Notarikon], 90

Passing the River characters, 57

Pentacle of Peter de Abano, 197

Pentacle of Solomon, 197

Phoebus, 170

Planetary angels, 77

Planetary governors, 169-171

Planetary Hour, length of, 164

Planetary Hours, names of, 183-186

Planetary table of the Cabala - English, 122

Planetary table of the Cabala - Hebrew, 123

Planetary trades & professions, 75

Planets, friendship and enmity, 48

Pliny, 95

Possession, against, 205

Proserpina, 171

Psalms, 215, 216

Quarters, names of, 182

Raphael, seal of, 65

Rules for drawing seals, 72

Samax Rex, 177

Saturn, Table of, 60

Sigil of Jupiter, 198

Sigil of Solis, 198

Sigils of the Planetary spirits, 68

Spatula, 311

Spirit of the World, 236

Stilbon, 170

Sun sigil, 198

Sun, Table of, 63

Table of Nine Chambers, 88

Talismans belonging to great men, 87-88

Talismans, 35-37, 97-100, 106-107, 111-119

Thurible design, 81

Transpositions, numerical, 126-129

Treasures, finding, 205-206

Vassago, 302-305, 311

Venus, Table of, 64

Witchcraft, against, 97

Zadkiel, seal of, 61

Zaphiel, seal of, 60